TRUE BLUE
The Loyalist Legend

Also by Walter Stewart

Shrug: Trudeau in Power
Divide and Con
Hard to Swallow
But Not in Canada
As They See Us
Strike
Paper Juggernaut
Canadian Newspapers: The Inside Story
Towers of Gold, Feet of Clay

TRUE BLUE
The Loyalist Legend

Walter Stewart

Collins
Toronto

First published 1985
by Collins Publishers
100 Lesmill Road, Don Mills, Ontario

Canadian Cataloguing in Publication Data

Stewart, Walter, 1931-
   True blue: the Loyalist legend

Includes index.
ISBN 0-00-217468-5

1. United Empire loyalists – Canada.   2. Canada
– History – 1763-1867.   I. Title.

FC423.S74 1985   971.02'4   C85-099394-6
E277.S74 1985

Printed in Canada by John Deyell Company

*For my wife, Joan,
whose family were Loyalists
(or late Loyalists)*

CONTENTS

TRUE BLUE
The Loyalist Legend

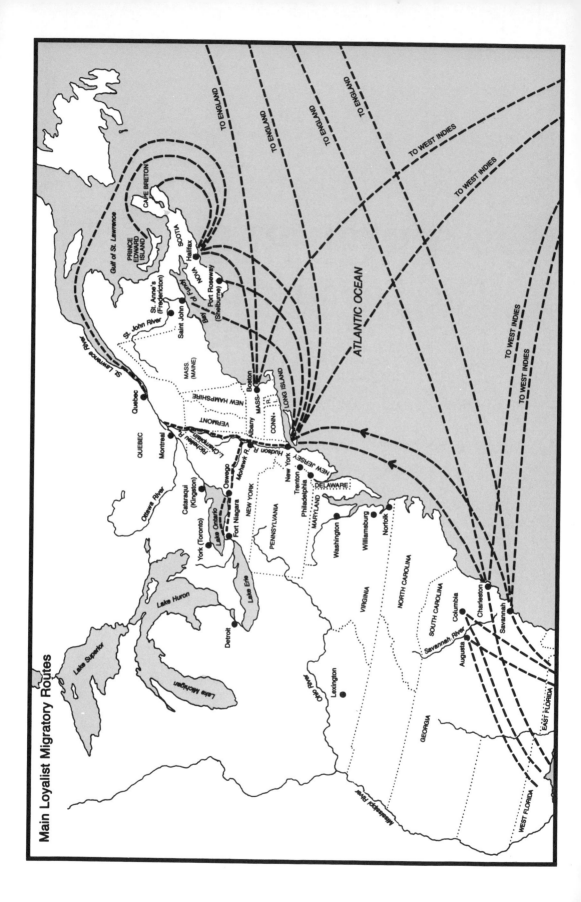

Main Loyalist Migratory Routes

Introduction

Let This Be Our Bond: To Hell With the Yankees

"Barring Catastrophe shocking to think of, this country must, to the End of time, be peopled by the Canadian Race, who have already taken such firm root, and got to so great a Height, that any new Stock transplanted will be totally hid, except in the Towns of Quebec and Montreal."

Guy Carleton,
governor in chief of North America, 1767

They poured across the border. They walked, they rowed, they sailed. They came on horseback, in carriages, in small boats and large ships. They came up the eastern seaboard, and along the rivers and through the wilderness. Many of them died along the way—of disease or despair, or as the victims of bullet and bayonet, tomahawk or bare fists. Some were rich, many were poor. A good many of them were soldiers or the families of miltary men, but there were also farmers, artisans, merchants, mariners, teachers, preachers, slaves and bums.

They were the Loyalists—tens of thousands of North Americans who were driven from their native hearths during the American Revolutionary War, because they would not embrace independence and republicanism.

Some of them were driven from their homes, tarred and feathered, publicly humiliated, ridden out of town on a rail. Some came skulking through the night, leaving property and even family behind, driven by the interdiction of a local committee of public safety. Some fled from the mob in blind panic, trailing their possessions. Some came in state, slowly, with dignity, surrounded by their belongings. Most came by ship, crowded together—men, women, children, cattle, pigs and chickens all crammed onto the decks and into the holds of His Majesty's overburdened ships.

There were Englishmen among them, and Scots and Irish, too. But there were also Hessians and Prussians, Swiss, Swedes, French, Dutch and a high proportion of people who had been born in the colonies, (as had their fathers and grandfathers), and who had begun to think of themselves, in the new term, as Americans. There were blacks, too—slaves, freed servants and former soldiers. Finally, some of the most loyal and the most suffering were Indians—the perpetrators and victims of one of the most gruesome and cruel guerrilla wars the world had known until that time.

George Washington described those who fled as "unhappy wretches! deluded mortals!" and suggested that "a great many ought to have . . . long ago committed suicide."[1] Emily Lady Tennyson described them as "A grand type of loyal, God-fearing men," and she suggested that "No country ever had such founders, no country in the world. No, not since the days of Abraham!"[2]

In truth, the Loyalists were mean and magnificent, steadfast and treacherous, law-abiding and law-breaking—just like their Patriot neighbors. The reasons for their loyalty were as varied as themselves. Some, like Thomas Hutchinson, the last royal governor of Massachusetts, were Loyalist by faith; their loyalty was as unshakable (if sometimes as uncomfortable) as belief in God Himself. Some, like Benedict Arnold, were turncoats and opportunists. Some were Loyalist by reason of geography, because their neighbors were loyal. Some became loyal by accident. John Walden Meyers, later to become the mayor of Meyers' Mill (now Belleville), came upon a group of the Sons of Liberty torturing an old man in a field, and he knew that, whatever side he was on, it was not on the side of torturers.[3]

There were a great many reluctant Loyalists whose minds were made up for them. When Joseph Brant, the Mohawk chieftain, appeared in the Mohawk Valley with a throng of painted and menacing warriors, he invited a number of settlers to go north with him or "to take their own risks."[4] Eying the circling braves, settlers discovered an affinity for George III hitherto hidden from them. There were others whose reluctance was not a matter of caution, but of politics. The missionary John Stuart, later the first rector of St. George's Church in Kingston, strenuously opposed the entire thrust of British policy from 1763 onward, but remained faithful to "the British connection."

The king was wrong, but he was still the king. For many of these people, it was only the outbreak of violence that finally stopped their streams of complaints about the stupidity, cupidity and tyranny of their British overlords. A contemporary account notes, "The word 'Rebellion' hath frozen them up, like fish in a pond."[5]

There were wealthy Loyalists, but wealth was not the determining factor; nor was education, breeding or family. Despite a persisting notion that the Loyalists represented the best and loftiest of the colonists, they were a cross-section. George Washington was as wealthy and as haughty as any Loyalist; his mother remained a Tory. She upbraided him for gallivanting off to fight for the Patriots instead of staying home to look after her and made no secret of her sympathy with the British government throughout the Revolution.[6] Benjamin Franklin was a renowned Patriot; his bastard son, William, royal governor of New Jersey, was a renowned Loyalist, and *his* bastard son, in turn, was a Patriot. When John Butler led his Rangers in a raid across the top of New York province, he fought, among others, his brother and his cousin.

The Loyalists were scattered throughout all Thirteen Colonies, but they were strongest in New York, New Jersey, Pennsylvania, the Carolinas and Georgia. They were weakest in Massachusetts and Virginia.[7] There were pockets of Loyalists in the other five states as well. But the reasons for the varying degrees of allegiance had more to do with local conditions and local personalities than with any common thread among the Loyalists.

At the time of the American Revolutionary War, the population of the Thirteen Colonies was about 2,500,000 and recent research suggests that about nineteen percent, or 500,000 were Loyalists.[8] The vast majority of these loyal people did what most people do when trouble looms—they kept their heads down and their mouths shut and waited for someone to blow the All Clear. But many of them—perhaps as many as 100,000— got out, or were kicked out. They fled home to Britain, to the West Indies or to Florida, and between 45,000 and 50,000 came to Canada, although not all were traceable through the written records of the time. (Many of them couldn't write, for one thing, and some who could never applied for aid and thus never got onto the official rolls.)[9] Nor were the blacks and Indians counted, although they probably comprised at least half as many as the official Loyalists.

More than half the Loyalists who made the lists were Scots, a large proportion were German, Irish or Scots-Irish, and only eight percent had been born in England.[10] (Again, these proportions change if the Indians and blacks are added in.) Major John Ross, who was in charge of helping Loyalists settle around Kingston, said it all when he said, "Strange is the collection of people here.[11]

Many of the Loyalists were soldiers or members of Loyalist regiments of one sort or another. At one point in the war there were 8,000 professed Loyalist soldiers under arms, compared to 9,000 in the continental army run by George Washington. But there was a lot of skulduggery and double-counting among these numbers, and the regimental lists, which should be such solid evidence, are suspect. Pay was drawn for many a soldier who never shouldered a gun.

In fact, it is not the numbers of the Loyalists, or their subdivisions by race, language or creed that count. The Loyalists were a tiny number, really. It is estimated that 700,000 have fled Cuba since the Castro Revolution, out of a population of 9,800,000.[12] But those 700,000 have disappeared into the maw of a North American population of 250 million, while the Loyalists landed, for the most part, in a land they could, and did, remake. If there were not many of them by modern count, there were a hell of a lot of them in proportion to the population on which they were dropped.

The coming of the Loyalists was the pivotal event in Canadian history—the end of our childhood, the commencement of our formation as a nation. It was the equivalent of the Norman invasion of England in 1066, but even more potent, because in much of the country, the invaders were in the majority. Today some 3.5 million Canadians are descendants of the original Loyalists.[13] But when the fleets came flooding into Nova Scotia in 1783, they decanted more Loyalists than there were existing colonists. A local population of about 20,000 in Atlantic Canada was buried in a transplanted population of 34,000. The area that is now Ontario was a wilderness almost bereft of white men, and the scattering of Indians and French traders was overwhelmed by somewhere between 7,500 and 12,000 newcomers who were fruitful, and multiplied.

If the Loyalists had anything in common as a group, it was this: For one reason or another, they were on the losing side of the Revolutionary War. Some historians have made much of the fact that Canada is a nation shaped by losers. In fact, it was shaped by losers who became winners; driven out of one country, they built another.

Or, to be more precise, they transformed another. On the eve of the Revolution, the northern half of North America consisted of two colonies—Nova Scotia and Quebec. Nova Scotia was made up of scattered outposts inhabited mainly by "neutral Yankees" who had drifted north from the New England provinces. These outposts were ruled, with careless contempt, from the muddy garrison town of Halifax. The portion of the country that counted most—Quebec—was destined (as Guy Carleton and all the wisest people knew for certain) to remain French, feudal and Catholic.

But fifteen years after the American Revolution and the influx of the Loyalists, Quebec was the contested territory of a dual people—"Two nations," as Lord Durham would later put it, "warring within the bosom of a single State"—with the dominant strain being English, Protestant and impatient. In the blink of an eye, historically speaking, Canada was transmogrified as dramatically, if not as handsomely, as a frog kissed into a prince.

Nova Scotia, the junior colony, was also transformed, although in a different way. The Loyalists brought with them not only an allegiance to the Crown and a distaste for things American; they brought as well the regrettable infection of self-government. Before long they were clamoring for more control over their own affairs. When the Loyalists came surging into Nova Scotia, there was bitter contest between the newcomers and the old office-holders. A contemporary account notes, "The old and new settlers at present struggle, and from the number of able, enterprising men in the latter class, I should think they are likely to prevail."[14] They did, too. Even the formation of three new provinces—Cape Breton, (later reabsorbed into Nova Scotia), New Brunswick and Upper Canada—could not contain the Loyalists' surging energy.

The Loyalists, quite simply, took Canada away from its original owners and rebuilt it. It was a conquest no less clear, though less bloody, than that of 1759. And, like the battle of the Plains of Abraham, it left a legacy of duality and bitterness, along with the greatness and glory.

In the sweep of history, what became crucial about the Loyalists was not their imagined superior morals and abilities, nor their much tainted British background, nor their religion, nor their training in the wicked doctrines of democracy. What proved vital was that they were anti-American by conviction and experience. The Earl of Carlisle wrote home to England from America on July 21, 1778, "The common people hate us in their hearts, notwithstanding all that is said of their secret attachment to the Mother Country. . . . In our present condition the only friends we have or are likely to have are those who are absolutely ruined for us."[15]

That was the reality of the loyal bond in the midst of the Revolution—hatred. People who have been driven from their homes, whose cattle have been mutilated, furniture smashed, daughters molested, people who have been brutalized, intimidated and robbed, do not make chummy neighbors. What the Revolutionary War did was to take many of the people who had been treated this way, lift them in a body to a neighboring country, and put them in charge of that country, with their hatred fresh and intact.

Until this time, North America north of the Spanish territories had been drifting into continental union. The attractions of continental union were so many and so manifest, that it was all but inevitable. Indeed, even during and after the Revolution, many Americans continued to be puzzled as to why it could not come about (for some, the puzzle persists to this day). They knew that many of the colonists in Quebec and Nova Scotia were as discontented as they were. They understood that the real reasons few of the northerners had joined in the attacks on British rule were, in Quebec, a fear of losing their religion and, in Nova Scotia, a fear of losing trade. It was not a spontaneous upwelling of affection that kept the northern provinces mainly loyal during the Revolution—it was the tug of special interest.

Then why, once the fighting had died down, shouldn't they all embrace the Noble Experiment? Because by then the northern provinces were in the hands of the new United States' mortal enemies, and the dream of continental union was finished. The Loyalists stood, not for England and King George, but for Unity of the Empire. Unity of the Empire stood for many things, but at heart it stood for one main conviction— To Hell with the Yanks.

A Tory poem of the time summed up the contemporary view of the United States in a fashion you will not find quoted in today's tourist brochures:

So vile a crew the world ne'er saw before,
And grant, Ye pitying Heavens, it may no more!
If ghosts from Hell infest our poisoned air
These ghosts have entered these base bodies here
Murder and blood is still their dear delight.[16]

Not, to put it another way, the kind of people you want to sign a continent-sharing deal with.

If Canada can be defined, it is as that part of northern North America which is not American. The credit for this goes to the Loyalists. The War of 1812, before which many Americans saw the conquest of Canada as "merely a matter of marching," would probably have been exactly that without the presence in Canada of the Loyalists. When Confederation finally came to Canada in 1867, it was not a continental union. It was a union of the British provinces—a union forced by the need to deal with the two major inheritances of the Loyalist influx— the duality of Canada, and the need to keep it from sliding into the American melting-pot.

Without the Loyalists, Canada would have the *Star-Spangled Banner* as its national anthem, and a president as its highest elected official.

If the coming of the Loyalists was arguably the single most important event in Canadian history, it was important in American history, too. While only a small proportion of the U.S. people became refugees, many many more were caught up in the conflict at home.

All of the colonies passed laws to deal with the traitors in their midst. They were called test acts, and they made oaths of allegiance mandatory. In many states, anyone charged with being a Tory became a non-person at law and could neither collect debts nor defend his person or his family. Tories—sometimes those merely accused of sympathy with the British— could be assaulted, insulted, blackmailed, slandered or robbed, with no remedy under the law. They could not buy land or transfer it. Particularly in smaller communities, this berserk justice meant the instant and often bloody confiscation of property from anyone who was regarded as a Tory. The lands, cattle, homes and even clothing of the victims were seized and auctioned off to the highest bidder, or in less-regulated instances they were simply taken by the mob.

Beating the Tories became a kind of blood sport—tolerated, if not encouraged, by the authorities. When General Israel Putnam saw Sons of Liberty parading Tories up and down the streets of New York on rails in 1776, he attempted to put a stop to the practice and was reprimanded by George Washington, who wrote that "To discourage such proceedings was to injure the cause of Liberty in which they were engaged, and that nobody would attempt it but an enemy to his country."[17] This was not a reign of terror comparable to that of the French Revolution, but it was—as must happen in every civil war—a time of bloody repression in the name of liberty.

Guilt by association, mob rule and lynch trial all came into flower during the treatment of the Loyalists in the United States, and while none of these was new, they acquired the sheen of nobility in those tormented years. The Ku Klux Klan and the penchant for home-brewed justice which still mark parts of the American system, had their roots in that time when patriotic fervor was joined with with blood-lust and ordinary greed. The Loyalists were not born; they were created. Their opinions, their faith and their loyalty itself were the results, not of some single, cataclysmic event that produced a particular vision of the world—with God and King George at the center—but of a whole series of disparate and often contradictory experiences that made up the American Revolutionary War.

After all, most of the Loyalists spent more of their lives in the Thirteen Colonies than they did in Canada, and all of them were shaped by their experiences before and during the Revolutionary War. That conflict was a long, bloody, civil war. It has been rendered neat and tidy by innumerable Walt Disney movies, but there was nothing neat about it. It may have lacked the scale of the Civil War, but it had that struggle's elements of bitterness and blood-feud, as well as some of the ersatz romance that was later attached to both wars.

History has dealt with the Loyalists in a skittish manner. For a time they were stalwart heroes in the eyes of every British or colonial historian, and rogues and traitors to the Americans. Then there came a kind of reversal, in which Canadian historians downgraded the Loyalists while the Americans upgraded them. Then in the period between the celebration of the American bicentennial in 1776 and the bicentennial of the Loyalist landings in Canada in 1783, a positive torrent of praise came pouring out of the presses on both sides of the border. You couldn't swing a cat without clouting some historian penning the exploits of Loyalist settlers hacking and hewing their way through the wilderness, carving out a new nation in Canada.

But the Loyalist legend, with its brave Ma, bold Pa and well-behaved kids, all dressed up to pose for a drawing by C.W. Jefferys, is not merely exaggerated. It is wrong, and misleading. The vision absorbed in history classes—the Loyalist as a tea-drinking, God-fearing, king-supporting, tree-hacking pioneer—does an injustice both to fact and to the Loyalists themselves. You will meet, in the following pages, Loyalists who do, in part, fit that vision, but you will meet far more who do not—Loyalists who were rogues, thieves, snobs, savages, slaves, proud warriors and pompous asses, as well as Loyalists who spoke little English and wouldn't have known King George if they had met him at a garden party. To understand what the Loyalists brought to Canada, why they behaved as they did once they reached this country, and what that behavior meant to every North American, it is necessary to meet them first in their homeland, and to follow them through the nearly two decades of strife that shaped them.

It is customary to meet these folks only as they step ashore from a boat in the harbor at Saint John, or stride through the forest at Niagara, or paddle up the St. Lawrence in a bateau on the way to Cataraqui or muddy York. But this truncated version of Loyalist history misses the main point about these people—the anti-Americanism that motivated many of them, as much as any attachment to God, King George or Great Britian. If we want to know what made the Loyalists tick, we have to spend some time dealing with them in the crucible of their formation—in the streets, taverns and assembly-houses of the Thirteen Colonies, and in the threatening forests and bloody fields of the revolutionary conflict.

These were not stalwart heroes who conquered a wilderness with a bible in one hand, a flag in the other and a needlework portrait of the king in their haversacks. In fact, as pioneers they had many advantages over future waves of settlers, who had none of the king's bounty that supported the Loyalists for years. I don't mean life was easy for them—indeed, for most of them it was bloody hard—but there was nothing unique about their struggle against the wilderness. What was unique about them was how they came to be in the wilderness, instead of in a warm drawing-room back home.

This, then, is a particular kind of book about that beleaguered, much studied but little understood species, and of their important and peculiar place not only in the history of Canada, but of North America. The Loyalists transformed one nation and scarred another; they fled as losers and arrived as heroes. They built, out of their own despair, a land of hope.

They were the damndest people Canada has ever seen. This is their story.

SECTION ONE
1765-1775

BLOWS MUST DECIDE

"I am not sorry that the line of conduct seems now chalked out, which the enclosed dispatches thoroughly justify; the New England governments are in a state of rebellion, blows must decide whether they are to be subject to this country or independent."

King George III,
November 18, 1774

SPECIAL NOTE

Five terms will be of particular concern during the course of this book: Whig, Tory, Patriot, Loyalist and Late Loyalist.

The word "Whig" comes from "Whiggamore," which originally meant a country bumpkin and later became attached to Scottish raiders. It was a term of derision, adopted as a term of pride (like "Yankee") and applied to more reform-minded or radical Britons when political parties began to form. The word crossed the Atlantic to the new colonies in America and was used to describe those in opposition to the royal government in those colonies.

"Tory" was the English version of the Gaelic "toraidhe," literally meaning a "pursued man." Irish bog-trotters and rascals were called "Tories." This derisive term was adopted as a badge of pride by the adherents to the government during the rise of parties in England and crossed the water with Whig. During most of the time leading up to the outbreak of hostilities between Britain and her colonies, Whig and Tory were the epithets used. But as war came rushing down, the people who had been calling themselves Whigs began to use "Patriot" instead. It had a ring to it, and Whig dropped out of American usage early in the 1770s. On the other side, "Loyalist" came to be the preferred term. It sounded better than Tory, in the first place, and in the second, it was more exact. Many of the people we now call Loyalists were not Tories at all and did not agree with most of British policy. It's just that, in the end, they were loyal, and wanted to know themselves as such. Again, as with Patriot, the name crept into the language; it was not formally adopted until the so-called "Loyalist Declaration of Independence" of November 28, 1776, but it was certainly used informally before then. In this book I have used both Loyalist and Tory in the section leading up to the War, depending on whether the context described someone then known as a government man, or what we would now recognize as a Loyalist.

"Late Loyalists" were a particular group who crossed the border into Canada after the Revolutionary War came to an end. Some were mere land-grabbers, others perfectly solid Loyalists who just happened not to get out of the new nation before it was a new nation.

1
The Mob Comes to Call

"The real authority of the government is at an end. Some of the principle ringleaders in the late riots walk the streets with impunity. No officer dares attack them, no attorney general prosecute them, no witness appear against them and no judge act upon them."

Massachusetts governor, Francis Bernard,
letter, November, 1765

It was a mystery why the mob came calling on Thomas Hutchinson, lieutenant governor of the province of Massachusetts, on that brutal night of August 26, 1765. Damn it all, he was on *their* side. Couldn't they see that? It was the Stamp Act that had them boiling through the streets of Boston. The Stamp Act seemed to be the excuse for every kind of hooliganism these days. But—and here was the point—Hutchinson was *against* the Stamp Act. Had been against it from the very start. He would make that point in court the next day, when he stood "with tears starting from his eyes." He put it in the extravagant prose of his day:

> I call my Maker to witness that I never, in New England or Old, in Great Britain or America, neither directly nor indirectly, was aiding, assisting or supporting, or in the least promoting or encouraging what is commonly called the Stamp Act, but on the contrary, did all in my power, and strove as much as in me lay, to prevent it.[1]

The sad thing is, though, that when you get a good-sized mob really rolling, it is not inclined to stand around debating the fine points. Especially once they get into the wine, as they did at Hutchinson's. They found a dozen pipes of wine in his cellar (a pipe was a measure equal to two hogsheads, or 126 wine gallons; a dozen pipes could lubricate quite a crowd), and, thus fortified, they took the place apart. Smashing down the front door as Hutchinson and his family fled the dinner table, they continued to smash everything smashable.

It was a fine house. Hutchinson had inherited it from his father, Colonel Thomas Hutchinson, who had got it from his father-in-law. It was one of the handsomest houses in the colony—a building beautifully designed (perhaps by Inigo Jones), featuring fine brick walls "adorned with Ionic pilasters."[2] Inside, the rooms were marked by wainscoting, wall hangings and fine furniture. Yet such was the fury of the mob that the furniture was destroyed, the wall hangings ripped down, the wainscoting chopped to bits. The inner walls were torn down, the library—one of the finest in the colony—scattered in the mud, and even Hutchinson's garden was torn up. The mob carried off all the family plate, along with £900 sterling. The next day money, plate and gold rings were found scattered along the streets, dropped by the more careless—or more drunken—members of the mob.

Why was Hutchinson's place attacked? He wasn't in charge. As lieutenant governor he was merely the province's administrative chief. Inquiries were instituted the next day while a crowd came to gawk at the ruins. Governor Sir Francis Bernard thought the level of savagery was due to the merging of two Boston gangs—the North End gang and the South End gang—but that didn't explain the target. Hutchinson himself thought he was the victim of an inflammatory sermon. The day before the riot, the Reverend Jonathan Mayhew, a notorious Whig, had preached on the text, "I would they were cut off which even trouble you,"[3] and Hutchinson was certainly one of the ones who troubled people. Some of the mob thought they were doing the work of God, with crowbar and ax.

Savagery Begins at Home

Although you could hardly expect Hutchinson to see it this way, the mob knew what it was doing when it decided to give the lieutenant governor the honor of having his house sacked. Bernard, the governor, was an English barrister placed in charge of Massachusetts by the patronage system of the British Empire. Hutchinson was something else again. He was a true "American," a Bostonian by birth (in 1711), a merchant by trade and a Tory by conviction. He knew the colonists, knew how the colony worked and made it work for him. The American Revolutionary War, which we must understand if we are to understand the United Empire Loyalists, was at base a civil war, not a revolution at all. As in most civil wars it reserved its worst savageries and greatest hatreds for friends, neighbors and relatives. Hutchinson qualified. Bernard hoped to retire back to England; Hutchinson expected to spend the rest of his days right here in his beloved Boston.

Hutchinson—a tall, serious, fussy man (he kept a careful account of every shilling he ever spent)—was a far greater danger to the movement for self-government now shaking the colonies than Bernard would ever be.

The Thirteen Colonies were such a damned irascible group. Indeed, cantankerousness may have been the only thing the thirteen had in common. The American colonies at this time were already clearly divided between north and south. In the north, while the farm remained the basic unit of life, urban centers were already assuming a major role. Four of the five great ports in America were in the north—Philadelphia, New York, Boston and Newport—while the south boasted one, Charleston, North Carolina. Philadelphia, the largest city, with a population of 40,000, was reckoned to be "as fine as any city on the globe," with "a market-place equal to any in Europe."[4]

New York's population was 25,000 and growing fast, while Boston, which lacked the rich hinterlands of either Philadelphia or New York, had stuck at 16,000 about the middle of the century. Newport held 11,000 people and Charleston 12,000. These were all, for their time, considerable urban areas. They were backed by such secondary towns as New Haven, Norwich, Norfolk, Baltimore and Salem—all in the north. Even in this predominantly rural country, the northern towns and cities held far more people than the huge sprawl of Quebec and Nova Scotia, and it was far more settled, with theatres, inns, universities and an intellectual life modeled on European centers. Philadelphia was larger than any English city except London, and its taverns, where news was exchanged and views broadened, were centers of sophisticated and disputatious politics.

In the south, while small freehold farms were still the rule, the great plantations held primacy in the economy, raising tobacco, indigo and rice (cotton was still a minor crop) for the European market. Slavery was vital to the south, of course, and its politics were in the hands of gentlemen like the Randolphs, Washingtons and Jeffersons of Virginia. In the north, sharp tradesmen like Benjamin Franklin and even ne'er-do-wells like Samuel Adams succeeded in elbowing their way to power.

The north's sea-bound urban centers were natural magnets for the large segment of unemployed who provided the raw material for the mobs. These mobs, often led by the outraged middle-class and ignited by politicians of whatever class, were as much a part of political life on both sides of the Atlantic as was the House of Lords or Magna Carta. Raising the mob was a political skill, and raising it while keeping control of it a greater skill—equivalent, perhaps, to today's requirement that a politician appear attractive on television. Mob rule, universally denounced, was a part of public life in the great cities throughout the British Empire. George III's biographer has written, "Every unpopular minister in the eighteenth century risked attack from the London mob. It was an occupational hazard of the trade."[5] Lord Bute, George III's parliamentary commander, wanted out of politics in 1762 because he was convinced his opponents had arranged to have him murdered by the mob. Early in 1765, the Duke of Bedford's house was assaulted, and soldiers were sent to guard him from further harm. Political life, at home or in the colonies, was lively.

Commercial life was booming, too. Directly or indirectly, commerce and shipping provided the bulk of the work of urban dwellers—as merchants, shopkeepers, artisans, mechanics, day laborers, longshoremen, sailors or fishermen. The commerce that was the cities' lifeblood was based on the English acts of trade and navigation, which conceived of all the colonies as markets for manufactured goods and sources of raw material, rather than as potential rivals for sales. Goods destined for North America, even if they came from Europe or India, had first to be transshipped to Britain and then forwarded.

In the northern colonies, what is now Canada, there were neither the large cities nor the highly developed commercial life that was the hallmark of the provinces (the colonies were properly provinces) to the south. Thus when Britain began to enforce the provisions of the acts of trade, especially in regard to smuggling, which was both common and profitable, that action bore much more harshly on the American colonies than it did on Canada.

The Thirteen Colonies had been founded under thirteen separate charters from the Crown, with thirteen different sets of rules. But by the 1760s some common ground rules had been established, and there were three main types of colony—Crown, proprietory and corporate. Pennsylvannia was a proprietory colony, held in trust by the heirs of William Penn; Massachusetts was a corporate colony, originally established as a straight business venture; the Carolinas were Crown colonies, established under the direct imprimatur of the monarch. All had become somewhat similar over the years. Eleven of them were ruled by governors appointed by the Crown (called "royal governors"). In Rhode Island and Connecticut the office was elective. All had councils appointed by the Crown (except in Massachusetts, Rhode Island and Connecticut, where election intervened). All had assemblies elected by qualified freemen. And all of them were rent by constant squabbles with the British lords of trade and plantation and the secretaries of state for colonial affairs. The British cabinet responded to these quarrels—mostly over trade rules and boundaries—by threatening to revoke charters, upon which the affected colonies would grudgingly give way.

New Rules for Old Smugglers

Hutchinson found himself saddled with the task of upholding the law under a new system of customs duties imposed to raise some of the money required for colonial defense. Beginning in April, 1764, the British Parliament passed a series of laws restructuring the trade of the colonies, which was beginning to become competitive with that of the merchants of London whose lobbies reached into Court and Parliament. That was one reason for imposing the duties. The other was that the end of the Seven Years' War in 1763 had left Britain badly in debt. Canada had been won, but only at great expense. The British thought that in the future, the colonies, who were great beneficiaries of the peace and wouldn't have to worry about the French ransacking their towns and farms any more, should pay at least part of the cost of defense.

So there were changes in the law. The first major change was in the Revenue Act, which asserted Parliament's authority to levy duties on colonial trade. Of course, it had always had such authority, but smuggling was rife and enforcement lax. (A chap named John Hancock, who would become the first signer of the Declaration of Independence and a respectable pillar of the new nation, made his fortune in smuggling.) That was all to change. The revenue collectors—nearly all of them appointees from England—were to get to work. The royal navy was to pitch in; the royal governors were to get on the ball. Old copies of the acts of trade were dusted off, and long lists of dutiable goods were drawn up to produce the cash required for colonial defense.

There was, for example, all that wine coming in from Portuguese Madeira—paid for mostly by bartering barrel staves for the wine. That had to stop. The wine was to be purchased through British shippers just as it said in the law, with duty paid. Gone was cheap wine; gone was a market for American barrel staves.

Worse was to come. In theory the colonists should have been paying a duty of a sixpence per gallon for molasses from the West Indies, which was made into rum. The duty was never collected, and colonial ships crammed with fish, lumber, naval stores and horses swarmed into the West Indies and came back laden down with molasses. Massachusetts alone imported two million gallons a year of the stuff, on which not a shilling of duty was forthcoming. The British generously decided to cut the duty in half, to threepence, and then ungenerously decided to collect it. What is more, they limited the trading area of the colonies to the British-held islands of the West Indies, apparently not knowing, or not caring, that this area could neither supply the amount required nor absorb the trade goods to pay for it. Molasses shot up in price, and scarce cash reserves disappeared to pay for the tiny quantities now available. The entire British West Indian output of molasses was about one-fifth of what the thirty distilleries around Narragansett Bay in Rhode Island required.

The colonies protested loudly, and each province established a committee of correspondence to communicate with the others and coordinate the protest. These committees swiftly became the nerve centers of defiance and seedbeds of radicalism. For example, the Massachussets assembly contended ominously that the new and renewed duties "violated the right of levying taxes conferred by Charter" on the colonial assembly itself.[6]

Thomas Hutchinson was caught right in the middle of this struggle. He was a local boy, not an appointed outsider. He was a trader—in tea, among other things—and he understood perfectly the colonial dismay over this sudden and disastrous change of policy. The sugar acts, as the new measures came to be called collectively (although the word "sugar" is barely mentioned in them, and although they were essentially changes in the Revenue Act and its regulations), were bad news for every colonial merchant.

And yet did the British Parliament or did it not have the right to impose such charges on the colonies? Hutchinson argued that it did, and he made the argument not out of false humility or self-serving sycophancy, but as the result of long study and debate. In brief, he argued, the colonies owed their very existence to Britain. They could not survive without Britain, and it was nonsense in the circumstances for them to try to place limits on what the British Parliament could do.

This was the point that turned Hutchinson and many others into Loyalists—not blind faith but close, if conservative, reasoning. Without the protection of the mother country, the colonies would quickly be gobbled up in a world of warring nation-states. It was therefore inevitable that they "should ever remain subject to the control of Britain and consequently must be bound by the determination of the supreme authority there, the British Parliament."[7]

That meant, Hutchinson acknowledged, that colonial subjects had fewer liberties than British subjects, who could not be taxed without being represented. "I doubt whether it is possible to project a system of government in which a colony 3,000 miles distant from the parent state shall enjoy all the liberties of the parent state."[8]

Supremacy Was Not Divisible

Hutchinson would not accept the argument raised by others, including his boss, Governor Bernard, that Parliament could impose customs duties but not internal taxes. This was nonsense, in Hutchinson's view. Parliamentary supremacy was not divisible. However, he was willing to accept any compromise, any subterfuge, that would meet the situation without engendering an outright breech. The important thing was to get past the present moment of danger.

It was Hutchinson's job as lieutenant governor to guide the deliberations of the colonial council and to maintain, as best he could, smooth relations with the elected assembly. The latter was no easy task, but the British government refused to budge, and the sugar acts remained in place.

The sugar acts became much less important, however, once word drifted across the ocean about the new money-raising scheme proposed by a new prime minister, George Grenville. This was the Stamp Act, about which rumors drifted through the colonies all during 1764, although the act was not actually passed until March 22, 1765. It imposed a direct tax on a wide range of legal papers, licenses and publications. The fees would be collected in the form of a stamp affixed to the paper. With the Stamp Act, gone was any metaphysical argument about internal or external taxes. This was an internal tax, plain and simple, specifically aimed—again—at raising revenue to pay defense costs by taxing the colonies. It was true that Britons were already required to buy stamps to conduct most business, but the distinction in colonial eyes was that Britons voted for the Parliament that did this to them, while the colonies did not.

Hutchinson was opposed to the Stamp Act not because it was illegal, as most of his neighbors contended, but because it was impolitic. It would unite two groups of people in opposition—the traders and merchants who had prospered under a system in which the rules were studiously ignored, and the leaders of the mobs. Hutchinson did not have a high opinion of the average colonial, who was under-educated, undernourished and underemployed. "The people," he wrote, "are absolutely without the use of reason."[9]

There he was dead wrong. The people had leaders who could reason very well—men like James Otis, leader of the radical wing in the assembly and chairman of its committee of correspondence. Otis saw the Stamp Act as another piece of the robe of tyranny being woven for the colony by Hutchinson and his friends, and he said so to the Boston town meeting and the Massachusetts assembly. Then there was Ebenezer Mackintosh, a gang leader who specialized in hanging and burning effigies and pulling down houses. The Stamp Act gave such men a perfect opportunity to lash out, and Hutchinson knew it.

Protests against the law began months before its passage, fed by the rumors flying about the colonies. In November, 1764, both houses of the Massachusetts legislature—the assembly and the legislative council—convened to draw up a petition against the proposed act, and the assembly put its case in high-blown language. Under Hutchinson's direction the council rejected the draft, so a joint committee—of which Hutchinson got himself appointed chairman—was drawn up to prepare a compromise. In meeting after meeting, through draft after draft, the assembly leaders demanded that the great principles of liberty and justice should be addressed, and the theory of government set down. Hutchinson would have none of this and kept them at it until, worn down, they finally agreed to a version which, while protesting the act, assumed that colonial control over taxation was a favor granted by Parliament, not an intrinsic right. Hutchinson was pleased.

But not for long. Reports from the other colonies began to pour in. Their petitions against the act, full of ringing phrases and high principles, made the Massachusetts assemblymen feel like pretty small cheese. Even Nova Scotia, that northern and hitherto silent colony, showed its outrage. The *Halifax Gazette*, a semiofficial journal, erupted in protest against the imposition of taxation without representation. The printer was discharged, which silenced him but not the protests, and when the act became law and stamp masters were appointed, the Halifax stamp master was hanged in effigy.[10] On another gallows the Haligonians strung an old boot, representing local sentiment toward Lord Bute, the king's closest adviser.

A Sense of Betrayal

If remote Nova Scotia could react with fire in its belly, the Massachusetts assembly felt it had been betrayed in going along with Hutchinson's mild prose. That sense of betrayal grew more pronounced when word reached the colonies not only that the act had been passed, which was bad enough, but that every colonial petition had been rejected out of hand. Politeness hadn't done Massachusetts any good. Indeed, it could be argued that by destroying the unanimity of rage embodied in the other colonial petitions, Massachusetts had undermined the other colonies.

From this it was a short step to assume that Hutchinson had acted with incredible cunning. By opposing the Stamp Act he had promoted it—which was said to be his secret wish—because his ostensible opposition persuaded the legislature to accept a moderate stance and avoid the argument of principle embraced by every other colony. Ergo, Hutchinson was a traitor to his country. When it was announced that the stamp master for Massachusetts was to be the colonial secretary, Andrew Oliver, who just happened to be Hutchinson's brother-in-law and protégé, the fat was truly in the fire.

Before long, James Otis was galvanizing public meetings with a claim that the Stamp Act had been dreamed up by Hutchinson and Governor Bernard, and that he, Otis, could point to the very house, nay, the very room, where the plot had been hatched. Hutchinson protested in vain. On the night of August 13, 1765, a mob ransacked Andrew Oliver's stamp office and attacked his house. The next night the same or another mob turned up at Hutchinson's place and demanded that he swear that he had never written to England in favor of the act. Hutchinson refused. Surely, he said, he was "not obliged to give an answer to all the questions that may be put to me by every lawless person."[11] Fortunately, an elderly bystander intervened and persuaded the crowd that Hutchinson was not the sort of man to do anything deliberately to hurt his country. The mob moved off sullenly and slowly.

Twelve days later it was back for the ransacking described at the beginning of this chapter. The mob was in the capable hands of Will Moore, the Patriot agitator who eschewed debate and got straight to work with ax and crowbar in what Hutchinson called, with pardonable exaggeration, "the most barbarous outrage which was ever committed in North America."[12]

Well, it was barbarous and it was an outrage, but it was not, as Hutchinson seemed to think, an insane frenzy. In the Massachusetts of his time, Hutchinson was a danger to the emerging political power—not so much because of his position, as because of his roots and his philosophy.

Governor Bernard wrote of the attack on Hutchinson: "This destroying all peace and order in the community—all will feel its effects. And I hope all will see how easily the people may be deluded, enflammed and carried away with madness against an innocent man. I pray GOD give us better hearts."[13]

Fine sentiments to be sure, but from the point of view of the majority of Hutchinson's fellow colonialists, he was hardly an innocent man. Even if he hadn't plotted against the colonies on behalf of Parliament—and most people believed he had—he had never made any secret of where his sympathies lay in any quarrel between Britain and America. They lay with Britain. The notion of independence was a long way off when the mob called on Thomas Hutchinson in 1765, but, instinctively, people were choosing up sides for the conflict to come. Instinctively, Hutchinson had chosen the side of a nation that was never his own—Great Britain. In the decade before such a name had even been coined, he was a Loyalist. In the decade ahead, that would become an inconvenient, and even dangerous, thing to be.

2
Heating Up the Tar

"The people seem to me to be in a state of absolute dementation."

Thomas Hutchinson,
letter, November, 1768

On the morning of September 7, 1768, between the hours of ten and eleven, an angry crowd swarmed onto the wharf at Salem, Massachusetts, and seized a customs official—called a waiter. His crime was that he had notified the authorities that a local merchant had hidden goods on board a ship to avoid paying the newly required customs duties. His punishment—there was no trial—was swift and painful. He was hustled off to Salem Common where, as the *Salem Gazette* reported, "His Head, Body and Limbs were covered with warm Tar, and then a large quantity of Feathers were applied to all Parts." After which he was paraded through the town on the front of a cart, bearing placards marked with the word "Informer" on his chest and back—a sight that drew from the crowd "Huzzahs and loud Acclamations."[1]

In point of fact, it was not tar that was normally used to tar and feather those on whom the mob had chosen to visit its displeasure. It was pine pitch. Both tar and pitch come from the pine tree, but the pitch is slightly more refined and even stickier than tar.

What happened, usually, was this. A mob would work itself up into a good rage at the feet of an orator—often one of the Sons of Liberty, as they came to be called (members of local, secret groups that sprang into being after the passage of the Stamp Act to organize resistance). The mob would then take after some Tory. He would be stripped, manhandled and then firmly held while the pitch was heated in a pot over an open fire before his eyes. This increased the natural terror the victim felt. Then the pitch, hot enough to flow and therefore almost boiling, would be lifted in a large ladle and poured over him, blistering the skin, smoldering the hair, sometimes blinding him. Large quantities of the scalding stuff were poured over his back, across his stomach and legs, sometimes on his private parts, while he was held screaming against the pain. Then he would be smeared with goose feathers gathered for the occasion or, if none were available, with ashes, and then placarded and paraded. Sometimes he was mounted on a cart, like the Salem customhouse waiter, but sometimes a rail from a fence was used, which could emasculate him. Throughout, he would be insulted, cuffed and spat upon by the crowd. If the ordeal did not kill him, he was left with the task of getting the pitch off. Skin often came off with the pitch, and infection was only to be expected.

It Was a Violent Age

The mere threat of this treatment was usually enough to make a Tory see the error of his ways. In the decade between the smashing of Thomas Hutchinson's house on August 26, 1765, and the outbreak of warfare on Lexington Common on April 18, 1775, tarring and feathering, threats, hanging in effigy, beatings, public denouncements, horse whippings and other expressions of disapproval became more and more frequent. It was, after all, a violent age, and there was not much of a police force to interfere. Until shortly before the Revolution, what policing there was fell to the lot of volunteer watchmen who walked the town at night with lanterns and bellowed a neighborly "All's well" at intervals. With the increasing urbanization had come some measures to hire regular constables, although they were not trained, and there were few of them. When anything went seriously wrong, the proper thing for a governor to do was to call out the military, but that could not be done when the major mobs of the 1770s began to roam the streets looking for trouble. There were not enough soldiers to quell a riot, and their presence was likely to provoke one. So the easiest and commonest course was to do nothing. Intimidation was much deplored but much practiced both on the Tories and by them, although tarring and feathering seems to have been exclusive to the Patriots, who controlled the mobs.

Looking back with the advantage of hindsight, the Revolution and its success seem natural and inevitable. But in considering the fortunes of the Loyalists, it is important to keep in mind that the notion of independence was not even formally introduced into the debate until late in 1774. At the first Continental Congress in October, 1774, when violent conflict seemed a certainty, the Patriots were demanding not separation from Britain, but "British liberties," and chorusing, "Independence— a hundred times No."[2] The turmoil in the time leading up to the outbreak of armed rebellion seemed part of a pattern of lawlessness, coercion and mob rule, which would all be straightened out in time when both sides came to their senses.

The problem for the "Friends of the King"—as some liked to call themselves before the term Loyalist came into vogue—was that the British policy that they were asked to support was, not to put too fine a point on it, a damned stupid policy.

Essentially, that policy was based on two contradictory notions. The first was that the colonies were too dependent; the second that they were too independent. In the one case, they needed to be made to stand on their own two feet; in the second, they needed to be brought to heel. This contradiction was perfectly enshrined in the proposal to maintain a standing army in the colonies, with the expenses to be met at first by the British taxpayer, but then transferred to the American taxpayer. The parliamentary opposition raised no objection when this proposal was first set down in 1763 at the end of the Seven Years' War. Former prime minister William Pitt, a staunch friend of the colonies, only worried that the 10,000 troops to be stationed in America might not be enough.[3] What if the French went to war again, he wondered.

The Americans, even many Americans who were heart and soul with the British government in most of its actions, saw this proposal in quite another light. A standing army in their midst, eating its head off at their expense, did not strike them as anything but a threat. The French had been defeated and driven from North America. Against whom then were the troops to be used? It could only be against themselves. The troops were not so much a standing army as a standing threat. As the colonists pressed this point, the British grew more insistent. The colonies' refusal to accept the troops proved the need for the army. The prophecy fulfilled itself.

All of the arguments returned to the same spot, to the unshakable fact that the colonies were the creation of the British Parliament, therefore both dependent upon it and, if they were wise, subservient to it. The taxes that were being levied were being put in place—as speaker after speaker rose in Westminster to point out—for the good of the colonists themselves, to help pay one small part of the necessary costs of their defense. Samuel Johnson put it crisply: "He that accepts protection, stipulates obedience. We have always protected the Americans; we may, therefore, subject them to government."[4]

This Fierce People

That was not how things seemed in the colonies themselves. There the British connection meant that the citizens of North Carolina or Virginia or Massachusetts had the rights of any Briton anywhere. Much was made of the glory of belonging to the British race, and, leaving out the inevitable racism and snobbery, there were some grounds for self-congratulation. In the colonial mind any diminution of American liberties was an attack on British liberties, and was to be rejected not on selfish local grounds, but on behalf of Britain itself. Britons could not be taxed except with their own consent. It followed that British subjects in the colonies could not be so taxed, or liberty itself was threatened. You couldn't station troops in the homes of the citizens of London and hand them the bill; so you couldn't station them in Boston or New York or Philadelphia. The colonists, as Edmund Burke put it, "Are not only devoted to liberty, but liberty according to English ideas and on English principles. . . . We cannot, I fear, falsify the pedigree of this fierce people, and persuade them that they are not sprung from a nation in whose veins the blood of freedom circulates."[5]

Thus, right up until the eve of war, both sides in the struggle claimed to be representing not merely Truth and Right—such is the staple of every war—but British Truth and British Right. The colonists saw themselves as warriors for everything good and fine, trying to appeal against a corrupt Parliament to the king. In vain, of course. George III, a conscientious monarch, accepted the best advice of his senior advisers, as he was bound under the constitution to do. It took some time for the colonists to realize this, and the "Glorious George" of their dinner toasts only gradually became "the sullen-tempered Pharoah" of Tom Paine's incendiary pamphlet, *Common Sense*.

Misunderstanding was the order of the day. No one in Britain seemed to think it might be a good idea to consult the colonies about a proposed military establishment. Why confer with local assemblies about something so clearly within the ambit of Parliament itself? The supremacy of Parliament was not something to be debated; it was the underpinning of the nation. Even Edmund Burke, the colonists' champion, assumed that Parliament "as from the throne of Heaven, superintends all the several inferior legislatures, and guides and controls them all."[6]

Was War Inevitable?

It is comfortable today to assume that the Revoluntary War was inevitable because it happened. The colonies had grown up. Therefore they would part from the mother country. Since the only way to do that was by bloody war, well, unhappily, bloody war was the consequence of maturity. In this approach to history, the Loyalists are accidental misfits who got caught on the wrong side of the line when war broke out. But surely it is possible to look at the Revolution another way. Britain in the middle of the eighteenth century was in the hands of a succession of particularly narrow and self-satisfied men at the center of a political system that had grown insensitive and corrupt.

George III, rather than being the oppressor the colonies came to despise, was the victim of a lot of bad advice. Because he was a vigorous king (when not in one of his fits of depression) he became the fountainhead of a policy that was inept and, as it turned out, inapplicable. Perhaps it was inevitable that once Parliament was defied in America, neither side could back off, and war had to follow. But it was far from inevitable that such a stalemate had to come. The Loyalists were not stupid or ill-informed or cowardly. A great many of them believed right up until 1776 that reason would come to prevail, and that the colonies would work out their relationships with Britain over time, with goodwill on both sides.

Was the war inevitable? It seems to me that it was not—that peaceable independence over time was as feasible for the Americans as it later became for Canadians. What brought on the bloodshed was a series of miscalculations on both sides (but surely more blame attaches to the British, who were in a position to know better) that produced a stalemate from which armed conflict was the only possible escape.

The Stamp Act was one such miscalculation. It was a chip knocked off the colonies' shoulder, and it quickly beame clear that the act could not be enforced. It was not only in Boston that the mobs broke out. The mob that attacked the stamp master in Charleston, South Carolina, contained—thinly disguised—friends and relatives of that worthy himself. In New

York, the rabble laid siege to the royal artillery garrison, holed up at the battery, burned the official coach of the lieutenant governor, Cadwallader Colden, and wrecked the home of the commander of the New York troops.[7] Men, who a few months earlier had begged for the lucrative post of stamp master, now begged to be excused. The sounds of dropped portfolios echoed across the colonies with a series of dull thuds.

In Williamsburg, Virginia, inspired by the windy rhetoric of Patrick Henry (who would later bellow, "Give me liberty or give me death," and much, much later, die peaceably in his bed) the elected house of burgesses, whose members included George Washington, engaged in a lively debate on the Stamp Act. The members agreed that "only Virginians had the right to tax Virginians," but they far from agreed on the language in which their protest should be embodied. Some were for the moderate approach, others for strident defiance. In the end the moderates won, and most of the inflammatory language that called on Virginians to "resist the yoke of tyranny" was pruned from the series of resolutions that passed the assembly.

However, even in their softened form, the Virginia Resolves proved too much for Joseph Royle, the Loyalist editor of the Virginia *Gazette*, which carried the official reports of debates in the House. Royle cut out not only the intemperate language that accompanied the debates, but the substance of the resolves. That was a blunder. The tough-tongued element promptly reproduced the colonial arguments in their original strident form and circulated every outrageous paragraph uttered in the house, as if all had been part of the finally approved action. The Newport *Mercury* published this version and the Rhode Island assembly passed, almost word for word, the resolves as, so it thought, the Virginians had worded them. Patrick Henry's unquestionably treasonable speech ("Caesar had his Brutus, Charles I his Cromwell, and George III—may profit by their example")[8] thus made it into the public realm.

The upshot was to stiffen the spines of other colonial assemblies, and that led to a call by the great and general court of Massachusetts for a congress of all the colonies to meet in New York in October, 1765. This meeting of the Stamp Act congress was attended by delegates from nine of the thirteen colonies (New York, New Jersey, Rhode Island, Massachusetts, Pennsylvania, Delaware, Maryland, South Carolina and Connecticut). Emboldened by delegate Christopher Gadsden's shouted claim that "There ought to be no more New England men, no New Yorkers, but all of us Americans!"[9] the delegates drew up a declaration of rights and grievances, which was duly dispatched to England, and duly denounced. The language of the declaration was unremarkable, even conciliatory, as it made the now-familiar argument that freeborn Englishmen could not be taxed without their consent. Therefore, any tax imposed on the colonies without prior approval was unconstitutional.

The Boycott Begins

There was a sting in the tail of the declaration of rights and grievances, as the delegates proposed a series of boycotts of British goods if their grievances were not redressed. At this point most people on both sides of the argument still thought a compromise could be worked out. It was not to be.

The Stamp Act, the British government declared, was law and as such must be obeyed. But that was not possible, not with mobs waiting with feathers, pitch and placards for anyone foolish enough to apply for the post of stamp master. Because almost nothing could be done legally without one of the stamped papers—which covered everything from birth certificates to ships' manifestos—commercial and social life threatened to grind to a halt. Then the colonists, acting on the proposal of the Stamp Act congress, began to set the wheels in motion to cease the importation of all British goods. Since the British had dealt themselves a monopoly on most manufactured products and made it illegal for the colonists to compete against them, this threatened a large and lucrative trade. Everything—from china to fine linens, tea to fine tools—was imported at monopoly prices. Britain could withstand the blow, of course (the colonies only represented a small portion of her trade), but those hurt would include a number of influential London merchants and many of the king's friends in the colonies, who had been given import licenses as reward for their loyalty.

A campaign of pressure—we would call it a business lobby—descended on yet another of Britain's fragile governments, a new ministry led by Lord Rockingham. In the spring of 1766 the Stamp Act was repealed. Then, in one of those acts of high principle and low intelligence for which Parliament was then notable, the Declaratory Act was passed. This stated that while Parliament was withdrawing the Stamp Act, it had an inalienable right to make laws binding on the American colonies, "in all cases whatsoever."[10]

In theory, the new act made perfect sense. It embodied the arguments that set forth the supremacy of Parliament. In fact, it was Parliament's inability to enforce its will, not its right, that came to be at issue. The mobs would not allow the taxes to be collected, so the Declaratory Act, which was supposed to be a face-saver, became merely a provocation. It blew up in Parliament's face, as it was bound to do. The goodwill that might have been won by withdrawal of the Stamp Act was undone and outweighed by the rage that broke along the co-lonial coast as it became clear that that act, or any other, might be reimposed at any time, and all the weary work to do again. The Declaratory Act was passed on March 18, 1766, but while the furore was still erupting over that, another battle broke out.

The Mutiny Act

In New York, a new governor, Sir Henry Moore, dredged up an old statute called the Mutiny Act, under which the colony could be required to pay for the stationing of troops. Moore presented a bill to the assembly. It was not well received. While it was undoubtedly a correct legal claim, it opened the possibility that the amount demanded could be increased year by year, giving Britain indirectly the access to colonial money it could not gain directly. The assembly simply ignored Moore's demand. In turn, the assembly was suspended until the money was forthcoming. But the colonials outsmarted Mother Parliament. The assembly voted the required supply of money for the troops, but worded the grant so that it appeared to come spontaneously from itself, rather than as the grudging outcome of a British demand. News of this coup spread gleefully up and down the coast, but it proved a temporary and hollow victory.

In England, Charles Townshend, the brilliant, erratic chan-cellor of the exchequer, had seized on the argument that had been advanced by some of the colonists when they thought they were contending with an internal tax. Townshend claimed that while it was wrong for Britain to impose internal levies, it was proper to establish duties on goods imported to the col-onies. He placed such charges on glass, lead, paint, paper and tea. Parliament passed them and, on June 29, 1767, the king signed into law a new Revenue Act which, in addition to es-tablishing these duties, provided for the direct payment of royal officials from the money raised.

You could hardly blame the British government for wanting to remove its officials from the control the colonies were able to exercise by shortening or cutting the purse-strings of officials. But the move was seen, inevitably, as yet another attempt to impose control on the colonies without consent.

Not surprisingly, the Townshend levies were given exactly the same reception as the stamp and sugar acts. The duties were avoided, and a boycott of British goods began. A board of commissioners of customs was created to enforce the new laws, and a fleet of cutters was sent out to catch smugglers. Each captain was commissioned as a customhouse official, and the admiral became, in effect, a revenue officer. Large rewards, to be paid out of the seized goods, were offered to the crews, and some captains went so far as to buy small vessels on their own, which they disguised and sent into coastal waters to collect evidence and make seizures. They had little success. Mounting such an impressive operation to catch smugglers, the colonists said, was "like burning a barn to roast an egg."[11]

Even if a smuggler were captured, no American jury would convict. That was why it had long been the custom to try all smuggling and revenue cases before an admiralty court, without a jury. Of course, in such courts the scales were weighted the other way, with the chances of acquittal low indeed. Besides, this system, which seemed so sensible to an increasingly frustrated administration in England, deprived the colonies of one of British law's proudest privileges—the right to trial by jury. The officers of the courts were paid out of the fines. So were informers and, in some cases, the colonial governor received part of the takings, too, "for the sake of encouraging them to greater diligence in executing the laws."[12] This was not, in brief, the kind of system that the British would have allowed to be imposed at home, but it seemed all right, in view of the fractious behavior of the colonies, to impose it in America. When smuggling regulations had been ignored, this point of principle had not mattered much to the colonists. But now the rules were to be enforced, and the tea hit the fan.

The board of commissioners of customs was headquartered in Boston, in part because it was a center of the smuggling trade, and in part because, in the words of one nineteenth-century historian, the people of Boston "seemed to be naturally riotous."[13] They certainly showed a penchant that way. When the sloop *Liberty*, owned by John Hancock, was seized for smuggling, the Boston mob rescued the vessel and smashed the windows of the houses of the customs officials, who fled, ignominiously, to the safety of the British man-of-war *Romney*.[14] In an English admiralty court, Hancock was fined £100,000 for smuggling , but he launched a counter-suit in Boston. His case dragged on until 1769, when all charges against him were dropped.

The Patriots reacted to every attempt to enforce the Townshend duties with fury—the kind of fury that springs from a combination of self-interest and strongly held opinion. They vented their rage on customs officers, like the poor wretch described at the beginning of this chapter, and on Loyalists. The Loyalists were in an increasingly difficult position. Most of them were in disagreement with the measures adopted by the British government, and many shared the contempt felt by their neighbors towards the corrupt English Parliament and, increasingly, toward the king himself.

"After all, he is the king," may make an acceptable political argument, but it is hardly a rallying cry. As the Loyalists were called upon to defend the quartering of troops, the new customs duties, the writs of assistance used by officers (which became virtual *cartes blanches* to search and seize), the arbitrariness of the admiralty courts, the arrogance—not to say dim-wittedness—of some of the colonial officials, they were increasingly on the defensive. Who wanted to sing the praises of Charles Townshend or of Lord North, when he became prime minister?

Increasingly, people were being asked to choose up sides, and, while it might be easy enough to plump for king and Parliament if you lived within shouting range of the barracks off Boston Common, it was not so easy for a Loyalist in, say, Elizabethtown, North Carolina, surrounded by Patriots. A patriot, invited to dinner in the home of a Loyalist, was asked to join in a toast to King George. He could hardly refuse, but, to indicate his true feelings, rose as soon as that toast was finished to propose a toast to "the Devil himself." There was an awkward pause while the Loyalist wondered what to do. Then his wife chimed in, "Dear, he drank a toast to your friend. You can do nothing less than to drink to his."

The business of choosing sides was aided by the newspapers that poured out of every city and town and combined great energy with strong views. At a time when there were few popular entertainments and time to kill, the impact of a letter of musings in a local newspaper was astonishing. In late 1767, the Pennsylvania *Chronicle* began to carry the essays of John Dickinson, a Philadelphia barrister and graduate of Middle Temple in London. The essays were grandly entitled, *Letters From A Farmer In Pennsylvania To The Inhabitants Of The British Colonies*. "Farmer John," as Dickinson signed himself, was in fact a member of the Pennsylvania assembly. He was a conservative and a Quaker and had tangled with Benjamin Franklin in an earlier battle over the rights of Pennsylvania's proprietors, which Franklin had attacked and Dickinson defended. In his letters Dickinson set forth the colonial position from a conservative view, supporting the right and duty of the colonies to boycott British goods until the Townshend duties were withdrawn. He argued that if the assembly of New York could be suspended by British Parliament, so could any legislature. His letters—there were twelve of them between December 2, 1767, and February 15, 1768—made Dickinson an instant hero. They were quickly copied in other colonial papers, reprinted as pamphlets in America and England, and translated in France. Dickinson was toasted by town meetings and grand juries and was viewed with alarm by those in authority as "calculated to excite the passions of the unthinking."[15]

Dickinson's arguments were pushed a good deal farther by Samuel Adams, that peculiar, passionate propagandist who failed as a businessman but succeeded brilliantly as a pamphleteer. Adams had in mind not merely the removal of duties from colonial imports, but the establishment of a new nation—a republic—in America, although that did not become clear until later. What was clear from the start was that he had the knack of putting the case against Britain in clear, understandable prose that rang in the hearts of aggrieved Americans like a tolling bell. ("Let us remember that if we suffer tamely a lawless attack upon our liberty, we encourage it, and involve others in our doom.")

Adams was the moving force behind the Massachusetts circular letter sent to the other twelve colonies in February, 1768. The letter denounced the Townshend duties, rejected the notion that colonial officials could be independent of the local legislatures and requested joint action by all the colonies. When news of the letter reached England, it arrived on the desk of Lord Hillsborough, who had replaced Townshend. (One of the many problems of this era was that the vagaries of British political life, which returned a new government about once a year, robbed policy of any consistency except, apparently, a determination sooner or later to establish Parliament's authority.) Hillsborough reacted with fury. Massachusetts was conspiring to promote "unjustifiable opposition to the constitutional authority of Parliament,"[16] and the assembly of that rash province was dissolved forthwith. It would remain dissolved until it repented its rash action. What is more, instructions went to the governors of all the other colonies to order their legislatures to ignore the letter, on pain of instant dissolution.

It is hard to imagine that Hillsborough could have done any-thing more likely to set the colonies on the boil. As assembly after assembly roared its approval of the Massachusetts letter, they were slammed shut, making a true prophet out of John Dickinson. It began to appear that armed resistance was the only course and, from Virginia, George Washington, a landed gentleman who had fought in the British army against the French, wrote that he was willing to take up arms to defend his native land.

It was in the midst of this agitation that a flotilla of British ships floated into Boston harbor in September, 1768, and troops began pouring ashore. They were to be quartered in the city, but Boston officials announced that there were no quarters available. Only one of the three regiments even possessed tents, so the troops forced entry into Faneuil Hall, the Boston town meeting hall, and even into the state house itself.

As tension grew, it was inevitable that those who sided with the British would find themselves under attack and, in the name of freedom and liberty, silenced. John Mein was the owner of a bookshop (the first circulating library in America) and a Bos-ton newspaper, the *Chronicle*. Mein remained carefully neutral until 1768 and then began increasingly to take the side of the royal government. He was warned pointblank by Samuel Ad-ams to halt "this opposition to an awakened, an enlightened, and determined continent,"[17] but he refused to be silenced. The *Chronicle* urged local merchants to break the trade boycott. The newspaper office was picketed; Mein was attacked on the street, but he escaped. His windows were shattered. He stood firm. And then one day the mob seized a man accused of in-forming on a smuggler. He was tarred and paraded through the town to the offices of the *Chronicle*, where he was held on display for Mein's benefit. Then Mein was presented with a blob of cold tar and a bundle of feathers. He was on the next ship out of Boston.

But there were others less movable than Mein who remained behind to face the mounting fury that would culminate in the Boston Massacre, the Tea Party and the outbreak of war.

3
The Rocky Road to Lexington

"It is difficult to know whether either party is in the right . . . I wish we had let alone strife before it was meddled with and followed things that make for peace."

Ben Franklin's sister, Jane Mecom,
letter, November, 1768

The British troops who marched ashore in Boston on a cool morning in late 1768 came in response to descriptions of impending chaos in the dispatches of the royal governor of Massachusetts, Sir Francis Bernard, and his lieutenant, Thomas Hutchinson. Illegality was becoming a way of life. Not only were the new customs laws flouted; so, apparently, was every other law. In August the Boston mob had celebrated the anniversary of the sacking of the home of Hutchinson's son-in-law, Andrew Oliver, the stamp officer. Prominent among the revelers was Will Moore, the man who had led the attack on Hutchinson's own home, and whose jail sentence for that effort had been remitted by a group of the Sons of Liberty who had broken into the prison to set him free.

"Government must be aided from without," Hutchinson wrote, "or else it must subside and suffer anarchy to rise in its place."[1] It was a familiar-enough dilemma. Should the government crack down on the dissidents or hope to win them over by moderation? In the end the policy followed was the worst possible—alternate bouts of harshness and weakness, bold talk and limited action. This confused the Loyalists and convinced the Patriots that they were on the right track.

Governor Bernard had tried to prepare the way for the arrival of two regiments in Boston by leaking the word that they were coming. He feared an immediate insurrection if they appeared

unannounced. In response, the radical leaders kept Boston in a
state of turmoil with protest meetings and denunciations, and
the Boston town meeting issued a (premature) call to arms.
When the troops arrived, conditions worsened for most Bostonians, although Hutchinson reported that he, for one, slept
better.[2]

The troops could extend no protection to those who were
increasingly harassed by their Patriot neighbors. Indeed, it was
all the soldiers could do to defend themselves. They were poorly
paid and underfed. Some of them were persuaded to desert,
while others were hired out for minimum wages to do menial
labor, which merely added to the rage of the average townsman
in an economy where unemployment was chronic. The locals
discovered that they could taunt the soldiers with impunity.
In return, the troops challenged Bostonians on the streets, forc-
ing them to identify themselves at numerous checkpoints, or
held impromptu band practices outside the Boston churches,
tootling their flutes and banging their drums through the ser-
monizing.

Who's Cowering?

The newly founded radical paper *Journal of the Times* painted
a picture of a city cowering in terror beneath a military dictatorship. In fact, it was as often as not the troops who did the
cowering. They were not, after all, the most prepossessing soldiers. Their ranks were jammed with the scourings of the London slums and city jails, and it must have puzzled some of
them to know that they were regarded as professional machines
of destruction. Yet to the Patriots they were just that.

With characteristic vigor, Samuel Adams got across the message that the real purpose of the troops was to establish a mil-
itary-backed autocracy with Thomas Hutchinson and his friends
at its head and to throttle liberty in Massachusetts once and
for all. Hutchinson dismissed the charges as "ravings,"[3] but
they did not seem that way to some people. So, those who
insisted on loyalty to the king, despite misgivings about his
policies (for a while they were called "royalists," but the term
didn't stick), found themselves labeled as the defenders of a
military dictatorship. Not that they were able to do much defending, at least in public. Newspapers that took the government line were rigorously suppressed throughout the colonies.
Joseph Royle, the editor of the Virginia *Gazette*, who had kept
all mention of the Virginia Resolves out of his paper, was re-

moved, and the paper taken over by a group of the Sons of Liberty.[4] Others like the unfortunate John Mein were driven right out of America. The Patriot press had the field pretty well to itself, and it made the most of its opportunities with a series of solemn warnings and a disregard for fact that kept America in turmoil. Throughout the autumn of 1768, while the colonies seethed, the Patriots gathered their forces. The Loyalists wondered what would happen next.

Then came 1769 and, in Parliament, the declaration that the colonies were "in a state of disobedience" (which was putting in mildly), followed by instructions to the governor of Massachusetts to obtain "the fullest information touching all treason or misprision of treason within his government."[5] The suspects were to be shipped off to England for trial. The man called on to carry out Parliament's wishes was Thomas Hutchinson; Sir Francis Bernard was gone. In April, letters Bernard had written to the secretary of state had come to light. They described conditions in Massachusetts and urged a change in the constitution to replace the elected assembly with an appointed body and to conduct a loyalty screening of all officials. The letters were exactly what the radicals feared—or hoped for—and Bernard's position became untenable. He was charged by the house with willful misrepresentation, character assassination and a lust for "exorbitant and uncontrollable power."[6] Samuel Adams got out a pamphlet in which he described Bernard's version of impending insurrection in the colony as "slanderous chit chat."[7] Bernard resigned, and Hutchinson took over.

Hutchinson inherited an impossible situation. Less than a month after he assumed office, a mob seized a sailor accused—falsely, as it turned out—of having informed on smugglers. The boys tarred and feathered him anyway and dragged him through the town, threatening along the way to smash every window in any house that did not display some symbol of support for the Patriot cause. Hutchinson asked his council—who alone had the power—to call out the troops. The council refused. Nor would the justices of the peace act. In the end the troops were worse than useless. You couldn't call out a regiment to patrol the streets if, when a riot broke out, there were not enough of them to put it down.[8]

Matters were moving to a climax elsewhere as well. In the spring session of the Virginia house of burgesses, Colonel George Washington had delivered a resounding attack on the ministry in England. He predicted, quite correctly, that Parliament would resurrect a two-hundred-year-old statute to bring dissidents to England to face trial. This was serious. Many of the men present

when Washington spoke knew they would be on any list of
troublemakers.

The house embodied Washington's complaint in a resolution.
In response Lord Botetourt, the royal governor, dissolved it.[9]
Members of the assembly straggled out to a meeting in the
Raleigh Tavern on Williamsburg's main street. Out of this and
subsequent meetings came a firm resolve to join Massachusetts
in a strict non-importation agreement. The new boycott was
to be more comprehensive than earlier ones, such as the Massachusetts informal boycott in 1764. It would embrace every
colony (as each assembly passed the required law) and last for
a year, unless Parliament gave in earlier. Word quickly spread
through the committees of correspondence. Soon every colony
but two—Pennsylvania and new Hampshire—had joined in.

These agreements were hard on everyone, but they were particularly hard on known Loyalists. After all, smuggling was a
way of life in the colonies, and much of what went on was
undetected. But the wharves and stores of known Loyalists were
subject to intense scrutiny, and, where British goods were found,
they were confiscated or destroyed. Sometimes the guilty Loyalist—who was merely acting within the law as he knew it—
was tarred and feathered.

One of the victims of the non-importation agreement was
Thomas Hutchinson. He was a silent partner in a trading business operated by his two sons. The business was not doing well
because the mob had forced the young men to deposit all of
their goods of English origin with a committee of Patriot merchants for the duration of the boycott agreement. When that
original agreement ended, the sons said they were going back
into business. A mob marched on their store, and a delegation
demanded that the governor order his sons to stop trying to
trade. He did, and they did.

Hillsborough Paint

Hutchinson's sons were luckier than Hutchinson's nephew,
Nathaniel Rogers, another Loyalist trader who opposed the
Townshend duties but resisted the importation ban. The Sons
of Liberty called on him, threatened him, smeared his house
with "Hillsborough paint"—a mixture of urine and human
feces—and dumped tubs of "ordure" on his doorstep. Soldiers
were stationed in his home but there was little they could do,
and he fled to New York. The committees of correspondence
went to work, and Sons of Liberty called on Rogers in New

York, where he was obliged to flee his house in the middle of the night. Finally he decided to mend his ways and forsake the royal cause, but before he could make his intentions known, he suffered a fatal seizure, although he was still a young man.[10]

Ironically, the treason trials Washington had warned of—and Parliament ordered—never came about. If Hutchinson was in no position to reestablish order in Massachusetts, neither were governors in other colonies. In North Carolina lawlessness had reached such a state that a group of men who called themselves "regulators" sprang up to enforce a form of rough justice. They rounded up the bands of roving robbers who were making life a misery and in some cases simply lynched them. Gradually, however, the regulators became allied to the Patriots. Instead of dispensing mere vigilante justice, they began to dispense Patriot justice which, from beneath a coat of steaming pitch, felt remarkably the same. They demanded the dismissal of the North Carolina assembly—for corruption—and insisted that North Carolinians only be required to pay "legitimate" (i.e., locally imposed) taxes. Governor William Tryon's secretary, Edmund Fanning, became the particular object of the regulators' rage. They claimed he was corrupt and demanded his punishment. When that was not forthcoming, they staged a series of bloody riots. These lost them the sympathy of the large property holders and the clergy (in slave country anything that smacked of a popular uprising made the gentry blanch), and in the end the regulators were put down and seven of their leaders executed. Fanning went on to lead Loyalist troops in the Revolutionary War. He wound up as lieutenant governor of Nova Scotia and, later, of Prince Edward Island.[11]

This was not the kind of atmosphere in which it was possible to round up Patriots and ask them if they were plotting insurrection. Except for exciting the colonists, not much came of Parliament's bold plans of early 1769. As the year wore on and the boycott on importations took hold, British merchants began to clamor for a remedy. Once more, Parliament gave way. All of the Townshend duties were withdrawn except one. To underline, once more, Parliament's right to impose such duties, a tiny tax was left on a single product. Tea.

At first the colonies thought their victory was complete, and associations that had been formed to police the boycott began to break up. Then there was, inevitably, more trouble. In New York ill-feeling between the military garrison and the Sons of Liberty resulted in a bloody brawl early in 1770. No one was killed in this "Battle of Golden Hill," but nerves were stretched taut once more. Then the British war office, in an attempt to appease the colonies, withdrew almost half the troops stationed in Boston and moved them to Halifax. This left behind a contingent too small to defend, but large enough to irritate.

Massachusetts was becoming ungovernable. When Harvard students gathered around a Liberty tree (any tree or pole with a Patriot cap on it) to complain that rules compelling them to attend exercises at the college were "unconstitutional," what had started as something of a lark quickly turned ugly. The students began to smash windows, and a handful were arrested. The rest instantly charged that they were being brutalized, and riots broke out. Three students were expelled for rioting and the entire freshman, sophomore and junior years immediately resigned. The seniors, a few months away from graduation, prudently put in for transfers to Yale.[12]

Snowballs vs Guns

Although Thomas Hutchinson had welcomed the troops to Boston, no one was more aware of the danger of a clash between the soldiers and civilians. When the general court of Massachusetts was due to meet in mid-March of 1770, Hutchinson feared that the gathering of royalist politicians would provoke unrest, especially if British troops were visibly on hand. So he asked the British military commander, General Thomas Gage, to remove the main guard by the fourteenth. That was exactly nine days too late. On the evening of March 5, a gang of waterfront rowdies gathered to taunt and bullyrag the British sentry on duty near the customhouse. When he failed to respond, they began to pelt him with sticks and snowballs. The duty guard turned out, and the mob began to pelt them, too. Captain Thomas Preston of the 29th Regiment arrived on the scene, shouting to his men, as later testimony would reveal, "Do not fire!" Whether his order was misunderstood or the troops simply panicked as the mob pressed closer is not known. What is known is that a ragged volley of muskets went off, and five Bostonians were dead in the snow.

The Revolutionary War might have begun at that instant, except for the cool actions of Preston and Hutchinson. Preston got his men under control. Hutchinson, in response to an agonized plea to "For God's sake, go to King Street," shoved his way through the fast-growing throng, making for State House. On his way through the mob, some brandishing cudgels and cutlasses, he paused to shout at Captain Preston, "How came you to fire without orders from a civil magistrate?"[13] Not a bad question; Preston's answer is lost to history. It probably amounted to, "Damned if I know." Hutchinson reached State House, dashed inside and quickly appeared on the balcony overlooking the street. From there he addressed the crowd, many of whom hated him and all he stood for, but none of whom doubted his word. He promised that the soldiers would be put on trial. With that assurance the mob broke up to go back to their homes, while the soldiers went back to their barracks. Hutchinson stayed up all night, fearful that the crowd would hunt down and lynch Captain Preston.

Eight soldiers, including Preston, were charged in what instantly became the Boston Massacre. They were defended by John Adams and Josiah Quincy, prominent Patriots who nevertheless believed that the men were entitled to a fair hearing and were unlikely to get it unless men like themselves stepped forward. In the teeth of a clamor for conviction and execution, the court returned acquittals in all cases but two, and those two soldiers received light sentences. However, the incident was far from over. It made perfect grist for Samuel Adams' propaganda mill. Very soon, broadsides and ballads of the cold-blooded murder of the brave martyrs of Boston were passing into history (where they remain, at least in the environs of Boston). After much agonizing, Hutchinson requested—he could not order—the removal of the troops to Castle William in Boston harbor, where they were dubbed "Sam Adams' Regiments." Hutchinson tendered his resignation (although he later withdrew it) because he could see that the lesson of the Boston Massacre was that mob violence worked and that no attempt to restore order was likely to succeed.

On the heels of this massive victory for the Patriots came a period of comparative calm, at least on the insurrection front. The Townshend duties had been withdrawn, the troops were locked up, and trade was beginning to revive. So the colonies went back for a time to fighting among themselves. Connecticut farmers clashed bloodily with their Pennsylvania neighbors over possession of the Wyoming Valley; battles over land claims broke out in the Hampshire Grants between New York and New Hampshire; the Carolina regulators were on the warpath. Some of the steam had gone out of the impending revolution.

Just when a measure of comparative calm seemed about to break out, the British schooner *Gaspee*, in hot pursuit of smugglers, ran aground in Narragansett Bay on the morning of June 9, 1772. Virtually the entire citizenry were engaged in smuggling, and they had been getting angrier and angrier over the previous two months as a result of the legitimate activities and haughty manners of the *Gaspee's* commander, one Lieutenant Dudington. A group of prominent citizens of nearby Providence, led by Captain Abraham Whipple, decided to burn the ship. On June 9 they swarmed onto the *Gaspee*, manhandled Dudington, captured his crew and burned his ship. The governor, Joseph Wanton, was in something of a pickle. Rhode Island was one of the colonies that elected a governor, so rigorous action to enforce the law seemed imprudent. Wanton therefore issued a proclamation asking citizens to come forward with information about the officially unknown perpetrators of this dark deed. When no one came forward, he washed his hands of the entire matter.[14]

Incidents like the burning of the *Gaspee* served to drive home to the Loyalists how vulnerable they were. If the British could not act to protect a schooner engaged in its duty, what chance did a fractious Loyalist stand? The heart went out of many of them, and the collector of customs for Rhode Island mourned, "There's an end to enforcing the acts of trade."

The *Gaspee* affair provided rich material for the committees of correspondence, which now assumed a regular and semiofficial role with a chain of riders—one of them a Boston silversmith named Paul Revere—to carry messages along the coastal roads.

The next steps in the onrushing tragedy came in 1773, and they occurred on both sides of the Atlantic.

In Boston, Governor Thomas Hutchinson announced that henceforth, his salary and those of his officials would be paid directly from England—removing him from local financial control.

In England, Lord North steered a special concession through Parliament to allow the faltering East India Company to ship tea directly to America, escaping additional duties and handling charges normally involved in importing, then re-exporting, the product. This would allow the company to undersell all other tea-trading firms and give it an effective monopoly. At the same time, the tea was to be consigned to a select group of merchants loyal to the Crown, making the monopoly a double one. However, there would still be an import duty on the tea when it reached America, a remnant from the perished Townshend duties. As historian Elizabeth McCaughney observes, "The Ministry seemed less concerned with quieting America than with saving the nearly bankrupt company."[15]

Many staunch Tories, at least among those who were not eligible for a consignment of tea, objected to the monopoly, if not to the tax. Those who supported both generally kept quiet about it. But this time there was to be no backing away. The tax was small, threepence a pound, but it would be paid. Lord North was sure that America's female tea addicts would not object to the "peppercorn of principle" involved. And if they did, well, too bad. "There was no purpose making objection," Lord North said, "the king would have it so."[16]

William Samuel Johnson, a staunch Connecticut Loyalist, wrote that the Tea Act (as the amendments came to be called) "has produced the most fatal and pernicious and violent effects."[17]

Johnson was one of those tough birds thrown up by the crisis. He was a lawyer, diplomat and politician who had served as Connecticut's agent in London and applied his considerable skills to combating British policy. However, when the final break came, he risked his life, career and property to combat independence. He got away with it—so highly was he regarded in the province that he lived unscathed throughout the war (and in later life became a United States senator and president of Columbia College). His case is typical of those staunch Tories who stood by the Crown but groaned at the stupidity of British policy. I have never seen an estimate of how many Tories or Loyalists managed to stay within the colonies while expressing strong views on the royal side. In some colonies where the authorities either chose not to enforce oaths of loyalty to the congress, when they became fashionable, or were unable to carry out the enforcement, no doubt many local Tories flourished.

The point Johnson made about the Tea Act was the crucial one. Parliament certainly had the right to levy a duty on tea, but doing so was bound to enrage the colonists without helping the government's supporters to deal with that rage.

Once again the fat was in the fire, and once again events conspired against that honorable but not always wise Loyalist, Thomas Hutchinson. Despite the problems his family had run into earlier with the colonial boycotters, he named his two sons as managers for the tea consigned to his trading firm. They refused to follow the lead of most other agents who, when a crowd of Patriots came calling, swiftly resigned their tea portfolios. That was bad; worse was to come.

Hutchinson had long been in correspondence with a man named Thomas Whately. Benjamin Franklin, at this time the agent of Massachusetts in England, got his hands on these letters and others written by Hutchinson's brother-in-law, the provincial secretary, Andrew Oliver. Whately, as secretary to the treasury under George Grenville, had been a key figure in the drafting of the Stamp Act. The letters revealed Hutchinson's inner thoughts on that still-festering subject, including his argument that the liberties of people three thousand miles away from their mother country were bound to be reduced. Franklin sent the letters, which had almost certainly been stolen from Whately's papers (he had died in 1772), to the speaker of the house in Boston, with a note asking that they be kept confidential. But whether he expected or even wished that condition to be kept is subject to some doubt.[18]

In any event, the letters were soon in the hands of the Boston committee of correspondence, and Samuel Adams was able to turn them into proof that Hutchinson had been plotting to rob the colony of its liberties all along. It has since become a staple of American history that the letters revealed that only one view, that of the Tories, was reaching Parliament while the Stamp Act crisis was brewing. But that is simply nonsense. The views of the colonies were placed before MPs early and often through letters, speeches, pamphlets and by the provincial agents in London.

However, that didn't matter. What mattered was that the letters were inevitably read as proof of a decade-long plot to bind the Americans in chains. Under the prodding of Adams, the Massachusetts house petitioned the king for the recall of Hutchinson and Andrew Oliver. The single most influential Loyalist in America was undone. Hutchinson did in fact leave the colony for England, but not before the Boston Tea Party had broken beneath his feet.

Dropping in for Tea

The much-told tale of the Boston Tea Party is now familiar. Merchants up and down the coast were warned of the consequences if they accepted any of the tainted tea, on which the tax would have to be paid before unloading, either by the ship's owner or the merchant (who were often one and the same). When three ships entered Boston harbor in defiance of the warnings, a large local mob—containing not merely the usual thugs, but some of the city's prominent citizens thinly disguised as Indians—swarmed onto Griffin's wharf and dumped 342 chests of tea into Boston harbor. An unsigned pamphlet handed out that morning called on "Every friend to his country" to meet at Faneuil Hall and advised, "The hour of destruction or manly opposition to the machinations of tyranny stare you in the face."[19] This mob action, about which Governor Hutchinson could do nothing effectual, caused Loyalist Peter Oliver to write: "This villainous Act soon grew into serious Consideration. Some of the Country Towns, as well as some of the inhabitants of Boston, thought that Justice demanded Indemnification to the owners of the Tea; but the Faction was great; and it prevailed; it had so repeated Success, in Impunity, from their other Disorders, that the Power of Great Britain did not weigh a Feather in their Consideration."[20]

But this time Britain did respond with a series of acts—the so-called coercive acts (the Americans called them the intolerable acts), which shot through the British Parliament in early 1774. Under one of these, the Boston Port Act, the port of Boston was ordered closed on June 1, 1774, and was to remain closed until the tea was paid for. General Gage took over Massachusetts as military commander, replacing Hutchinson, the civil governor. The colonial charter was revoked, and a new Quartering Act required the colony to provide barracks and supplies to British troops.

The tea monopoly, wrote Samuel Adams, had gone a long way to quell the natural disposition of the colonies to quarrel with each other: "The Ministry could not have devised a more effectual measure to unite the Colonies. Old Jealousies are removed and perfect Harmony subsists between them."[21] If the monopoly was a boon for the Patriots, the intolerable acts were a Godsend. Riders fanned out across the colonies carrying handbills marked with mourning wreaths, skulls and crossbones and Liberty caps (which were tuques, usually knitted in the Patriot colors—red, white and blue). They soon brought back feisty responses from New York, South Carolina and Pennsylvania. New Yorkers dumped their tea, too, while those in Philadelphia allowed the chests to be landed and to rot in the warehouses. In Charleston the tea was sold at public auction and the proceeds put into a Patriot war chest. Food, money and other supplies poured into Boston.

Of course not everyone reacted with such zeal. In New York a meeting was held in Fraunces Tavern to select a bipartisan committee of fifty-one to correspond with other colonies (New York, as primarily Loyalist, did not yet have an official committee of correspondence). Isaac Low, a prominent merchant and eventual Loyalist, was chosen as chairman. Low told the meeting, "Zeal in a good cause is laudable, but when it transports beyond the bounds of reason it often leaves room for bitter reflection."[22]

Low managed to direct the committee to toss the whole contentious issue into the laps of a proposed meeting of all thirteen colonies—the First Continental Congress—and kept from de-claring himself except to say that, like so many who remained loyal to Britain, he did not agree with the mother country's actions. (Later, Low was sent as a delegate to the First Conti-nental Congress, but he would not embrace independence. He was proscribed as a Loyalist and lost all his property in New York.)

Elsewhere it was not possible to slide sideways, even tem-porarily. Every colony set aside a day of fasting on June 1, 1774, to mark the date the intolerable acts took effect. In Pennsyl-vania, Quakers who refused to observe the day for religious reasons found themselves condemned as "Enemies to the Country." The newspapers began to print lists of such enemies, which included, along with known Tories or Loyalists, some whose offense was merely to drink tea. In Connecticut a tough old Tory, the Reverend Samuel Peters, persuaded the towns of Hebron and Hartford not to support the Boston relief fund. But he couldn't prevent the Sons of Liberty in Farmington from burning a copy of the Boston Port Act, "For which vile con-duct," Peters complained, "they have not been styled a pest to Connecticut and enemies to common sense either by His Honor (the Governor) or any king's attorney or in any town meeting."[23]

It was a hard time to be a Tory. It would get harder. On June 22, George III gave royal assent to the Quebec Act, a forward-looking piece of legislation which among other things formally granted religious freedom to Catholics—in effect, to nearly all French Canadians—and, while specifying English criminal law for the province, retained French civil law.

These provisions were read in the paranoid southern colonies as the beginnings of an attempt to foist an established church, perhaps even the hated Catholic church, upon them.

However, it was the boundary provisions that did the real damage. The Quebec Act redrew the boundaries of Quebec, extending them south and west to the Ohio River, effectively blocking the westward expansion of the thirteen southern col-onies. There were sound political and strategic reasons for the Quebec Act, including the fact that according to the Procla-mation of 1763, under which the province was then being ruled, Quebec had no civil government, only military rule.

Well, of course, that was the point. There was all that land out there waiting to be grabbed and without any law. Schemes, plots and stratagems to develop this were under way, and not only by Patriots, either. One of the schemers was William Franklin, the bastard son of Benjamin Franklin. With the help of his father's influence, William had become royal governor of the province of New Jersey. He was a shrewd and able leader, but broke. To retain popularity in his fractious province, he lived on a meager salary and eschewed the fancy formal palace he was entitled to at Perth Amboy for humbler digs at Burlington, a mere seventeen miles down the river from Philadelphia, where his law practice and his friends were.

Franklin was a Whig—a political reformer—even though he was a Loyalist. He would become a high Tory, but only under the impetus of the onrushing Revolution. He was one of the many backers of a scheme to unite all the British provinces of America, and a backer of another scheme that would make him rich—to develop a new province, to be called Vandalia, in what is now much of Indiana and Illinois. His father, Benjamin, was one of the backers of Vandalia. The Quebec Act put paid to any such projects, and you didn't have to be a Patriot to resent it. William Eddes of Annapolis, Maryland, a customs surveyor and Loyalist, wrote, "The Canada Bill [as the Quebec Act was often called] is as unpopular here as the Boston Port Bill and adds greatly to the universal discontent." A man with a neat turn of phrase, Eddes blamed the Canada Bill for the fact that "All America is in a Flame!"[24]

Well, perhaps not all, but enough to be getting on with. In Williamsburg, that sunny, troublesome southern capital of Virginia, the house of burgesses had passed another resolution calling for "A Congress . . . from all the Colonies to concert a uniform and general plan for the defense and preservation of our common rights." This congress should—humbly and dutifully, of course—petition the king for redress of the colonial grievance. If King George failed to respond, well, the colonies would know what to do about that: "From our Sovreign there can be but one appeal"—which is to say, to force of arms.[25]

The First Continental Congress met in Philadelphia at the Carpenters Hall. Joseph Galloway, one of the conservative delegates (and author of one of the more imaginative of the continental-union plans), wanted the meeting in State House, but he was overruled. Delegates were there from every colony. Many of them were Loyalists—though few were Tories like Galloway—who became increasingly uneasy as the talk turned from the usual recitation of the wickedness of Parliament to talk of what to do about it. The congress became bogged down in debate between conservatives and radicals. Old Sam Adams was nearly beside himself with anxiety that the meeting would produce nothing more than another remonstrance, when in rode Paul Revere at the end of a lathering journey from Suffolk County, Massachusetts, bearing a copy of a statement endorsed there—the "Suffolk Resolves."

These declared all the intolerable acts (to which the Quebec Act had been added) unconstitutional and without legal force. But that was just for starters. The people of Massachusetts were enjoined to form their own provincial congress to replace the dissolved assembly, with the power to collect taxes and withhold them until the intolerable acts were repealed. People were to gather arms and form a militia, while the economic boycott of British goods was to remain in force.

The Suffolk Resolves, read aloud by Peyton Randolph of Virginia, swept the congress, which formally adopted them without a comma changed. The conservatives and Loyalists were bludgeoned into silence, although the congress had not yet gone so far as to opt for independence. In a private meeting later, John Adams asserted, "There is no man among us that would not be happy to see accommodation with Britain" (he did not consult Samuel Adams, who was at his elbow), and another Patriot, Robert Paine, added, "Independence? A hundred times no!"[25]

To implement the congressional resolves, a continental association was formed with committees in every town, city and county to enforce the trade boycott. There were to be no imports whatever from Britain as of December 1, 1774. In stunned silence Joseph Galloway, Loyalist, signed the document along with the cheering Patriots.

Loyalists Should "Lick the Dust"

Hectoring Loyalists had now become well-nigh respectable. In Virginia the new governor, Lord Dunmore, complained, "There is not a justice of the peace that acts, except as a Committeeman." A Son of Liberty wrote in the *New London Gazette* that Loyalists were "the Guy Fawks of the present day ..." who should be made "to bow ... and lick the Dust." The Loyalists were somehow transformed into the aggressors. They had "combined to subvert our civil government, to plunder and murder us," and therefore should be denied "protection in their persons or properties."[26]

In Massachusetts the provincial congress called for in the Suffolk Resolves was established with John Hancock as president. This congress ruled virtually all the province outside of Boston, and it decreed that all officials who refused to renounce their offices were "infamous betrayers of their country" and as such fair game. The organized persecution of Loyalists had not yet begun, however—that was to await the outbreak of war.

It was not long coming. By the time the First Continental Congress adjourned on October 26, 1774, the local committees in every colony had become parallel governments. When the merchant vessel *Peggy Stewart* arrived in Annapolis, Maryland, with a cargo of tea on which tax had been paid, her captain was forced to burn his own ship. In response to the continental congress call, local militia or "Minute Men" were soon arming themselves—from British stores—all across the colonies. On December 9 they seized weapons at Newport, Rhode Island, and carried them to Providence. On December 14 one hundred barrels of powder were seized from Castle William and Mary in New Hampshire. Similar actions followed in other colonies.

It was not until February 26, 1775, that the British army struck back. That day, troops were landed by sea at Marblehead to destroy stores gathered by Massachusetts Patriots. There was a tense confrontation with the militia of Salem and a scuffle that led to some bloodshed but no deaths. On March 23, Patrick Henry delivered his famous "Liberty or Death" speech to the Virginia convention meeting in lieu of the banned assembly, and the convention resolved to put the colony onto an official policy of defense (for which read offense).

On April 15, a reinforced British army went on maneuvers with twenty-three companies from eleven regiments detached for "separate training." Actually, they were deployed to crush the rebels, and on April 18 in the late evening, they moved out of Boston to destroy rebel stores at nearby Concord. Paul Revere, Samuel Prescott and William Dawes were dispatched on horseback to alert militiamen along the line of March. This was the famous ride on which Revere's future fame was mainly staked, although in fact he lost his horse and never reached Concord, the end of his planned route.[27] (Not his fault; he fell into the hands of the British. Actually, Dawes did more than Revere on this memorable night, but it was Revere whose story attracted the attention of William Wadsworth Longfellow and went into history for his midnight ride.)

On the morning of April 19, just as day was breaking, Major John Pitcairn of the royal marines led the British column past Munroe's Tavern and onto the Green at the small town of Lexington, Massachusetts, about twenty miles from Boston. Two companies of militia under Captain John Parker were already on the Green, and more were in the nearby woods and fields. Pitcairn, under the explicit instructions of General Gage,

ordered his troops "on no account to fire," but someone did—
probably an American straggler near the edge of the Green. That
was the shot heard around the world. The British troops replied
with several volleys, and the outnumbered militia fell back.

The British went on to Concord and destroyed the stores as
ordered, but all the way back to Boston they were subjected to
sniper fire from rebel militia who dodged from tree to tree and
hid behind fence posts, rocks and any cover available. By the
time the day was done, 4,000 militia and 1,800 British troops
were engaged; the British lost 270 and the rebels 95.[28]

The war was on, but it was not yet a war on the Loyalists.
It soon would be.

Section Two
1775-1783

THE CIVIL WAR

*"Neighbor was against neighbor, father against the son,
and he that would not thrust his own blade through his
brother's heart was called an infamous villain."*

Stephen Gorham,
July 22, 1777

4
Low, Private Revenge

"Farewell, unhappy land, for which my heart bleeds in pity. Little does it signify to you who are the conquered or who the victorious; you are devoted to ruin, whoever succeeds."

Janet Schaw,
on leaving America, October, 1775

Shots had been fired in anger, hundreds had died at Lexington and Concord on April 19, 1775, but many on both sides of the conflict thought it was not too late somehow to restore the peace and patch up the quarrel between the mother country and the colonies. When the Second Continental Congress met in the state house (now Independence Hall), Philadelphia, two weeks after Lexington, most of the delegates hoped that the fighting was over. Every province but Georgia (largely Loyalist at this time) sent delegates to this congress, which produced the "Olive Branch Petition," restating the colonists' grievances against Parliament, but professing continued loyalty to the king. We can work this out, the petition said in effect; call off your dogs and let's talk.

But it was far too late for that. George III by this time had the bit in his teeth. He welcomed the opportunity to put the bumptious rebels in their place once and for all. "The die is now cast," he harrumphed. "The colonists must either submit or triumph."[1] Actually, what he had in mind was that they would submit, not triumph, and in that he was acting on the best available advice—that of his courtiers, advisers and military men.

His advisers included men such as the Earl of Sandwich, first lord of the admiralty. He was an energetic if corrupt gentleman who succeeded in getting named after him both a new kind of meal (meat between two slices of bread, which could be eaten standing up at the gaming tables) and the Sandwich Islands (but the name was later changed to the Hawaiian Islands). Sandwich once confessed to Lord North that "I never could understand the real state of the fleet,"[2] but he was sure that, whatever its state, it would soon sink the rebels. They couldn't fight a lick, as everyone knew. In a speech to the House of Lords, the earl laid it on with a trowel, in the accepted manner of his time: "Suppose the colonies do abound in men, what does that signify? They are raw, undisciplined, cowardly men." In fact, instead of the forty or fifty thousand colonial troops it was expected that congress would put into the field, Sandwich hoped they would produce "at least two hundred thousand; the more the better, the easier the conquest; if they did not run away, they would starve themselves into compliance with our measures."[3]

Of course it was easier for the House of Lords to heap scorn on the colonials than it was for the Loyalists in Boston, Philadelphia or Savannah. The Loyalists were already under severe strictures. The continental association of 1774, which had mounted the continental congresses, had called for the establishment of local committees of public safety, because, as General Charles Lee said of the Tories on Long Island, "Not to crush these serpents before their rattles are grown would be ruinous."[4]

These committees of safety had already swung into action with the usual enthusiasm of their breed. Under test acts passed by every province, the committees required those suspected of Tory sympathies to proclaim allegiance to congress, foreswear the king or, sometimes, merely recant for having drunk tea. Complaints were laid before the committee members. If a majority on the committee were satisfied of the accused's guilt, "the truth of the case" was published in a local newspaper. Often the truth of the case was not a matter of proof, but opinion, suspicion and hearsay. No matter—once the names were published, the suspects were fair game.

In Windham, Connecticut, Francis Green was driven out of town by the mob and fled to nearby Norwich, where he took shelter in the inn. "Out with him!" shouted the mob, and he was pulled from his shelter, tumbled into his carriage and angry men lashed his horses to send him on his way. Green left the area, never to return. His crime was that he had been one of the signatories to a farewell address to Governor Thomas Hutchinson of Massachusetts.[5]

They Poisoned His Other Horse

In Berkshire, Massachusetts, David Ingersoll was driven from his house, and his fences were pulled down. Daniel Leonard's home was riddled with bullets; he fled to Boston. A man named Ruggles fought off an attack, but the mob painted his horse and cut off its mane and tail. Later they came back, robbed his house and "poisoned his other horse."[6] There was no point in laying a complaint before the courts. The mob had prudently forced the judges from their benches and closed the courthouse. At nearby Worcester, an armed mob forced the judges, sheriffs and lawyers present to march up and down, caps in their hands, and to read—thirty times—a promise never to hold court again under Parliament.

Besides tarring and feathering and riding their victims on rails, the Patriots had dreamed up other punishments. Some suspects were bound and gagged for days at a time. Others were pelted with stones or locked into a room with a fireplace, with the chimney stopped up, to "smoke them clean." Their houses or ships were burned if they had been named for trading with the British. In some cases, their silverplate was confiscated— to be held "as surety for good behavior"—and never returned. A man named Dunbar who, although not a Loyalist, had committed the sin of buying a cow from someone who was, was stuffed into the carcass of an ox and publicly paraded. Then he was fined four head of cattle and one horse.[7]

To smoke out the Tories, committees of safety opened private papers, spied on suspects and used informers. An incautious or over-bold word could lead to variable consequences. At Kennebec, Massachusetts, the committee sentenced a man to be buried alive "for wishing success to the king's troops." The sentence was carried out, too. So much for free speech. Elsewhere milder punishments sufficed. In Augusta, Georgia, William Davis, who announced publicly that he opposed the Sons of Liberty (though not the congress) was drummed around a Liberty tree three times. In Boston, Daniel Leonard, who called the Boston committee of correspondence "the foulest, subtlest and most venemous serpent that ever issued from the eggs of sedition' " was merely forced to sit on a cake of ice "to cool his loyalty."[8]

The capriciousness of the Patriots was perhaps the most frightening thing for the Loyalists. Stephen Resco of Stockbridge, Massachusetts, was captured by British troops and held prisoner for a few days, then released on his promise to remain peacefully on his farm. Why was he released, the Patriots asked.

He must be a Loyalist, they answered. So Resco was seized, tarred and feathered, crowned with "an Owl which had been killed for that purpose" and driven to the county convention— which turned him loose and rebuked the zealots.[9]

A Scottish visitor to a farm near Wilmington, North Carolina, described the usual procedure this way: "An officer or committeeman enters a plantation with his posse. The Alternative is proposed: Agree to join us, and your persons and properties are safe; you have a shilling sterling a day; your duty is no more than once a month appearing under Arms at Wilmington, where you will have as much grog as you can drink. But if you refuse, we are directly to cut up your corn, shoot your pigs, burn your houses, seize your Negroes and perhaps tar and feather yourself."

The writer noted that this technique usually worked "with the lower sort,"[10] but that was just part of the innate snobbery of the day. In fact it worked with nearly every sort nearly every time. When Dr. Joseph Clarke was seized by the Hartford, Connecticut, mob and ridden about on a rail, he fainted several times during the ordeal. When examined by a Dr. Tidmarsh, Clarke was found "to be injured in a Manner unfit for Description in a Newspaper" (newspapers were more squeamish in those days; Clarke was emasculated). His crime had been "Speaking in Terms of Respect of the King and of his Government." The doctor who treated him was also threatened, but not manhandled.

In a pioneer community where local ties were strong and where, especially in the towns, privacy was almost unknown, the pressure to conform was great. But it was not a pressure that applied much on the king's behalf. After all, only the most devout and narrow Tory supported most of the actions of Parliament. William Smith, chief justice of New York (and later chief justice of Quebec), was at this time known as "Patriotic Billy" because his denunciations of British policy were so strong. He had married a Livingstone, a member of one of the wealthiest families in New York province, as well as one of the strongest supporters of the colonial cause.[11] Unless he wanted a battle at home, he was not about to attack his neighbors for maintaining what he himself believed—that Parliament was an ass.

Many men like Smith became Loyalists only later, when the issue was independence, not defiance. Peter Van Schaak, one of New York's most respected attorneys, continued to support the Patriots until he became convinced that Britain's behavior was due to "human frailty" and not, as the Patriots argued, "a pre-concerted plan to enslave us."[12] Van Schaack did not become a Loyalist, but he wouldn't swear the allegiance to congress demanded by the the test oaths, either, and he was forced to seek refuge in England until after the war.

It was becoming harder and harder to be a neutral. John Adams' contention that the First Continental Congress itself consisted of "one third Tories, another Whigs and the rest Mongrels"[13] may have been an accurate description, but that didn't help much when the mob came to call.

What did you do when that angry noise at the front door turned out to be a motley crew of the Sons of Liberty, carrying tar, feathers, a fence rail, clubs, a hungry look and the latest copy of the local paper, in which you had been named as "an enemy to the Congress," or a "king's man," or a tea drinker? If you were prudent, you swore whatever oaths were required and threw yourself on the mercy of the mob.

Not every committee of safety acted in an arbitrary manner, although most did. The committee of Cumberland County, New Jersey, spent "much time," as its minutes complain, "in vain" trying to convince Silas Newcombe of his error in drinking tea, before naming him "an enemy of liberty." Alexander Miller of Augusta County, Virginia, was found guilty of "having called the Americans rebels." George McMurtie of Sussex County, New Jersey, "spoke very contemptuously and disrespectfully of the Contintental and Provincial Congresses," and Eleazar Bradshaw was branded a Tory in Waltham, Massachusetts. But in each case the punishment was not more than a boycott on business with the offender "until there appears a reformation in his behavior."[14]

The disparity of the treatment was not due so much to the tenderness or otherwise of the committees as it was to the presence or absence of either British troops or other Tories in the neighborhood. The quality of mercy was generally strained, or not, according to the view of the neighbors. There was also the danger that a too-vigorous committee or a too-brutal mob would create sympathy for the victims and harm the Patriot cause, creating Tories out of potential Patriots.

That is what apparently happened in the case of William Franklin, the governor of New Jersey, whose early sympathies were clearly Whig (that is, reformist). When the stamps required under the Stamp Act first arrived for his province, Franklin (perhaps under the persuasion of eight hundred Sons of Liberty who turned up for the occasion) refused to let them be landed and then asked New York's lieutenant governor, Cadwallader Colden, to store them in Fort George. Colden replied that there was no room in the fort—it was full of troops. It didn't matter, anyway, because the New Jersey stamp commissioner, William Coxe, resigned after he was refused as a tenant in a house unless he could provide a guarantee that the house wouldn't be pulled down by the mob. So far, Franklin was on the side of the Patriot angels.

"I Shold Be Very Much Afrunted"

In September, 1765, an incident occurred that began to change his views. William and his famous father, Benjamin, were publicly and wrongly accused of having fostered the Stamp Act. A mob descended on the Franklin home in Philadelphia, where Ben's redoubtable wife, Deborah, and his daughter, William's half-sister (she was legitimate), barricaded themselves in the house along with a gaggle of cousins and two guns. Deborah was not the kind to scare easily, and when the mob suggested she should leave her house, she refused to budge. As she wrote to her husband, with fine spirit and atrocious spelling, "I ordored some sorte of defens up Stairs such as I cold manaig my self," adding, "if aney one came to disturbe me I wold show a proper resentment and I shold be very much afrunted."[15] Philadelphia was still a divided city, and a group of Franklin adherents (a counter-mob, if you like) sent the rioters packing from the Franklin house.

The incident shook William Franklin, who was afraid that his own house "would be pulled down about my ears," but when the Stamp Act was repealed, he joined the celebrations, firing off two cannons on his lawn and drinking eighteen toasts.[16]

Franklin was a populist in an age before the term was used. He called the citizens "the people," and not "the mob"; and he chided the New Jersey assembly for not moving quickly enough on his programs of public works and crop bounties. What finally pushed him into the Loyalist camp began as a minor incident in 1773, when a passel of thieves—the Samuel Ford gang—broke into the home of the provincial treasurer, Stephen Skinner, and made off with £7,854. Franklin had the gang rounded up, but the assembly insisted that Skinner, who was wealthy, aristocratic and unpopular, had been negligent in storing the money. The assembly refused to allow the prosecution of the gang and demanded Skinner's resignation instead.

After a five-month struggle, Skinner did resign, and Franklin took the symbolic step of moving from his own modest home at Burlington to the magnificent Proprietory House (New Jersey was a proprietory colony) at Perth Amboy, which featured a deer park, orchards, a lake, stables for twelve carriage horses and Tories for neighbors. He quarrelled with his father, apparently because he thought that the excesses of the Sons of Liberty and Benjamin's notoriety had cost him a post as governor of Barbados, the birthplace of his ailing wife. By 1775 he had become a staunch Tory and Loyalist. (He was later arrested, paraded through his former province in custody and imprisoned. He finally escaped to England, where he lived until his death in 1813.)

The urge to be among sympathetic neighbors was a moving force for Franklin. For others it was often the crucial factor. Lord Dartmouth told Benjamin Franklin that social isolation, not violence, was the major factor in blocking the growth of what he called "the royalist party" in Massachusetts. Royalists, he noted, were "held in Contempt, and People don't care to incur the Disesteem and Displeasure of their Neighbours."[17]

Especially when it costs money. Baltimore merchant James Christie, charged with royalist sympathies, was locked into his house, fined five hundred pounds "for the defence of America," and was then ordered to pay nine shillings a day to each of his guards.

The desire for loot may have fuelled the attack on Reverend Samuel Seabury, first Episcopal bishop in the United States. He was seized by a mob that invaded his house, threatened his two daughters—some mob members thrust bayonets through the girls' caps—and then took all his money and silverplate. Seabury was paraded through the streets of new Haven, then imprisoned for a month. When he got out, he went into hiding with other Loyalists and lived in a secret room in a friend's house where, for some months, he was fed through the trapdoor in the floor.[18]

All of this took place, in effect, before the actual outbreak of formal fighting at Lexington. Once the war began, whatever tolerance had previously existed in places mostly vanished. The Loyalists were now seen as "a nest of locusts," "a band of traitors" and a threat—as some certainly were—to every Patriot.

Loyalists found themselves in an intolerable situation—compelled to choose between their principles of loyalty and their affection for their friends and neighbors. Such a man was Isaac Wilkins of Westchester County, New York. He made himself known as a Tory by backing a motion in the New York assembly, which was dominated by Loyalists, to refuse to send delegates to the Second Continental Congress. The Patriots were able to get around this by appealing over the heads of the assembly directly to the citizens. The Patriot faction proposed a new legislative body, a provincial convention, which was to meet on April 20—the day after Lexington. The battle lines were then drawn over whether or not to send delegates to this new body. The Patriots were for it; the Loyalists, naturally, opposed.

The two groups met separately in White Plains taverns. Then the Patriots sneaked off to the courthouse to a secret meeting to appoint delegates to the new legislature. The Loyalists got wind of this and a group of them, led by Isaac Wilkins and Frederick Philipse, called around at the courthouse to register a protest. It went unheeded. The Patriots appointed deputies to the provincial convention and passed resolutions of thanks to the continental congress. Two weeks later, Wilkins, a popular man with ingratiating manners, said a sad farewell to his country. He wrote in the *Rivington Gazette* of May 11, 1775, "I leave America and every endearing connection because I will not raise my hand against my Sovreign, nor will I draw my sword against my Country. When I can conscientiously draw it in her favour, my life shall be cheerfully devoted to her service."[19] Wilkins sat out the war behind British lines on Long Island, then emigrated to Shelburne, Nova Scotia, before moving on to Lunenburg, where we will meet him again. He was one of the few Loyalists (no one has kept track of the numbers, since most of these people did their utmost to efface themselves) able to return successfully to former haunts. In 1799 he came back to Westchester and served as clergymen there for thirty-one years. He died at age eighty-nine, full of honor.

His Wife Had a "Hysterik Fit"

The lines were being drawn more clearly and more harshly. They ran through the middle of families other than the Franklins. Samuel Curwen was a Tory, his wife Abigaill a Whig, and when he was driven out of Salem, Massachusetts, she refused to go with him. Curwen had been a merchant, deputy judge and—fatefully—a collector of import duties for the Crown. He fled to Philadelphia, but, as he later noted in a petition to the Loyalist claims commission after the war, "the political phrenzy there had risen to equal height with New England," and he was forced to flee again, to England. When he finally returned to America after the war, his wife "had a hysterik fit." Curwen knew what to do about that. He wrote instructions to a friend:

"It is my express and peremptory order, command and injunction to my heirs that on no consideration her dead body be entombed with my late niece or any of my family, being unwilling that her dust should be mixed with a family to which she bore enmity; and I should be not a little deranged in the Resurrection Morning to find Abigaill Curwen starting up by my side."[20] Curwen wound up back in Salem, where he died in 1802, aged eighty-six. There is a portrait of Samuel and Abigaill in the Essex Institute at Salem, and they are a tough-looking couple. You can almost imagine him saying, What's this about the Patriots? and her replying, What's it to you?

From the onset of the fighting, the major events of the Revolutionary War became a tolling bell of doom for the Loyalists, although no one knew this at the time. When the war went badly for the Patriots, the Tories felt the rebels' rage. When it went well, they felt the rebels' scorn.

After the British forces withdrew from Philadelphia and the Patriots took over, Loyalists Abraham Carlisle and John Roberts were charged with treason. Carlisle, a carpenter, had helped guard one of the city gates, while Roberts, a miller, had enlisted with the British and urged others to do the same. They were found guilty. But the jury recommended mercy for Roberts and a reprieve for Carlisle. As it became clear that the men were to be hung despite the recommendations, petitions were drawn up on their behalf and forwarded to the executive council, the appointed provincial cabinet. Five clergymen and 387 other Philadelphians, including several of high military rank, signed the petitions. But the council decided it was necessary to hang the men to appease popular demand and to terrify the Pennsylvania Quakers, who refused to show any enthusiasm for the Patriot cause. The hangings were carried out despite the appeals of Roberts' wife, who brought her ten children to the gallows to beg for their father's life. Carlisle, who had been quite ill, said nothing at his execution, but Roberts made a moving speech, which Joseph Humphreys, owner of the *Pennsylvania Ledger*, recorded: "He told his Audience that his Conscience acquitted him of Guilt; that he suffered for doing his duty to his Sovereign; That his Blood would one day be demanded at their hands—and then, turning to his children, charged & exhorted them to remember his Principles, for which he died and to adhere to them while they had Breath."[21]

The executions were widely reported, and the image of Roberts calmly addressing his ten assembled children before mounting the gallows created something of a sensation, but it was soon forgotten as other outrages on both sides captured public attention. It was, wrote James Allen of Philadelphia, "A fine time to gratify low private revenge." Allen's complaint was that his tenants, who were supposed to pay him in sterling, switched instead to the new continental money (which would be worthless if the rebels lost) and, as he said, "I am as much robbed of five-sixths of my property, as if it was taken out of a drawer."[22] Allen was a Whig who wanted no part of the Loyalists, but he became a Tory.

Low, private revenge was also dished out in 1775 to Philip Skene, the patentee of Skenesborough, a 34,000-acre township laid out along the shores of a creek near Lake Champlain in northern New York province. Skene was a Scottish Jacobite who had once fought for Bonnie Prince Charlie, but he became a Loyalist in North America. He was known as "Lord Skene" or "Old Skene," and he was not popular with his neighbors. He carried the title of Lieutenant Governor of Forts Ticonderoga and Crown Point, the forts guarding the inland route to Canada. Around Skenesborough it became a game to ask children whether they would rather meet "Old Skene or the devil," and for the children to reply, "the devil."

When Ethan Allen's Green Mountain boys marched on Fort Ticonderoga—which they surrounded and captured with ridiculous ease, and never a shot fired—a group stopped off to capture Skenesborough. Skene was not there at the time—he was on the way home from England—but his sister and daughters were captured and taken off to Connecticut. The estate was seized along with "about 40 negros' " i.e., slaves. The attack also turned up the body of Skene's wife, laid in "a very nice wooden coffin," which was in turn laid within a lead coffin in a small room partitioned off from the cellar. The locals believed (although the story was never verified) that she had made a marriage contract to pay a handsome annual sum to her husband "as long as she was above ground," and the canny Scot chose this method of keeping the funds flowing.[23] Skene himself was seized when he landed at Philadelphia and was paroled on a promise of good behavior. But when the parole expired, he refused to promise to remain peaceable, and was thrown into jail. Exchanged in 1776, he served with Burgoyne's invading British army.

Loyalists Paid for British Blunders

It was, all in all, a weird war. The British strategy, if that's the word for it, was concocted in the main by three men: Lord

North, first lord of the treasury, the Earl of Sandwich, first lord of the admiralty, and Lord George Germain (later Viscount Sackville), who was in charge of the colonial office and directly responsible for the conduct of the war. They were quite a trio. North noted, "On military matters, I speak ignorantly," and he never spoke a truer word. He was a dillydallier. "Damn him!" spluttered Lord Chancellor Thurlow on one occasion, "nothing can goad him forward."[24] Germain at least had a military background. He had been cashiered out of the army after the Battle of Minden, for disobeying orers, and was pronounced "unfit to serve in any military capacity whatever."[25] The Earl of Sandwich was able—when he wan't wenching or gambling—but his arrogant dismissal of the colonials, and the contempt all three of the strategists shared for the capacities of the Loyalists to fight on their own behalf, contributed to the series of blunders that marked the British effort. The Loyalists paid for the blunders. North, Germain and Sandwich were all heaped with honors for their part in the war.

The one who had it right was Lord Chatham—formerly the great commoner, William Pitt—who thundered in the House of Lords:

> You cannot, I venture to say it, you cannot conquer America. . . . You may swell every expense, traffic and barter with every little pitiful German prince that sells his subjects to the shambles of a foreign power; your efforts are forever vain and impotent; doubly so from this mercenary aid on which you rely, for it irritates to an incurable resentment the minds of your enemies. To overrun them with the mercenary sons of rapine and plunder; devoting them and their possessions to the rapacity of hireling cruelty! If I were an American, as I am an Englishman, while a foreign troop was landed in my country, I would never lay down my arms—never—never—never![26]

Chatham was an old man—what did he know? Subduing the rebels was going to be easy. The British plan, at least at first, was to land a large army in America and thereafter accept the surrender of the locals, who would be overawed. They weren't, as it happened, and after Bunker Hill—a technical victory for the British troops, but a battle that showed how easy it was to massacre the redcoats marching in file—the rebels got it up their noses that they could lick the assembling armies by taking the offense. The march on Quebec over the winter of 1775-1776, ending in the bloody repulsion of the invaders by Sir Guy

Carleton, with a small corps of British troops and a larger one of Loyalist militia, cooled out that notion for a time. The rebels were content to mount a six-month siege on Boston, bottling up six thousand troops and a mob of civilians that started at seven thousand and grew every month as Loyalist and Tory stragglers came in from the surrounding countryside.

General Thomas Gage, in charge of military matters in the colonies at this time, had a couple of shrewd ideas. One was that Carleton, now that he had licked the rebels around Quebec and driven them out of Montreal, should come down Lake Champlain and, "raising all the Canadians and Indians in his power, attack them in his turn." He dashed off a note to Carleton telling him to do that, but Carleton, who had only a few hundred Canadians and Indians in his power—none of them anxious to take on New York—declined. Then, said Gage in a letter to the war office, "You must have large armies, making diversions on different sides to divide their force." Which was true, no doubt, but did not explain where the large armies were to come from. No, no, said the war office, "the true way to reduce America is by sea only."[27]

The General and the Sultana

Gage didn't care. He was out of it, resigning to be replaced by General William Howe as commander in chief in the colonies. Carleton became the commander in Canada; that is, he was to report directly to England, not through Howe. Howe settled down comfortably in Boston with his mistress, the Loyalist Mrs. Deborah Loring, also known as "the sultana." There were card games—Mrs. Loring dropped three hundred guineas in a single evening—banquets and parties. (After the later defeat at Saratoga, a Patriot wag wrote: "Sir William, he, snug as a flea,/ Lay all this time a snoring/Nor dreamed of harm as he lay warm/In bed with Mrs. Loring.")[28]

The British officers wore wigs and left calling cards, and a relatively fine time was had by all until the American army, lugging cannon captured at Fort Ticonderoga and elsewhere, very inconveniently set them up on Dorchester Heights overlooking central Boston, which Howe had neglected to fortify. On the night of March 4, 1776, the American Army began to bombard the town. A contemporary account notes, "You could see shells sometimes seven at a time in the air, and as to cannon, the continual shaking of the earth by cannonading dried up our wells."[29]

Boston had become indefensible at a stroke, and there was nothing Howe could do but withdraw. Howe made an arrangement with Washington, who had been named commander in chief of the continental army. If the rebels refrained from firing on his army as it withdrew, he would refrain from destroying the town. On March 17, Howe and his troops withdrew to Halifax, and with them went 1,100 Loyalists, fleeing for their lives.

A Whig wrote, "Nothing can be more diverting than to see the town in its present situation; all is uproar and confusion; carts, trucks, wheelbarrows, handbarrows, coaches, chaises all driving as if the very devil was after them."

A Tory wrote, "Neither Hell, Hull nor Halifax can afford worse shelter than Boston."[30] One man, John Taylor, committed suicide—leading George Washington to give his opinion that all Loyalists should follow Taylor's example.[31]

The fleeing Loyalists were crammed into every vessel that could be found. In the emergency, even class distinctions went out the porthole. Benjamin Hallowell's cabin afforded shelter for "thirty-seven persons—men, women and children; servants, masters and mistresses—obliged to pig together on the floor, there being no berths." Furniture, furnishings and clothing were disposed of overboard, and the Loyalists watched in dismay as their cherished possessions bobbed around Boston harbor or sank soggily to the bottom.[32]

This ragtag fleet took six stormy days to reach Halifax, and then General Howe turned south again for New York, which was still in British hands. A few Loyalists went with him, and more stayed in Halifax, but the bulk of this first band of refugees—mostly those who could afford to—went to England after spending a season or so in the inhospitable clime of Halifax. In England they formed a sort of lobby, pressing successive administrations for more belligerence in America. At first they were well received, but later they became a bit of a bore as the British became more and more uncertain about the war. (There was an element of the same divisiveness that would split the Americans over Vietnam nearly two centuries later.) Some of them also spent much of their energy pushing for preferment for that inevitable day when the war ended. They wanted their jobs, or better ones, back in America. John Wentworth, the royal governor of New Hampshire, got himself lined up for the post of surveyor-general of the king's woods and eventually became lieutenant governor of Nova Scotia.

For every Loyalist who escaped Boston with the British, perhaps five were left behind. Most of these quickly found or assumed a new enthusiasm for the works of congress, even when that body, emboldened by the easy victory at Boston, turned its thoughts to independence.

The rebellion was turning into a revolution, and independence, oft-shunned, became first fancy and then fact. On April 12, 1776, the provincial congress of North Carolina instructed its delegates to the continental congress "to concur with the Delegates of the other Colonies in declaring Independence." A month later, Richard Lee of Virginia moved a resolution "That these United Colonies are, and of a right ought to be, free and independent." By July 1 the Declaration of Independence, largely written by Thomas Jefferson, had been adopted.

Some Loyalists were annoyed, some defiant, some terrified. Joseph Galloway, William Franklin's friend and author of one of the plans of union for British North America, saw the Declaration of Independence as a knavish trick that proved that the Patriots had been lying all along: "The independent faction, having obtained by their arts sufficient power, were not afraid to acknowledge that they had deceived the people from the beginning of their opposition to Government; and that notwithstanding all their solemn professions to the contrary, they ever had independence in their view."[33]

Henry Hulton, former commissioner of customs for Boston, exulted—from the safety of England, whence he had fled—that "London alone is worth ten Americas." Jacob Duche, rector of Christ Church in Philadelphia, who had "rashly" accepted a post as chaplain to the continental congress, advised Washington in a letter to rescind the "Hasty and ill-advised Declaration of Independency."[34]

Recant or Die

Independence was the Rubicon and everyone knew it. It led to the stepping-up of the activities of the committees of safety and the redoubling of the pressures on Loyalists who were told in plain language to "Recant or Die." John Hopkins, the Savannah mariner to whom this advice was given, had been heard to mutter "Damnation to America" in a tavern. He was tarred and feathered and carted to the now-familiar Liberty tree, where a man named Bunner acknowledged that he was "rather fat," but not too fat to shinny up the tree and hang Hopkins unless he shouted "Damnation to all Tories and Success to American Liberty." Hopkins complied, but his heart wasn't in it, and he later asked for recompense for his sufferings as a Loyalist.[35]

The Tories were always being urged by the British—and later by historians—to stand up and fight against this persecution, and to organize. Why didn't they organize, the historians like to ask. Sometimes they did, and their fellow Loyalists may have wished they had left well enough alone. After the Battle of White Plains on October 28, 1776 (which the British won with the usual heavy losses), both sides withdrew and Westchester County became a no-man's land. It was here that James De-Lancey, scion of one of the key families of politicians, soldiers and merchants in New York, established his band of West-chester refugees. More commonly called "DeLancey's Cow-boys," they went out raiding the Patriots. Inevitably there sprang up a counter-group, the Skinners, so called because they often robbed and murdered their victims. These two groups did not battle each other—a risky business—but instead preyed on the farms of the so-called "Neutral ground." In theory, the Cow-boys were Loyalists and the Skinners Patriots, but as Washington Irving would write later, "Neither Cowboys nor Skinners stopped to ask the politics of horse or cow which they drove into captivity; nor, when they wrung the neck of a rooster did they trouble their heads to ascertain whether he were crowing for Congress or King George."[36]

Obviously some freelance looting went on on both sides under the cover of military operations. The British army, on its march through Westchester, reportedly treated Loyalists, Patriots and Neutrals without discrimination: "The general distinction of Whig and Tory has been lost here in one general scene of ravage and desolation." The locals might have been forgiven for wishing the whole lot of them would quietly drift away.

Life was far easier when Loyalists took the line adopted by Beverley Robinson of Virginia, head of one of the most famous Loyalist families. He was called on by his local committee and asked to swear an oath of loyalty. He responded with the soft answer that turneth away tar and feathers, neither swearing nor refusing to swear. "I have kept myself a prisoner on my Farm," he said, "in order to keep myself from a necessity of expressing my sentiments."[37] He wound up by inviting everybody over to his place "some Sunday," by which time he would be willing to give the committee of safety a definite answer. The stall worked, and while the Patriots were still wondering whether the right Sunday had come along, Robinson scampered away from under their noses and reached the British lines. He went on to raise the Loyal American Regiment, which he commanded throughout the conflict.

However, the problem most Loyalists faced in the early stages of the war was that for the British soldiery war was still part of the old, gentlemanly game, while for them and for the Patriots, it was a matter of life and death. Lord Rawdon, writing from Long Island at the time of the successful British siege of the place, remarked that "The fair nymphs of this isle" were unhappy, because "the fresh meat our men have got here had made them as riotous as satyrs." A girl could hardly step into a bush to pluck a rose without danger of being ravished, "and they are so little accustomed to these methods that they don't bear them with the proper resignation."[38]

They Resolved to Cut Out the Preacher's Tongue

That was one man's war. Not far away, the Reverend John Beach of Newtown, Connecticut, was dragged from his pulpit because he refused to cease praying for the king, as ordered by the continental congress. His was the only loyal church to remain open, and to make an example of him the local committee resolved to cut out his tongue. "If my blood must be shed," the redoubtable old man said, "let it not be done in the house of God." So he was dragged outside, where he knelt down and begged God's forgiveness for his enemies, for "They know not what they do." The speech so moved his persecutors that his life was spared. He died peaceably six months later.[39]

Persecution of the Loyalist clergy was common, especially when they were Anglicans, for that was the established church of England, autocracy and the king. The religious aspect added to the bitterness of the times. When Moses Dunbar of Connecticut switched from the Congregational church—the accepted Patriot church—to the Anglicans, he was seized by the mob, beaten and thrown into jail as a suspected Loyalist. When he was released he fled to the British lines and joined a Loyalist regiment. When he returned to Connecticut on a private trip, he was betrayed by a friend (make that former friend) to the local committee, charged with treason and hanged at the site of the present Trinity College in Hartford. At the gallows he prayed "from the bottom of my heart" for all his enemies, and asked God "to forgive them all."[40]

As the war gathered momentum, strictures became ever tougher on the Loyalists. Massachusetts made it a crime punishable by death to "adhere to Great Britain." It was no longer necessary to prove treason; mere disloyalty was enough to attract the rope.

As if there weren't enough elements of enmity loose in the population, the behavior of the troops on both sides added a dollop of anger. The British army was famous for its discipline, which meant that British troops, often the scourings of the London jails and city slums, could be bullied and beaten into performing marching drills with machine-like precision and into lining up in serried ranks to take a hail of enemy fire. Off the drill square and the parade route they behaved much as armies do everywhere in a strange land—namely, they stole everything that wasn't nailed down, drank anything that gurgled and molested the civilian population whenever possible. The hired mercenaries were not much better. Throughout the war the ordinary soldiers on both sides were underfed, underpaid and forced to live in appalling conditions—often conditions that had nothing to do with the fighting, but were imposed by the parsimony of the authorities on both sides. They reacted, as soldiers will, by taking out their grievances on the defenseless.

British troops under the command of Lord Cornwallis near Pennytown, Pennsylvania, went on a rampage one day in late 1776. "Sixteen young women who had fled to the woods to avoid brutality . . . were seized and carried off," according to the report of the Pennsylvania council of safety. One man who may or may not have been a Loyalist—no one bothered to ask— reported that his wife and ten-year-old daughter were raped. A thirteen-year-old was taken from her father's house to a barn and raped six times. Furniture was destroyed, windows and doors smashed and "the houses left uninhabitable," while everything edible was carried off, including every horse, cow, ox, hog and chicken in the town. A blind old gentleman, plundered of everything he owned, was left with nothing but a message scrawled on his door: "Capt. Wills of the Royal Irish did this."[41]

Inevitably the Loyalists became the beneficiaries of the rage this sort of conduct engendered, and their homes, cattle and families bore the brunt of colonial anger. No one even pretended that the continental troops were disciplined. Their commander in chief, George Washington, in a private letter to his brother, wrote of his own army, "Their officers generally speaking are the most indifferent kind of people I ever saw. . . . I daresay the men would fight very well (if properly officered) although they are an exceedingly dirty and nasty people."[42] When Baron Friedrich von Steuben, who claimed to have been a lieutenant general on the staff of Frederick the Great, but who had been in fact a mere captain, arrived to try to instill military methods into the Patriot troops, he flew into constant towering rages. His English was minimal, his French passable and his meaning clear when he cursed: "Sacre! Goddamn de gaucheries of dese badouts! Je ne puis plus. I can curse dem no more!"[43]

Gentleman Johnny Comes to Crush the Rebels

Lieutenant General Burgoyne had already served in America, so King George III was prepared to listen when the bluff, cheerful, outgoing soldier came to call on him to outline his grand scheme. The king was so impressed that he asked Burgoyne to put his ideas in writing and lay them before Lord George Germain. Thus was born "Thoughts for Conducting the War from the Side of Canada." It was a sound scheme with one tiny flaw. The idea was to split the colonies by a double thrust. Burgoyne, with a force of eight thousand regulars aided by Indians and Tories, would charge down Lake Champlain to the Hudson. As he went, thousands of unhappy locals would join his army to put down this unjust and unaccountable revolution. At the same time, General William Howe would drive north from New York to meet Burgoyne at Albany. The American armies would be crushed, the colony split and the rebellion ended.[44]

The tiny flaw in the scheme was that it depended on perfect timing and the coordination of two armies separated by a wilderness. Never mind; Burgoyne was so sure of success that he made a wager, with Charles James Fox, recorded in the books of Brook's Club in London, that "he will be home victorious from America by Christmas Day, 1777." The bet was for fifty guineas.[45]

Germain gave his blessings, and Burgoyne sailed for Quebec. In the early summer of 1777 he set out down the Richelieu with his mistress riding in one of his carriages along with his supply of wines and several chests of uniforms. Burgoyne insisted on taking 138 cannon, which slowed the grand march to about one mile a day and allowed the Patriots lots of time to prepare.

The Loyalists did not come forth in the required numbers, and he didn't think much of those he got. "Sullen," he found them, and "spiritless." Then one of his Indian allies murdered Jane McCrae, the beautiful wife of a Loyalist, and Burgoyne was forced to pardon the murderer for fear of losing the other Indians.[46] That sent a message to the locals, who began to join the army, all right, but the wrong army. They signed up with the Patriots.

As Burgoyne drove south he became increasingly impeded by his own baggage, and began to lose cannon, supplies and skirmishes. Near Bennington, Vermont, he sent off a body of 650 hired Hessian mercenaries, with some Loyalists, under a commander who spoke not a word of English. They were supposed to round up horses. What they got instead was the Patriot militia under Colonel John Stark. The regulars, wearing jackboots that weighed twelve pounds a pair, along with heavy woolen coats and waistcoats, were not at their best in brush-fighting, and the fight was soon over, with 201 of Burgoyne's mixed force killed and 700 captured. The German prisoners were treated as prisoners of war and speedily exchanged. The Loyalists were treated as traitors. They were tied in pairs to horses and led through a jeering crowd to prison.

Burgoyne pressed on. He discovered, too late, that Lord Germain had forgotten to send the plan for his joint maneuver to Howe. It had been left in a pigeon-hole in his office one weekend when Germain took off for a holiday in Sussex, and it missed the packet-boat for America.[47] Howe, unknowing, sailed south from New York instead of north, and retook Philadelphia while Burgoyne's battalion was being cut to pieces north of Albany. Gentleman Johnny finally threw his troops into repeated charges against entrenched rebels at Saratoga. The British were decimated, and he was forced to surrender six thousand men. Never mind; Burgoyne was exchanged swiftly and returned across the ocean to write plays, of which *The Heiress* was the best known. For some people it was that kind of war.

The Turning Point

But for the Loyalists there were no exchanges, no wagon trains of baggage and no going home. Saratoga was not much of a win in military terms but it is generally considered to be the turning point in the war because it convinced France that the uppity new country that had declared itself independent was in fact to be taken seriously. Even if the Americans didn't win, they would make life miserable for the British, and that was enough for the French. On May 4, 1778, congress ratified a treaty of alliance with France, but long before that the French had begun to send men, arms and advisers like the engaging and effective Marquis de Lafayette.

With successes such as Saratoga came prisoners. As at Bennington, army prisoners were exchanged, but Loyalists found fighting side by side with the troops were often treated as spies and executed, beaten or imprisoned. There were no proper prisons on either side. The British used the rotting hulk of the *Jersey*, anchored in Wallabout Bay. The most notorious of the rebel prisons were the abandoned Simsbury copper mines near the town of East Granby, Connecticut. The place is now a museum. Even today, its dank, black cells over one hundred feet below ground inspire trepidation and a strong inclination to whistle Yankee Doodle. This was where hundreds of Loyalists were crammed to sicken and die of scurvy, dysentery, untreated disease and "Gaol fever." Many attempted escape, preferring to die in a bid for freedom rather than to remain and rot.

A contemporary description notes, "The prisoners are let down on a windlass into this dismal cavern, through a hole, which answers the triple purpose of conveying them food, air and—I was going to say light, but it scarcely reaches them. In a few months, the prisoners are released by death."[48]

Not every Loyalist was intimidated by Simsbury mines. The Reverend Simeon Baxter, confined in a brutal section of the place called "Orcus," preached a sermon through a barred grate to his fellow Tories outside, advising them that it was their Christian duty to assassinate George Washington and members of the congress. Baxter heaped scorn on those nice nellies who would "scruple to kill their oppressors in the dark." He survived the war, did old Baxter, and had his discourse published in London.[49]

But many did not survive the war, and the deaths were most common in the guerrilla campaign along the frontier. Here occurred some of the most savage episodes of the fighting, in which Loyalists were both aggressors and victims.

5
Tomahawk Tories

"To: MR. CARR
"P.S. I hear that Cherry Valley people is very bold,
and intend to make nothing of us. They call us wild
geese, but I know the contrary."

Joseph Brant,
letter, July, 1778

In May, 1778, a marauding band of 1,200 Tories and Indians, led by Colonel John Butler and his irregular corps of Butler's Rangers, slipped out of Fort Niagara at the mouth of the Niagara River. Moving swiftly southeast in a flotilla of war canoes, they swooped down the Mohawk and into the Wyoming Valley in Northeast Pennsylvania, descending on the settlements around Fort Wilkes-Barre.

Many of the Tories, including Butler, a prosperous farmer and merchant before the war, had been driven from their homes by the rebels, who called themselves Patriots and were in a murderous mood. Many of the Indians—Mohawks and Senecas mostly—had seen their villages smashed, their crops destroyed, their families slain. This was, as much as anything else, a raid of reprisal, and as such it was spectacularly successful, and bloody. Today a modest cement pillar stands in a small patch of grass overlooking the Susquehanna River in downtown Wilkes-Barre. Pedestrians amble past with never a glance at its stark summation, all in capital letters, of the slaughter that took place here two centuries ago: NUMERICAL SUPERIORITY ALONE GAVE SUCCESS TO THE INVADER AND WIDE-SPREAD HAVOC, DESOLATION AND RUIN MARKED HIS SAVAGE AND BLOODY FOOTSTEPS THROUGH THE VALLEY.

And that is a fair enough way to put it. In a single battle, on July 5, at least 450 American militia were killed trying to defend their homes against a force nearly three times their size. The Tory and Indian losses were eleven. The day before that battle an Indian leader, Queen Esther, had brained eleven revolutionary prisoners with a war club to revenge the slaying of her son. The revolutionaries were trussed up, stood up and battered to death. This was not a war of march and counter-march, with set-piece battles and brave bugles. It was, on both sides, a war of stealth and slaughter, a grim guerrilla campaign in which the massacre of innocents took place not by accident, but by design.

As Butler's Rangers and his Indian allies withdrew, they left behind the smoldering ruins of homes, barns and sheds won from the wilderness with years of unremitting toil, along with the bodies of men, women and children whose fatal crime was to be in the wrong place at the wrong time. Cattle were butchered, horses mutilated and left to stagger in blind pain around the scalped bodies of their owners. It became a polite fiction to pretend that all the truly savage work was done by Indians, rather than by the Loyalists.

"Tho' much pain has been taken," a British officer wrote later, "it is impossible to bring them [the Indians] to leave women and children unmolested and as for the Rest it must be expected that they will regard all White People alike." In fact there are many recorded instances of the cruelest barbarities being committed by the whites on both sides. Indians didn't rape, for one thing, and whites did.

When the marauders headed back north, they were carrying so much loot that it took them nine days to paddle back to a staging-point at Tioga, New York—normally a two- or three-day trip.

On the heels of the Wyoming Massacre, as it came to be called, a Loyalist named Joseph Wilson was seized by a group of his neighbors who charged that he had harbored some of the invading Tories in his home, a charge he heatedly and repeatedly denied. "I am no stranger, no unknown person," he argued, "you well know that I am a home-staying man, laborious and peaceable. Would you destroy me on a hearsay?" Apparently they would. Wilson was hanged by his thumbs and toes to wring a confession from him, and he fainted during the ordeal. He was cut down, revived and once more commanded to confess. When he again denied his guilt, he was strung up again, this time by the neck, and hanged.

High Talk and Low Blows

This is what all the high-flown talk of liberty and self-government on the one hand, and of loyalty and God's will on the
other, came to in the end—agonizing death. In one incident a
group of Tories were ambushed by Patriot militia, surrounded
and shot to death. "That was your brother you just shot," one
of the militia was told. He replied, grimly, "I know." In another
incident some Patriots were driven into a river. As one of them
swam up to an island and, he hoped, safety, he suddenly noticed
Tory soldiers on it and turned away. One of them called to him,
"Come back, Charles, it's me, your old neighbor." So it was,
and so he came back. As he clambered out of the water his old
neighbor shot him through the head.

From 1776 to 1783, bloody civil war raged along the borders
of New York, Vermont and Pennsylvania. There was nothing
nice about it; there was no attempt to bring equal armies into
battle against each other and may the best man win. It was a
war of ambush, subterfuge and treachery. Out of the night a
massive force would pour into an Indian village or a Patriot
town, and the people would be slain, their homes put to the
torch. A force of Tories and Indians captured a group of militiamen who had ventured out of a stockade near a place called
Forty Fort, just north of Fort Wilkes-Barre. Forty Fort appeared
immune to the raiders, who lacked cannon to pierce the stockade. So, in something of a pet, they tied their captives to trees
within hearing distance of their wives, children and neighbors
and, all night long, tortured and then burned them while their
horrified relatives wept and raged.

When the war was over it was these incidents that stuck in
the craw. For those who were involved on either side of the
frontier war, there would be no forgiving and forgetting.

The man most responsible for bringing the Indians into the
war and ensuring that most of them were Loyalists was William
Johnson, who was dead—of syphilis among other things—before it began. Johnson is one of the towering figures of North
American history—not a nice man, but an important one. With
his Indian allies—including Joseph Brant and his sister, Molly—
he played a pivotal role in everything that happened along the
frontier for more than four decades. His son, Sir John Johnson,
was to become the most influential United Empire Loyalist of
them all.

During the North American battles of the Seven Years War
(1756-1763), William Johnson had won a reputation as an en-

ergetic fighting-man among whites as well as Indians when he led a British force of provincial militia to victory over the French at Fort George. He was knighted for this act and became Sir William Johnson. But in fact his most important role was not in battle; rather, it was his long, successful struggle to keep the Iroquois neutral. (The League of the Iroquois was made up of the Six Nations—the Seneca, Cayuga, Onondaga, Mohawk, Oneida and Tuscarora.) The strong inclination on the part of most Iroquois was to pitch into the battle on the side of the French, who treated them better and didn't constantly steal their land, as the British and Dutch colonists were wont to do, under treaties whose terms seldom outlasted the council fire.

To keep the Indians from following this natural inclination to join the French took great skill, handsome gifts and, perhaps most important, the constant aid of Johnson's consort, whose Mohawk name was Degonwadonti. She had moved in with William in 1756, three years after the death of his first wife, Catherine, and she ruled as the chatelaine of Johnson Hall, near Johnstown, New York. She was the granddaughter of one of the most powerful of the Mohawk chiefs, Sagayeanquarashtow, generally known as Chief Brant (easier to spell, among other things), and her English name was Mary Brant, although Johnson called her Molly. She was handsome, shrewd, energetic and a politician to her fingertips. She knew the native alliances, who made them, who broke them, how they shifted.

Molly Brant gained great prestige through her liaison with Johnson. He gained at least as much through his liaison with her, for she was respected in her own right as a power in the Iroquois council. She ensured that her younger brother, Thayendaneaga—Joseph Brant—received a white man's education at Moor Charity School of Lebanon, Connecticut, under Dr. Eleazar Wheelock, as well as an Indian education in the arts of war.

Molly Brant bore William Johnson eight children and was accepted by many of his friends as his wife, although her relations with her stepson, John, were never close.

Father and Son

John was a strange bird, a combination of drawing-room dandy and sturdy soldier, a nob and a snob despite his upbringing in the wilderness. He was thoroughly intimidated by his towering father. John had an affair with one of his Mohawk Valley neighbors, Clarissa Putnam, and wanted to marry her, but Sir William squashed that idea flat. Let him take Clarissa as his mistress, if he wanted (he did) but let him marry someone really useful.

So John married Mary Watts, daughter of one of New York's prominent Tories. Clarissa Putnam had two children by John, whom he acknowledged publicly as his own. He maintained a relationship with her that lasted forty-five years and sent her money for her support, until he got into financial difficulty, when he sent her instead a whining note begging her not to think harshly of him. With Mary Watts, John had fourteen children and an apparently happy marriage. Johnsons, father and son, were both devils with the ladies; but one difference between them is that it is hard to imagine William being told whom to marry, and swallowing the order.

Well, John had been raised differently. He was sent to school in England and became a baronet in his own right—he was Sir John, and Mary became Lady Mary—largely through the influence of friends he made there. Returning to his father's wilderness empire, he proved an adept-enough manager, but he didn't care to mingle too much with his father's tawny friends. As for putting on a breech-clout and dancing around a fire whooping and hollering the way William did, my dear, *jamais*. On Sir William's death in July, 1774 (he was only fifty-nine), Sir John inherited Johnson Hall and ordered Molly Brant to move out at once. Later he relented and let her move to Fort Johnson, Sir William's first home, where John and Lady Mary had been living. Sir John got to rule as feudal lord over the lives of 150 disbanded Catholic Highlanders, veterans of the French and Indian wars whom Sir William had settled around Johnson Hall to farm the land and form his own army. What he did not get was his father's job as superintendent of Indians. Sir William didn't think he was the man for it, and he was probably right. Instead, Guy Johnson, Sir William's nephew, a rough-and-tumble frontiersman (also, alas, something of a drunk) became superintendent.

As the Revolution came rushing down upon America, Johnson Hall, slashed from a primal wilderness, had become part of Tryon County, New York, a contentious and trouble-making county if ever there was one. It was divided between the Whigs of Palatine, Canajoharie, German Flats and Kingsland in the west, and the Tory Catholic Highlanders around Johnson Hall. The two sides had been glowering at each other for years, and, when a committee of public safety (Whig, of course) was established for Tryon County, one of its first moves was to pay a call at Johnson Hall.

Molly Ran a Spy Network

The committee wanted to raise with Sir John and his cousin Guy a matter of road patrols. Acting on information received by Molly Brant, who operated what would today be called an intelligence network, the Johnsons anticipated a move against them by arming the Highlanders and the Indians, fortifying Johnson Hall, and sending out patrols to stop and search travelers on the king's highway. The committee wanted all that stopped and wanted all the Johnsons to show a proper respect to the Patriot cause. What they got was the old brush-off.

On May 20, 1775, Guy Johnson sent the committee a letter to deny "idle and ridiculous" reports (which happened to be perfectly true) that he was inciting the Indians to attack his Patriot neighbors. In light of the reports Molly Brant had picked up that the committee was planning to move on Johnson Hall, Guy Johnson thought it wise to warn the boys that the Indians would take it amiss if their friend and superintendent, which is to say, himself, were to be molested in any way. The Indians would wreak "dreadful revenge," Johnson said. Not an altogether reassuring note. Guy followed it with another letter, equally misleading, on June 25, to say that he had called the Indians together at Johnson Hall merely for a conference, and not to measure their neighbors for the scalp-ring.

Tension continued to mount in the valley. The sheriff of Tryon County, Alexander White, a royal appointee and not a tactful man, came across a Liberty tree at German Flats. He cut it down and arrested a popular Whig named John Fonda. A Patriot mob marched on the jail, released Fonda and then went calling on Sheriff White. They thought it might be a good idea to dip him in a vat of tar and see if he liked it. Sir John Johnson arrived on the scene before this could happen and threatened to turn his Indian allies on the Patriots unless they released White.

They did that, but no one could make them like it, especially when White remarked that he hoped to have "the pleasure of hanging a good many yet for their Resistance against the Acts of Parliament." In due course the Tryon County committee of public safety turned the matter of Sheriff White over to the state committee at Albany and he was stripped of his office and—once the Indians were safely out of the way—slapped into prison.

There was a lot of bravado on the frontier, but there was an element of caution, too. Further to the south and east, armies were marching, and the issues were clearer cut. But here in the backwoods, it was hard to tell who was in charge. Sir John Johnson was the titular head of the Tryon County militia—it was a royal appointment—and what the Tryon County militia wanted more than anything in the world was Sir John's head on a convenient fence post. In the circumstances, he found it wise not to show up for parades.

No More Stalling

This polite sparring came to an end in January, 1776, when two companies of continental troops and three thousand local militia marched on Johnson Hall. Sir John, first thoughtfully ordering the burial of the family silver plate and other valuables in the garden, surrendered. Perhaps if he had kept in better with Molly Brant, she'd have tipped him off that the Patriots were on the move (she warned Guy in plenty of time for him to clear off for Montreal). So Sir John was arrested by his own militia.

Lady Johnson was taken into protective custody in Albany, while Sir John was taken to Fishkill for questioning. Then, in the custom of the day, he was paroled on a promise to behave himself—which he had not the slightest intention of honoring—and he went dashing back to Johnson Hall. There he dug up the silver plate and began to round up supporters, including about sixty Mohawks—the remnants of the tribe who remained in the area after the main body had moved off to avoid the gathering storm. He planned to strike north with Lady Mary, who had also been paroled, towards British territory. However, word of his activities got back to the committee of public safety, and Colonel Elias Dayton was sent out with orders to "Go arrest that damned fool again."

Johnson got away at the last minute, leaving Lady Mary behind. She was sick and, Sir John feared, might not survive the flight northwards. At least, that's the way he told it. Once again it is hard to imagine Sir William saying, "Well, goodbye, Hon, I'm off; don't let any strangers in." In any event, when the militia arrived, Johnson Hall was occupied by Lady Mary, a few slaves and her infant son, William. Once more Lady Mary was taken into custody in Albany, while the Johnson estates were confiscated. Sir John reached Montreal after a scramble through the wilderness that took three weeks and left him and his band of followers exhausted and near starvation.

Lady Mary was sent to the home of Cadwallader Colden, the former lieutenant governor of New York. Soon after, one of Sir John's loyal tenants spirited away Lady Mary, her sister and three small children, and carried them across a bleak winter landscape to the British lines at Paulus Hook, New Jersey. The youngest child died during the rigorous trip, and a second soon after they reached safety. Sir John joined them at Paulus Hook and took them to New York and then Canada. Now he was free to return to the Mohawk Valley without fear of reprisals on his immediate family.

The Royal Greens

He set to work at once to form the King's Royal Regiment of New York, known as Johnson's Royal Greens. In early 1777 he launched the first of a series of raids down the Mohawk and Schorharie valleys, in the pattern that was to become familiar throughout the war of raid and counter-raid, reprisal and counter-reprisal.

Some of the fighting on the Loyalist side fell to the lot of the provincials, as they were called—the regiments raised among the displaced Tories. Properly, they were the Provincial Corps of the British Army, Northern Division, and there were seven regiments in all.[1]

They Saw Red, and Shot

The provincials wore green uniforms to distinguish them from the regular corps, who wore red. Later the provincials were deemed to have earned the right to wear red and were issued with red coats. However, their commanders noted that the red merely made them easier targets for the sharp-shooting rebels, and they went back to green.

The provincials were given picket-duty at first, or were used as scouts or stationed in the camps around Niagara, Sorel and Chambly to guard supplies. One regiment, Jessup's Corps, seemed to spend most of its time on garrison duty along the St. Lawrence or in outposts along the Richelieu. Perhaps it was just as well; to get his regiment up to strength, Jessup took all comers—children, old men, German regulars whose enlistments had lapsed, escaped slaves—everyone. This was because a full strength regiment gained certain advantages, not the least of which was that its officers received half-pay once the war was over. Johnson's Royal Greens spent much of their time building houses for refugees (Frederick Haldimand, the man who succeeded Guy Carleton as British commander, said they were "better with the ax than with the firelock"). The Loyal Americans spent much of the war around Sorel, foraging for hay and building homes for displaced fellow Loyalists. The King's Rangers seemed to have an unusually large number of officers who spent most of their time working for the secret service.

By and large, the Loyalists were the most under-utilized resource available to the British, who seemed to think they would only get in the way. Gradually, however, it began to dawn on the authorities that the Loyalists were more highly motivated than their own lads (personal mayhem on a loved one concentrates the faculties). A conscious attempt was made to give them a more important role, especially on the raids into the Mohawk Valley and down the Susquehanna, where many of them came from.

These troops were often recruited from the midst of such towns as Albany by recruiters who stayed in "safe," i.e., Tory, houses until they had rounded up a band of men who had accepted the king's shilling. Then they were led north to one of the assembling points. The recruiters were paid. John Walden Meyers, perhaps the most famous of these recruiters, earned a guinea for each recruit delivered to Colonel Gabriel Ludlow, who was rounding up soldiers for DeLancey's Cowboys in Westchester County. He was also paid a shilling a day for delivering dispatches and other spy work.

It is hardly surprising that a level of paranoia prevailed along the frontier when almost anyone could be a spy, with the possible exception of the non-English speaking German mercenaries. Part of the bitterness that marked this period came from the inevitable concern that a friend or neighbor might, on the one hand, shortly spring out with a dozen Tories and smash you down or, on the other, go running to the local committee of safety to report that you had spoken disrespectfully of congress and were probably an agent. Spies were constantly being discovered on both sides throughout the war and were usually given short shrift.

Nathan Hale, dressed as a Dutch schoolmaster in a brown suit and broad-rimmed hat, was spotted checking up on British troops and was turned in by his own cousin, a Tory. He was executed the next morning. (Incidentally, Hale did not say, "I only regret that I have but one life to lose for my country." That was a line from a play by Addison that was carved on Hale's statue on the old campus at Yale, as appropriate for the case.) On the other side, Sergeant Thomas Hickey, one of George

Washington's own guard, was revealed as a spy and hanged in front of the troops. He said he had been led into the business by "lewd women."

No One Could Be Trusted

The soldier-spies were one sort—a normal hazard of war. But the civilian recruiters of provincial regiments were something new. It could truly be said that almost no one could be trusted in the contested zone along the frontier. That became appallingly clear when the raids of Butler's Rangers began to sweep down the Mohawk, and Johnson's Loyal Greens came pouring down the Richelieu. Legends quickly sprang up of the savagery of the Tories and their Indian allies, especially of that monster, Joseph Brant, whose Mohawks were not only ferocious, but unfairly intelligent. During the siege of Fort Stanwix, not far from Johnson Hall, Brant intercepted a rescue column of Patriot militia, lured them into an ambush by having his Indians pretend to flee in terror, and then slaughtered them. Brant became a name to frighten children with; he was credited with exploits with which he had no concern (for example, he turns up constantly in references to the Wyoming Massacre, although he was nowhere near the fighting).

However, he was certainly involved in the attack on Cherry Valley, a village about fifty miles west of Albany, in November, 1778. Brant was in command of five hundred Indians in a force that also included about fifty British regulars and two hundred Tories from the ranks of Butler's Rangers and Johnson's Royal Greens. The overall command was held by Walter Butler, John Butler's son and, by all accounts, a nasty packet of goods. The locals had been agitating for a long time for more protection and were advised by the authorities in Albany to raise a force of militia. So they did that, and it was promptly commandeered for use elsewhere. When the attack came, the small band of continental regulars barricaded themselves in Fort Alden (named for Colonel Ichabod Alden, a cloth-head who built the fort, named it after himself, refused to take any threat of attack seriously, and got himself killed trying to make it into the safety of his own stockade) and left the locals to shift for themselves. The Tories and Indians raged through the area. A Boston newspaper later carried an account of the slaughter that read, in part: "The enemy killed, scalp't, and most barbarously murdered thirty-two women and children . . . burnt twenty-four houses with all the grain, &c., took above sixty inhabitants prisoners, part of whom they released on going off. They committed the most inhumane barbarities on most of the dead: Robert Henderson's head was cut off, his skull bone cut out with his scalp—Mr. Willis's sister was rip't up, a child of Mr. Willis's, two months old, scalp't and arm cut off—the clergyman's wife's leg and arm cut off, and many others as cruelly treated.''

Ironically, the one dash of humanity shown in this barbarity came when Brant stationed Mohawks around the home of some people he knew, named Shankland, to prevent Senecas from murdering Katy Shankland and her five daughters. Walter Butler personally led a group of Rangers into the home of the Wells family, where he tomahawked and scalped Robert Wells, while six other family members, one a teenaged girl, and three servants were slaughtered.

Not surprisingly, the slaughters in the Wyoming and Cherry valleys led to a cry for vengeance. After due delays to round up the necessary troops and equipment, a punitive expedition was mounted in mid-1779 under General John Sullivan (General Horatio Gates was offered the command, but refused it). With four thousand troops, the largest army ever assembled in the western sector of the war, Sullivan marched into the Wyoming Valley to execute a direct order from congress "upon an expedition of an extensive nature against the hostile tribes of the Indians of the Six Nations." The country from the Susquehanna to the New York border and then along the Mohawk Valley was not to be "merely overrun but destroyed."

The Boots Were Made of Skin

And so, to a large extent, it was. The provincials had mostly withdrawn, and the local Tories lay low. The only resistance offered to Sullivan's massive force came from Brant's Mohawks, who tried to make a stand at New Town on August 29, 1779, before fleeing before Sullivan's overwhelming force, leaving behind their dead. "How many we killed I could never exactly ascertain," wrote Nathan Davis, an officer with Sullivan's corps, "but some were killed and one scalped to my knowledge, and much blood was seen on their track." Lieutenant William Barton wrote that troops sent out to count dead Indians "Found them and skinned two of them from their hips down for boot legs; one pair for the Major and the other for myself."

The Indian villages were overrun and, whether the inhabitants had taken any part in the war or not, destroyed. There were not many immediate casualties, as the Indians fled before the advancing white horde, but the next winter many starved to death because their crops and stores were all gone. The soldiers were so busy looting that one officer, coming upon his men who were supposed to be getting ready to attack Seneca Town, complained bitterly when he saw them marching about with pumpkins on their bayonets, for easier carrying. According to Major Jeremiah Fogg, who was keeping an account for congress, the officer shouted, "You damned unmilitary set of rascals! What, are you going to storm the town with pumpkins?"

The soldiers of the continental army were duly impressed with the quality of Indian agriculture—corn stalks grew as high as eighteen feet with ears of corn nearly two feet long, and there was squash, pumpkins, beans and fruits of every variety—and with the neat, well-ordered Indian villages, which contained, instead of the expected wigwams, well-built wooden huts, longhouses and chapels. Everything was smashed, and all the growing crops that could not be carried off were burned or buried. Even the graveyards were looted for trinkets, and a patch of destruction slashed across the Indian lands. Kanadasaga, the capital of the Seneca nation, was occupied and put to the torch without a shot being fired. After New Town, the Indians were unwilling to put themselves in battle against Sullivan's army, and the Rangers had vanished in their boats to Fort Niagara.

Brant's attempts to rally the Indian warriors came to nothing, and village after village was put to the torch, until at last the ravaging army came to Chenussio, the largest and finest Indian center in North America. It was burned to the ground, the stores torched or carried off, the surrounding fields devastated.

Driven to Loyalty

The overwhelming majority of Indians whose homes were smashed had nothing to do with the Loyalists; some Onondagas, whose tribe fought with the Patriots, were victims, too. In turn, any white suspected of being a Tory or harboring a Tory or a hostile Indian had his home torn down around his ears, and his cattle maimed, slaughtered or driven off. The net result was to drive many neutrals to the British lines, where they in turn became Loyalists.

On September 30, 1779, Major Jeremiah Fogg took pen in hand to report to congress. He was able to congratulate himself and the rest of Sullivan's army for "having fulfilled the expectations of our country by beating the enemies and penetrating and destroying their whole country." More than fifty villages had been smashed, nearly fifty thousand bushels of crops from potatoes to parsnips were ruined, some ten thousand apple, peach and plum trees were girdled, uprooted or felled. This had come about, Fogg was pleased to note, by "the special hand and smiles of Providence," which, as usual, had come down on the side of the big battalions. But Fogg was not entirely satisfied. Unlike Sullivan, who in his own report claimed that "We have not left a single settlement nor an acre of corn in the country of the Five Nations [should have been Six, but let it go], or is there even the appearance of an Indian on this side of Niagara." Sullivan, the pompous ass, missed the point that Fogg made: "The nests are destroyed, but the birds are still on the wing."

With every new outrage, every slaying on either side, the bitterness was driven in deeper to lodge and fester. That was inevitable, but what made it most poignant for the Loyalists was that they were no longer fighting to preserve Parliament, or even their homes. As the weight of the war began to shift against the British, it was their very lives that came to be at stake. They had taken a stand in what they saw as a battle to restore order and preserve the Empire. Now they faced a future that seemed to threaten them with uprooting, if not death. As the focus of the war swung into the south in 1778, it was becoming evident that, whatever happened in the wilderness war along the frontier, the final victory was going to go to the Patriots. It was also becoming evident that when the war was over, the victors were not going to be in a forgiving mood.

6

It's Damned Unfair, Damned Unfair

"If a stop cannot be put to these massacres, the country will be depopulated, as neither Whig nor Tory can live."

General Nathaniel Greene,
*in 1780, on arriving to take over
the Patriot army in the south*

At three o'clock on the afternoon of Saturday, October 7, 1780, a force of nine hundred Patriots assembled among the rain-drenched trees at the foot of Kings Mountain, South Carolina. Atop the mountain 1,100 Tories were grouped under the leadership of a single British officer, Major Patrick Ferguson. Ferguson chose to go to the ridge atop the hill (it really is no mountain) because he had great contempt for the Patriots and envisioned them charging up, only to flee back down again when he turned loose his combined force of South Carolina militia and "American volunteers" from the hills of North Carolina. It didn't work out that way. Instead, the Patriots, most of them the clannish Over-Mountain men from Virginia and Burke County, North Carolina, picked off the Tories and provincials with their rifles. General Light Horse Harry Lee (Robert E.'s father) later wrote, "Kings Mountain proved to be more assailable by the rifle than defensible with the bayonet."

In a little less than an hour, the Tories were decimated. Major Ferguson had three horses shot out from under him and kept on fighting; he was wounded twice and kept on fighting; then he was shot through the head—that ended his fighting. All across the mountaintop white handkerchiefs were tied to rifle barrels and thrust aloft. The Patriots ignored them and continued to fire. "Quarter! Quarter!" the Tories cried. "Damn you, if you want quarter, throw down your arms," replied Colonel

Isaac Shelby, a rebel commander. But when the Tories complied, the firing continued anyway.

The only thing that distinguished Loyalist from Patriot in this massacre—since neither side boasted many uniforms—was that the Patriots shoved slips of paper in their hats, and the Tories wore twigs in theirs. They came from the same backgrounds; they grew up in small settlements as alike as peas in a pod. They talked and walked the same way, sang the same songs, enjoyed the same food and, when the time came, slaughtered each other with that frantic hatred that seems the special prerogative of civil wars.

Young Joseph Sevier, whose father John was one of the rebel heroes, shouted, "The damned rascals have killed my father, and I'll keep loading and shooting till I kill every son of a bitch of them!" He only lowered his gun when his father appeared unharmed on horseback. Finally a Virginian, Colonel Campbell, shouted at his own troops, "For God's sake, don't shoot! It's murder to kill them now!" And Captain Abraham DePeyster, a Loyalist who assumed command of the Tories when Ferguson died, rode over to Campbell to lodge his protest. "It's damned unfair," he shouted, "damned unfair!"

But fairness had nothing to do with it; never had. Kings Mountain was about vengeance and blood hatreds. It was a battle among neighbors. Major Ferguson was the only British soldier engaged—all the rest were Loyalists or Patriots. In the fighting the Patriots suffered seventy casualties, dead and wounded; the loss on the Loyalist side was 157 dead, 163 wounded and 698 prisoners. The dead were hastily buried in shallow graves or pulled into piles and covered with logs, bark and rocks. Many of the corpses were devoured by wild hogs.

James Collins, one of the Patriots who helped bury the dead, later recalled, "The scene was really distressing. The wives and children of the poor Tories came in, in great numbers. Their husbands, fathers and brothers lay dead in heaps, while others lay wounded, a melancholy sight indeed!"

Among the Tory officers who survived that day were Abraham DePeyster (whose life was saved when a doubloon in his vest pocket stopped a rifle ball), Samuel Ryerson, John Taylor, Anthony Allaire, William Stevens and Duncan Fletcher, all of whom would become part of the Loyalist migration to Canada. They carried with them a sheaf of searing memories that would last a lifetime and help to form the attitudes of their new nation to the north.

One of those memories was the looting that was an inevitable part of any such victory, when the horses, guns and valuables were stripped from the prisoners. (It was a proud moment for a Patriot who snatched up Major Ferguson's watch, "as round as a turnip.") Another memory was of the brutal, exhausting march to Hillsborough, North Carolina, about two hundred miles to the northeast, where there was a rebel encampment. The healthy Tories were forced to carry two rifles each (after the Patriots had prudently removed the flints) throughout the long, weary march. The wounded were transported on hastily improvised horse-litters. Many of them died along the way.

The journey became a nightmare. There was little to eat for either victors or vanquished, although at Broad River, the deserted plantation of a Tory provided a feed of sweet potatoes roasted over a fire made of the Tory's fence rails. The weather was raw, the trail rough. Green pumpkin, sliced and fried, provided a staple for the Patriots, while the prisoners lived mainly on raw corn and pumpkin thrown into their midst "as if they were farmer's swine." After a week on the road, the straggling procession had covered only about forty miles, and the Patriots were in a savage mood. The citizen-soldiers were anxious to get home and impatient of the delays imposed by military procedures. Their commander, Colonel Campbell, felt compelled to issue a statement: "I must request the officers of all ranks in the army to endeavour to restrain the disorderly manner of slaughtering and disturbing the prisoners."

The Sentence Was Death

Instead, there would be an orderly slaughter. On Saturday, October 14, one week after the battle of Kings Mountain, the Patriots halted to hold a show-trial of the Tories and brought thirty-six of them before a makeshift court whose twelve-man jury consisted entirely of Patriot officers. All thirty-six were speedily convicted of "breaking open houses, killing the men, turning the women and children out of doors, and burning the houses." The sentence was death, to be carried out on the spot.

That night, from the limb of a giant oak tree just outside Gilbert Town, North Carolina, the Over-Mountain men gathered and, under the light of pine-knot torches, began to string up their hapless prisoners three at a time. However, after the third triple hanging, the festive air went out of the occasion. Some of the Patriots were appalled, although one bitter Tory-hater pointed to the nine bodies swinging in a row and growled, "Would to God every tree in the wilderness bore such fruit as that!" For most, however, the job was done. The other twenty-seven condemned were untied and rejoined their comrades on the long, cold march to prison in Hillsborough.

Kings Mountain was not a major battle, but it is popular with historians because it marks one of those handy turningpoints in a war. The British offense in the south was stalled, and Sir Henry Clinton, one of the many ineffective British commanders, would later write, "The instant I heard of Major Ferguson's defeat, I foresaw most of the consequences likely to result from it. The check so encouraged the spirit of rebellion in the Carolinas that it could never afterwards be humbled . . . [It] was the first in a chain of evils that followed each other in regular succession until they at last ended in the total loss of America."

Destroyed by Damned Driblets

The main shape of the southern campaign was less complex than the rambling, in-and-out affair of march and counter-march above the Virginia line.

The British tried to take Charleston, South Carolina, the most important southern city, in 1776 and were bloodily repulsed. There were no major battles for two years, until in late 1778 it was becoming clear that the war in the north was not running to form. The British had the troops, but could never pin that rascal Washington down. "Our army will be destroyed by damned driblets," complained Adjutant General Edward Harvey. So Lord George Germain came up with another of his brilliant schemes: shift the war to the south, take Charleston, then drive north to pin the villains down between two British armies. South Carolina could then be reestablished as a royal colony, which would lead to the capitulation of North Carolina, which in turn was "but the road to Virginia."

On paper the thing was a snip, and Germain must have wondered why he had to pay generals to think things up. But, like his terrific plan to capture the north with Gentleman Johnny Burgoyne's thrust to Saratoga, this plan tended to come unstuck. Sir Henry Clinton had succeeded the hapless William Howe as supreme commander in North America (a Loyalist wrote at the time that Howe's reward for his services in the war ought to be a hangman's noose—there's no pleasing some people), so Germain wrote to Clinton to tell him how it would be:

"So very contemptible is the rebel force now . . . that no resistance . . . is to be apprehended that can materially obstruct the speedy suppression of the rebellion. The American levies in the King's service are more in number than the whole of enlisted troops in the service of the Congress."

This is known as the light-at-the-end-of-the-tunnel school of military planning, but it was based on the fact that the Americans were indeed suffering from lapsed enlistments and general fatigue with the war, while the Loyalists were indeed capable of playing a much more active role in the campaigning. This fact was now being pointed out to the British high command by those Loyalists who had gone scurrying back to Britain after the fall of Boston, and spent their days chivvying the generals to get on with it so they could go home again. The Loyalist lobby in England was a constant reminder to the administration, when it wanted to turn its attention to other matters, that there was a war to be won.

Arnold Offers a Bargain

The British were also braced by the fact that Benedict Arnold, one of the most effective of the American commanders, had changed sides and offered to sell them West Point, of which he was in command. He started the bidding at £20,000 ("Money is this man's God," one of his enemies commented, and he hit the nail on the head), but eventually settled for less than £7,000. The plot was uncovered by accident when Arnold's go-between, Major John André, was captured while carrying incriminating papers. He was hanged, and didn't like it much. He drew back at the gallows. When an officer at his side asked—rather stupidly, I've always thought—"Why this emotion, Sir?" André replied, "I am reconciled to my death, but I detest the mode."

Arnold heard about the capture and knew the jig was up. He escaped and became an instant Loyalist. Later he would move to Canada, but in the meantime his defection rocked the rebels to the core. "Treason! treason! treason! black as Hell!" wrote Washington's chief of intelligence. "We are all astonishment— each peeping at his next neighbour to see if any treason was hanging about him."

All in all, despite the series of disasters that had befallen the British, it looked as if something might be done. So Sir Henry Clinton gathered his army and sailed out of New York for the south. Savannah and then Augusta had fallen with comparative ease to other commanders and, after a bloody, six-week siege, Clinton retook Charleston on May 12, 1780. Right, he said in effect, that's that; and he sailed back home, leaving Charles, Lord Cornwallis, to get on with the job of mopping up the

Carolinas. Cornwallis was a trained soldier who could line up his troops to fire off uniform salvos with the best of them, but he was not the man to cope with the guerrilla war in which he found himself embroiled. For more than a year he stumbled around the south wasting his army in vain attempts to catch up to the rebels, led by that shrewd and elusive Quaker, Nathaniel Greene.

Kings Mountain was the beginning of the end for Cornwallis. It wiped out his western wing, and he turned north, staggering eventually to Yorktown, Virginia, where he was outsmarted, outnumbered and outgunned. George Washington, in one of his brilliant military strokes, left the north and hustled south in time to pin Cornwallis down while Sir Henry Clinton was still stooging around New York wondering whether the south was captured yet. Cornwallis surrended on October 19, 1781, and the major fighting of the war was over. (No blame, needless to say, was assigned to Cornwallis; he was named governor general of India. Clinton merely got Gibraltar, and the two men exchanged insults and charges as to who was to blame for what, until Clinton died in 1795.)

That is the formal, military side of the southern campaign. But the side that has to do with the Loyalists was nothing so tidy as this thrust, counter-thrust, slip and fall. As in the north, the Loyalist fortunes in the south were tied to those of the military, but the Loyalists had little control over the battlefields where their fates were wrestled out. Theirs was for the most part a war of small brutalities, fought from town to town and door to door and transformed into a legacy of hatred on both sides that far outlasted the echoes of shot and shell at Yorktown.

Take the custom of "spicketting," which joined tarring and feathering as one of the ways to deal with a Loyalist or suspected Loyalist. The victim was bound, stood with one foot on a sharpened stake, and then whirled around, driving the stake into his foot and, quite often, crippling him for life. A man who has been spicketted and then moved to Canada is not the kind of person likely to say after a few years, Oh, well, what the hell, boys will be boys; we really should try to be better neighbors with the Americans.

Some You Win, Some You Lose

As in the north, the persecutions began early and ended late in the south, and had the twin and offsetting effects of frightening some neutrals into the Patriot camp on the one hand, and driving some into the Loyalist camp on the other.

That is what happened to Thomas Browne, an independent-minded inhabitant of New Richmond, South Carolina, near the Georgia border. Some of the Sons of Liberty in Georgia got it into their heads that Browne was the illegitimate son of Lord North, dedicated to subverting the Patriot cause. So in August, 1775, they paid him a visit. Browne was asked to go to Augusta to defend himself against charges that he had "ridiculed the Whigs in toasts," but he declined. "Whereupon," the Georgia *Gazette* reported, "they politely escorted him into Augusta, where they presented him with a genteel and fashionable suit of tar and feathers." In fact, the genteel suit of pitch was so roughly applied that Browne lost several of his toes. Browne, under the threat of future torture, swore "that he would for the future, at the hazard of his life and fortune, protect and support the rights and liberties of America." He was only kidding. When he subsequently escaped, he exacted his vengeance by leading the Florida Rangers on ravaging expeditions against his former neighbors. He became Indian superintendent in the province of Florida and helped to persuade the southern tribes—Cherokees, Choctaws, Chickasaws and Upper Creeks—to join the British. In 1780 he was with the British force, under Major General Benjamin Lincoln, that occupied Augusta. According to some accounts—which Browne denied—he allowed troops under his command to slaughter injured rebel prisoners. Obviously a sorehead.

Georgia was perhaps the most loyal of the southern provinces, but there were strong Loyalist settlements in the Carolinas, too—not only along the seacoast, which remained in British hands throughout the war, but in the up-country as well. Some of the Loyalists suffered appallingly.

One of the many grisly episodes of the war began when a group of Tories ambushed and killed six rebels at Piney Bottom in Cumberland County, North Carolina. In response, a troop of one hundred rebels under a "Colonel Wade and Captain Culp," captured and beat Daniel Patterson, described only as "an aged piper," until he revealed the names of the Tory miscreants. Then the Patriots attacked seven Loyalists—only two of whom were named by Patterson or had anything to do with the Piney Bottom killings—and murdered them.

One account reads: "Daniel McMillan came into the house begging for his life, with the blood streaming from his side, his hunting shirt on fire, where he had been shot in the shoulder, his wrist cut and broken by a sword, his arm shattered and torn by a musket ball, two or three musket balls having passed through his body; but revenge was not yet satisfied, and another ball through his breast near the left shoulder, soon put an end to his suffering."

The house into which McMillan came running in this passage was the home of a neighbor, Mrs. Allan McSwene, who with her child was still reeling from this horror when her own husband—a Tory, but not a participant in the Piney Bottom killings—was bound and slaughtered in front of her, and Mrs. McSwene was "jerked prostrate to the floor."

The ties that bound neighbors together were now as deadly as a noose, as Major John Eliot, a North Carolina Tory, discovered. At Wilmington while visiting a prison ship, he found that a Colonel Dugan, a rebel and his friend and neighbor, was about to be hanged for fomenting revolt. Eliot spoke up for Dugan so warmly and so effectively that the authorities became convinced that a mistake had been made, and they released Dugan instead of hanging him. Soon after, a band under the leadership of this same Colonel Dugan went on the rampage to revenge the slaying of one of its members. Dugan and his men seized, summarily tried and hanged three Loyalists. One of them was Major John Eliot.

Liberty to Some Slaves

Throughout the south an extra edge was given to the war of neighbor upon neighbor by the British policy of freeing the black slaves. Every large planter carried in his head a worry that one day his field hands would revolt. The British authorities decided very early in the war to harness this fear. On November 5, 1775, Lord Dunmore, the royal governor of Virginia, issued a proclamation freeing any slave in Virginia who would sign up to fight on the British side. Later the policy was extended to every southern province, phrased in such a way that only the blacks belonging to rebels were freed, while those owned by Britons and Loyalists remained in bondage. Many of the Loyalists' slaves, euphemistically dubbed "servants," were shipped north to Canada at war's end, where they formed the basis of the sizable black population of Nova Scotia. The emancipation policy, with its heady whiff of hypocrisy, outraged the sensibilities of the south. But it worked. By December Lord Dunmore had three hundred black soldiers under his command, each with "Liberty to the Slaves" emblazoned on his uniform (properly, the banners should have read, "Liberty to Some Slaves"). The latent paranoia of southern whites was fanned into flame, but the feared insurrection never came to pass. Just the same, emancipation was cited as a justification for the harsh treatment meted out to the Loyalists.

Will Ye No Come Back Again? No.

Some of the bitterest fighting of the war took place in those provinces like North Carolina where there was a fairly equal balance of Patriots and Loyalists. Such was the case in the area around Cape Fear, where one of the early engagements of the conflict involved that redoubtable Scots heroine famed in song and story, Flora Macdonald.

After her rescue of Bonnie Prince Charlie in the Jacobite Rebellion of 1745, Flora married, confusingly enough, a man named Allan MacDonald and moved to America. They settled among other Highlanders on the Carolina coast.

In February, 1776, a Loyalist force of 1,400 mustered to the sound of the pibroch at Cross Creek and began a march toward Wilmington to join up with Sir Henry Clinton. Allan MacDonald was the senior officer, and Flora went along with her husband to lend her famous name to the cause. (Another who went along was Alexander Legate. He had been named a member of the committee of public safety for Bladen County, and was supposed to devote his energies to smashing Loyalists, not joining them. It was a confusing war.)

Two units of Patriot militia and Minute Men marched north from Wilmington and positioned themselves across the Loyalists' route of march. There was going to be a battle. Flora, mounted on a white horse, addressed the assembled Loyalists in Gaelic. On the morning of February 27, the Loyalists came up to where the Patriots were waiting for them, at what was known as Widow Moore's Creek. General MacDonald, Flora's husband, had fallen ill, and the command was taken by Colonel Donald McLeod, an impetuous Scot, but not a brilliant strategist, who conceived the idea of charging across the creek into the cannon thoughtfully mounted by the Patriots on the far side. It was not a good idea. The rebels, rather unfairly, stripped the timbers from the Moore's Creek Bridge, leaving only the siderails. When the Loyalists came charging down, they were embarrassed to discover that only a few could scramble across the water at a time—just about as many, as it happened, as the cannon could dispatch in a single loading. The battle lasted three minutes, during which seventy Loyalists and two Patriots fell. Then the Loyalists surrendered and 850 of them were rounded up.

Part of the Patriot loot from this engagement was General MacDonald's muster lists. At a time when no one knew which side his neighbor was on, and when it had become common practice to slip away from the house for a few days to join one side or the other and the slip back with no one the wiser, the muster lists were invaluable. Presence on such a list constituted irrefutable evidence of treason, and the home of every man so documented became fair game for Patriot looters. So did the home of every one of the 850 Loyalist prisoners, including General MacDonald. His place was ransacked and Flora's two daughters were robbed, even to the rings on their fingers. Flora herself, captured at Moore's Creek with her husband, was paroled and took no further part in the war. At the general's death in 1778, she returned to the Isle of Skye, where she died in 1790.

For Every Tit, a Tat

In the aftermath of Moore's Creek Bridge, Patriot mobs roamed the countryside rooting out Loyalists and robbing them. It was inevitable. For every tit in this bloody war, there had to be a tat. When the rebels ran Lord Dunmore out of Williamsburg—he took shelter, as did many royal governors, on a king's ship—he ordered in retaliation "the destruction of Virginia." That was asking a bit much, but the British navy did its best to comply by lining up offshore from the town of Norfolk and cannonading that peaceable port to pieces. Norfolk was reckoned to be the home of many rebels and thus a fit object for such destruction. The eleven-hour cannonade reduced most of the town to rubble, but one section was purposely spared. That was where most of the Loyalists lived. Outraged Patriots descended on the area with torches and burned every house to the ground. When they and the fleet were done, no more than a dozen houses were left standing in all the town, out of several hundred original buildings.

It was never the kind of war where rules counted for much. The British officers were reluctant to turn the Loyalists loose (lot of damned amateurs), and sometimes the Loyalists chafed under the inaction. So one day, having nothing better to do, two of the Loyalist militia colonels, Hector McNeil and David Fanning (brother of the aristocratic and hated Edmund Fanning) called together five hundred of their men, mostly Highlanders, and swooped down on the rebel stronghold of Hillsborough, North Carolina. They caught the Patriots completely by surprise and released a jailhouse full of Tory prisoners. They also captured two hundred Patriots, among them the Patriot governor, Thomas Burke. How embarrassing.

Life Was Tricky for Traitors

What made life really tricky for both Patriots and Tories was when a town was taken and then retaken, as happened in Charleston. One week the British were on top and staging balls, parades and cotillions. Just about everybody, it turned out, was strong for the king, always had been, and where the pesky rebels got their recruits was a real puzzle. Then the British were gone, and the rebels took over and began to check around for Tories and spies. It turned out that all but a handful of the townsmen were Patriot to the core, always had been, and to hell with King George. Then, curse it, the British came back, and there was all that weary work to do again.

The British rounded up more than one hundred suspects—anyone who would not swear an oath to the king became a suspect, along with his family—and shoved them into a makeshift prison in the basement of the Exchange Building in downtown Charleston. Called the Provost Dungeon, it had been used as a jail for pirates in the early eighteenth century. The place is a museum today, and it has been cuted up, but you can see that with scores of men, women and children crowded into the dank basement for weeks on end, it must have been appalling.

One of those confined there was Isaac Hayne, a handsome, rich, thirty-six-year-old plantation owner at Hayne Hall on the Pon Pon River, not far from Charleston. His story, with its mixture of high honor and low brutality, of the fine points of debate and the rough knot of a hangman's noose, says something about the conditions of that time, which laid the ground for enmities that lasted long after poor Isaac was moldering in the grave.

Hayne had come to town in June, 1780, to get a doctor and medicines for his wife and children, who had smallpox. He was suspected of having been on the rebel side in the siege of Charleston, and there is some evidence that he was. Certainly he was in the Colleton County militia, which was not on the British side. In any event he was confronted, and swore an oath that he would agree to act as a British subject as long as the British controlled the area. He resigned his militia commission and was allowed to go home. By May of the next year, a series of British defeats changed the situation, and the British found their Loyalist militia deserting or, worse still, switching sides in large numbers.

In the circumstances, with only Charleston still in British hands, Hayne felt it right—or at least safe—to forget his oath. He argued that "Allegiance due to a conqueror ceased with his expulsion from the subdued territory." So he reassumed his commission and in July, 1781, he was in command of a troop that captured a Loyalist, General Andrew Williamson.

The British commander in Charleston, suspecting that Williamson might be hanged as a traitor, quickly dispatched a rescue mission which caught up to the inexperienced Hayne, killed thirteen of his men, freed Williamson, and brought Hayne back to Charleston. He was slammed into the Provost Dungeon and ordered before a court of enquiry with no charge specified.

A hastily assembled court of army officers examined Hayne about his oath of loyalty, which they thought he had violated, and which he thought had been rendered null and void by the fact that the British no longer controlled the area. He was convicted of "having been found under arms . . . though he had become a subject and had accepted the protection of the government after the reduction of Charleston." The sentence was death.

On the morning of August 4, Hayne was removed from the dungeon and "escorted by a party of soldiers to a gallows erected without the lines of the town with his hands tied behind, and there hung up till he was dead."

He died well, quietly and bravely, and even put on his own blindfold when the executioner fumbled with it. His death was apparently ordered to frighten the wavering in Charleston, but it was a major blunder. It had repercussions far beyond South Carolina, because of the incivility and unfairness of the so-called "trial." In Britain, such a furore erupted over Hayne's hanging that it almost led to a duel between the Duke of Richmond and Lord Rawdon. Whatever its merits or demerits as a matter of military protocol, hanging Hayne was a tactical blunder, especially in view of Britain's deteriorating position in the war. Before long the British would have to pull out of the city again. Worse than that, Cornwallis and his army were lurching northward into Virginia and the defeat two months later at Yorktown. Many of the rebels wanted Cornwallis strung up for Hayne.

Retaliation Was Promised

Nathaniel Greene, the southern rebel commander, promised retaliation for Hayne's execution and sent the Patriot guerrilla leader, Francis Marion, into the Pon Pon area where he ambushed Major Thomas Fraser and his Loyalists—Fraser was the man who had captured Hayne—and killed and wounded more than a hundred of his troops. On September 8, the battle of Eutaw Springs, another Patriot victory, brought dozens of British officers into American hands, and Greene was urged to string some of them up. But he stalled; he was weary of the game of tit for tat.

The British regulars could exhibit a maddening insensitivity toward the Loyalists. When Tory militia were captured by the Patriots, they were treated as traitors and subject to imprisonment or execution by their former friends and neighbors. However, the British insisted on treating all Patriot prisoners as prisoners of war who were entitled to the courtesies of exchange and parole. So the Loyalists stood by in rage while the men who had robbed and ravaged their homes were paroled to freedom.

"In this war," one Tory writer noted, "only those who are loyal are treated as rebels."

7
Vindictive Victory

"Was ever an instance, can history produce one, where such a number of the best human beings were deserted by the government they have sacrificed their all for?"

Sally Winslow,
Loyalist, April 10, 1783

The British surrender at Yorktown, Virginia, took place on October 19, 1781, but it was almost two years later, on September 3, 1783, that the formal peace treaties were signed. There were no more set-piece battles, although there were many attacks and counter-attacks all through 1782. But the outcome of the war was no longer in doubt. The rascally rabble had defeated the British and Tories expressly against the best advice of the day and in sublime ignorance of the fact that God was on the side of royalty. Victory adjusts the cloak of righteousness on the shoulders of the victors and leaves the losers mother-naked. This is always hard for the clergy on the wrong side to explain. It is even harder for their parishioners to live with.

On February 27, 1782, the House of Commons, acknowledging the news from Yorktown, petitioned George III to end the war. But it did not end. Commissioners from the new United States, and from Britain, met in Paris to sample the delights of that capital and debate (and debate and debate) details of the many treaties it would take to sort out all the combatants in Europe and America. While the delegates danced and dined and debated in Paris, Loyalists died along the coasts and across the back country of America.

Indeed for many Loyalists the two years between the disaster at Yorktown and the final arrival of peace were the worst time of all. They were fair game, and their tormentors took full advantage of the fact.

Consider the case of Isabella McDonald, a North Carolina widow whose husband, Captain James McDonald, was killed in the brutal bush warfare of the Carolina uplands. Her neighbors became concerned, after Yorktown, that any peace treaty would contain a provision making it illegal to loot the property of Loyalists. So they rushed right over to the McDonald plantation and cleaned out everything worth stealing, down to the widow's clothes and rings.

As the war wound down, the British began to evacuate the southern ports they still held, and to which the Loyalists had flocked for protection—places like Wilmington, Charleston and Savannah. The result was to expose those Loyalists left behind—who were mainly those too poor, ill or old to flee—to the mercy of their most intimate enemies. British troops were withdrawn from Savannah in July, 1782, and from Charleston five months later, with predictable results. The commanders in each case dragged out the evacuations as long as possible to allow Loyalists to escape—and many did—to St. Augustine in British-held East Florida, to the West Indies, to England and to Canada. But there were many who could not leave, and their plight was recorded this way: "Such a number were still left behind, that properly to describe their situation upon the evacuations is scarcely possible. There were old grey-headed men and women, husbands and wives with large families of little children, women with infants at their breasts, poor widows whose husbands had lost their lives in the service of their King and country, with half a dozen half-starved bantlings at their skirts, taking leave of their friends."

When the ships parted, the looting started. At Charleston the mobs poured in from the outlying countryside and began to harry the Tories. Some were seized and whipped, others were thrown into the Provost Dungeon where, not long before, Patriots had laid in their own filth. Some were tarred and feathered, others dragged to horse water troughs and held under until they were nearly or completely dead. Loyalists were bundled into carts and whipped around the city bearing placards that read, simply, "Tory"—for there was no worse epithet. Finally a gallows was erected at the waterfront, and twenty-four of the most prominent remaining Loyalists were hung in sight of the retreating fleet. The last vision many of the escapees had was of their friends being trussed and strangled along the Charleston waterfront.

Legal Looting of the Loyalists

Every state—the provinces were states now—had passed laws of varying severity to deal with the cancer in their midst represented by the Loyalists. It has not always been possible to enforce such acts in the midst of an ongoing war, especially when it was unclear how that war would come out. Now it was. Loyalists were ordered to swear oaths of allegiance under the early test acts and were punished for refusal. In New York, early in the war, of one thousand Loyalists arrested for refusal to take the oath, six hundred were freed on their promise to behave themselves. General Washington was having great difficulty holding together his army as peace approached and home beckoned, so Tories and suspected Tories were ordered to enlist and were fined if they refused. If they tried to hire substitutes to take their places—an acceptable practice at that time—they were fined for that, and the substitutes rejected. Any manifestation of loyalty brought a fine on the errant Tories.

In New York and in South Carolina, special laws were passed to make the Loyalists liable for all robberies committed in their areas, on the logic that robbers must be on the king's side. Tories were subject to double and triple taxation, and then, as the financial situation of the states continued to be desperate, their lands and goods were seized and sold. The continental congress invited the states to confiscate property and invest the proceeds in continental loan certificates—the war bonds of their time. In New York State alone, £3,600,000 found its way into state coffers this way, while probably at least as much again was absorbed by corruption along the way.

Horses, cattle, crops and personal goods, from food to clothing, jewels and even cutlery, were seized and sold in this "legal" way, as opposed to merely being ravaged by the mob. On both sides slaves, who were among the most valuable property, were snapped up, loaded on ships and dispatched to the West Indies for sale to plantation owners there, in the name of liberty or loyalty or both.

Bills of attainder were passed by local legislatures, singling out individuals for punishment. Once named, that individual became a non-person in law and could be denied any protection, including the right to a trial before punishment. The bills were not the invention of the Patriots, but had formerly been used only against those who had been convicted of treason. ("Attainder" comes from a French word that carries the implication of dishonour; my dictionary calls it "extinction of the civil rights and capacities of a person upon sentence of death or outlawry, usually after a conviction of treason.") But in the murderous mood of 1781-83, no such conviction was necessary. All that was required was the naming of an individual before the local government.

There was some revulsion among the Patriots over the use of these bills, and when the Americans drew up their Bill of Rights in 1791, its first paragraph outlawed such proceedings. That was too late for the Loyalists. The records show that almost five hundred bills of attainder were passed against individuals, most of them late in the war.

Loyalists Became Non-Persons

The next and inevitable step was to treat Loyalists as outlaws even if they had not been named in a bill. The moment a man refused an oath of allegiance to congress, he became an outlaw. If his neighbors owed him money, he could not go to court to collect (although, ironically, he could if he were a British citizen). He could neither buy nor sell land. He could be libeled, slandered, insulted, blackmailed or assaulted, and he had no remedy under law. He could not be a guardian, nor the executor of another's estate. He was, in short, a non-person. New York passed another law under which all debts owed to Loyalists were canceled on condition that the state treasury be paid one-fortieth of the amount owing. So if you owed a Loyalist a lot of money, you could get him named as a traitorous Tory, then pay a fraction of what you owed over to the state, thus getting rid of the debt cheaply—with the joint side-benefit of beggaring the lender. That might make you feel worthier than if you simply refused to acknowledge the debt, knowing no court would enforce its payment.

Not all Loyalists were ill-treated, of course. In many places away from the fighting, Tories lived side by side with Patriots throughout the war and came to no harm. The province of Delaware, in June, 1778, produced a list of forty-six "exceptionally objectionable" Tories who were to be excluded from any future pardon. (The list, to show what a cross-section the Tories comprised, included three doctors, one lawyer, seven officeholders—i.e., royal appointees—nine husbandmen, one bricklayer, one saddler, three shallopmen, one hatter and two innkeepers.) The total population of Delaware at that time was 59,096, so there were probably more than 10,000 Tory sympathizers in the province. Most of these would have held their tongues, but in other cases neighbors must have known of their views and let them be. Of course, these are not the cases that went into history, so it is easy to forget that alongside the terror there was tolerance.

What made life more complex was the fact that the Revolution became overlaid in some places with local feuds. One story concerns a Patriot group called the Retaliators and a Loyalist bunch called the King's Bravoes—also known as the Pine Robbers. They both operated out of Monmouth County, New Jersey, which was tough luck for the people of the county. You could get your horse stolen or your throat cut in the name of the king or congress; neutrality didn't count. This was a bloody enough business all through the war, but at the tag end the Bravoes and Retaliators got into a tangle that almost ended the peace negotiations taking place four thousand miles away in France.

It began in March, 1782, five months after Yorktown, when the King's Bravoes, on one of their regular raids, swept up a Retaliator named Joshua Huddy. As it happened, they had Huddy on their list of people-to-get-even-with. He had earlier hanged one of his neighbors who was one of the King's Bravoes (but whose name has not come down to us). In addition, the Bravoes charged that Huddy was the man who had murdered another of their number, one Philip White, who was reportedly slain "while resisting arrest."

Huddy was taken before the New York associated board of Loyalists, which happened to be chaired by William Franklin, sometime royal governor of New Jersey. Huddy was able to prove that the time of the death of Philip White, he was in the hands of the King's Bravoes and had been for six days. That gave the board of Loyalists some pause, and they decided to exchange Huddy for a Tory prisoner. He was removed from his prison in one of the hulks in New York harbor and escorted back to Monmouth County by Richard Lippincott, a Loyalist militia officer.

However, he was not exchanged. When the escort arrived at Sandy Hook on the road to Monmouth, a band of local Loyalists, who had heard countless tales of the murder of their Tory friends by the Patriots, took Huddy away from Lippincott and his escort (apparently without resistance) and hanged him. His body was left dangling with a placard that read, "Up Goes Huddy For Philip White," and was signed, "The Refugees." The fine point that Huddy had nothing to do with the death of White apparently did not appeal to the mob.

That was on April 12, 1782. Within hours news of the hanging had spread through the countryside, unleashing a torrent of rage. Three days later, a Presbyterian fire-breather, the Reverend John Woddall, spoke to a crowd of Patriots assembled on the steps of an inn at Monmouth, demanding that they wreak revenge on every Loyalist within reach. More than four hundred Patriots, many of them militiamen recently back from the fighting, signed a petition of protest. It said, in effect, that if the authorities did not exact vengeance from the Tories for the murder of Huddy, they would. The petition was sent to General George Washington, and it stirred him like a whisk. He was becoming more and more concerned with the tendency of the mob to take matters into its own hands, a tendency that might continue after the peace if not curbed now. This petition seemed to suggest slaughter on a more-or-less wholesale scale, right when peace negotiations were beginning to bear fruit.

Washington Wants Somebody to Hang

Washington sat down and dashed off a letter to Sir Henry Clinton, then in charge of the British forces (and waiting impatiently to be relieved by Sir Guy Carleton). Clinton was to turn the militia officer, Lippincott, over to him. Washington would hang Lippincott for the death of Huddy, and the slate would be wiped clean. Clinton had no sooner received Washington's demand, when he began to get counter-petitions from the Loyalists. One of them made a telling point. It said, "By a strange fatality, the Loyalists are the only People who have been treated as Rebels during this unhappy War."

That gave Clinton pause. Not long before, the British had refused point-blank to exchange Benedict Arnold to the Americans, who were willing to give up Arnold's spy-contact, Major John André, in his place. If the British now gave up Lippincott, what did that say to the Loyalists? Clinton wrote back to Washington promising to look into the matter. Then he sailed for home, leaving his successor, Carleton, to wrestle with it.

Carleton wouldn't surrender Lippincott, either. Instead, he was brought before a military court-martial to answer for Huddy's death. The court-martial speedily exonerated Lippincott, returning the ball to the Patriot court. By this time a comparatively minor case had become a *cause célèbre*, and the exoneration of Lippincott did not sit well with the Patriots. It didn't sit well with Washington, either. He decided that if the

British wouldn't give him someone to hang, he'd pick one himself. He ordered Brigadier General Moses Hazen, the man in charge of the Yorktown captives (and, incidentally, a native Quebecker who had joined the invading American army in his own province in 1775), to pick out, by lot, someone suitable for hanging "from among all the British Captains who are prisoners."

The articles of capitulation signed at Yorktown expressly forbade this kind of reprisal, but Washington had lost his temper by now and was not inclined to pay any attention to trifles. Hazen held the lottery and the choice fell on a downy-cheeked, handsome, seventeen-year-old sprig of British nobility. Captain Charles Asgill of the First Foot Guards drew the slip that read, "Unfortunate."

Asgill took it like a man. No one else did. Washington (the record doesn't show this, but we can guess) probably kicked his waste basket around the room a few times. With all the boozy old bums in the British army he has to draw a kid with fair hair, a firm jaw and seventeen summers to string up. The French authorities launched an immediate protest. They were signatories to the Yorktown articles, which expressly outlawed such action. They could not stand idly by and watch this happen; it was too much. The British public, too, was outraged, especially after the boy's mother, Lady Asgill, wrote a heart-rending letter to Washington to beg for her son's life, and the letter was made public. The British informed the Americans that if Lippincott was hanged, the peace talks would come to an end.

Washington must have wished he was back at Valley Forge, where all you had to worry about was death, cold and starvation. He would hold firm. The boy must hang. Well, wait a minute, he would not hold firm. Yes, he would. Finally he tried to dump the whole matter in the lap of congress. Congress would decide the boy's fate, he said. No, it wouldn't. Congress sent the papers straight back to Washington. He knew when he was licked. He released Asgill, who stayed in the army and eventually became a lieutenant general.

The peace talks resumed, and, ironically, that was about the last time anything that even touched on the Loyalists resulted in anything good. The truth is that the British were weary of war and ready to settle on any terms. The earlier stance, that the Loyalists must not be abandoned no matter what, had softened to the point of disappearing. The Loyalists were not such a boon now. In fact, if we wanted to get really frank about it, they were a bit of a pain, always asking for things—a home, an army, a victory. Besides, the British were not in a position to deliver for the Loyalists, even if they wanted to.

"Oh, God! It Is All Over"

When Lord Germain first brought word of the surrender at Yorktown to Lord North, the prime minister staggered and cried, "Oh, God! It is all over." So it was for him. He was driven from office, and a ministry headed by the Earl of Rockingham (and on his swift death soon after, the Earl of Shelburne) took over. Shelburne was one of the most consistently liberal and consistently unpopular politicians of his time. He had been a colleague of William Pitt and had resigned when neither Lord North nor George III would modify Britain's policies towards the colonies in 1768.

Shelburne wanted peace, and he was willing to grant it at almost any price. Britain was at war with France, the Netherlands and Spain as well as its own colonies, and it was being bled dry. The Americans had a different set of priorities. They wanted independence, and nothing less would do. The American negotiating team in Paris consisted of Benjamin Franklin, John Jay—a slab-sided, dour New York lawyer—John Adams and Henry Laurens, former president of the continental congress.

There were no Loyalists at or near the Paris negotiations, although William Franklin was in England, applying such pressure as he could to Lord Shelburne in hopes of protecting his former friends and neighbors in America. Shelburne promised much but delivered nothing. In fact, the Loyalists who had fled to Britain were becoming more and more unpopular as the negotiations dragged on. They were accused of having led the British government astray by exaggerating Loyalist sentiment in America and underestimating the Patriots. Now they were clamoring for help and compensation, and they were becoming a damn nuisance. George III, in an unguarded moment, said he "wished the Nation rid of their Importunities," a strange description of the plight of so many who had suffered on his behalf.

There were many vexed questions to be settled in the negotiations, starting with whether the British were dealing with an independent nation or agents of rebellious colonies. The point was semantic but crucial, and John Jay found a way around it by devising a formula in which independence was implied but never stated. Boundaries had to be settled—and fishing rights and trading rights—but the key issues were independence and treatment of the Loyalists. On both the British, after much shadow-boxing, gave way.

Benjamin Franklin, on America's behalf, asked that Canada (i.e., Quebec) should be turned over to the new United States. John Adams added that Nova Scotia should be thrown into the pot, too. But that was mere poker-playing. However, when it came to the British claim that the Loyalists should be paid compensation for their lost and stolen property as part of the treaty, Franklin flew into a rage. He said the fair way to do it was for the British to draw up a list of the damages done to American property throughout the war (he listed the destruction of Norfolk in a catalogue of a dozen atrocities) and then both sides would cast accounts. If the Loyalists were owed more, congress would pay it, but if the ledger showed that more damage had been done to Americans than Loyalists, well, then, Britain would have to foot the bill.

It would be cheaper, the American negotiators argued, for Britain to compensate the Loyalists themselves. Besides, they pointed out in a shrewd thrust, if a country had to pay off for harm done to enemies within its border, when were the British going to come across with money for the dispersal of the Acadians?

"National Honour, Bosh!"

When one of the French negotiators tried to soften up John Adams by pointing out that royal governors must look after their adherents as a matter of national honor, Adams exploded. "National honour, bosh!" he replied. He went on to accuse the Loyalists of deceiving the British and bringing their own country to "almost irretrievable ruin." He said that it defied logic that any nation would be honor bound to "compensate its dishonourers and destroyers." Besides, he argued, switching swiftly to a lawyer's ground, "the confiscation of property is an affair of the states individually."

It was that legal quibble that eventually settled the matter. The treaty between the Americans and the British, as it was finally drafted, left the Loyalists high and dry. Confiscations of their property were to end, and Loyalist prisoners were to be released. There was to be "no lawful impediment" to the attempts of individuals to recover debts; and congress was to "earnestly recommend to the legislatures of the respective states" a policy of amnesty and restitution. With those promises and a florin, you could take a stagecoach ride.

Could the British have done more? The point is debatable. Even if the American peace commissioners had been less bloody-minded, American public opinion was determined on revenge. But the commissioners were bloody-minded; they embodied much of the venom so nicely stirred up during the war. Benjamin Franklin wrote an aggrieved letter to his son, William, in which he stated, "Nothing has ever hurt me so much and affected me with such keen Sensations, as to find myself deserted in my old Age by my only Son; and not only deserted, but to find him taking up Arms against me, in a Cause wherein my Good Fame, Fortune and Life were all at stake."

Of course, that was an argument that cut both ways and through many families. Had the British won, it might have been a telling point for William, but they did not win. Franklin reminded the negotiators of that. Americans would never have conceded compensation to the Loyalists even if the rebels had lost the war, he said, and added grimly, "But we did not lose."

Jay warned that if the British insisted on pressing the Loyalist claims, the American commissioners would have to send back to congress for new instructions, which would take about nine months and, he was sure, would not change anything. America would go back to war, he said, rather than concede on this point. While some of the British negotiating team thought that was a bluff, others did not. Thus the Loyalists, who never dreamed they were about to be so deserted, were presented with a *fait accompli*—a peace treaty that provided almost no protection for them against the rage of their victorious neighbors.

When the provisional peace treaty was signed on November 30, 1782 (it would take ten more months to conclude final treaties with all the belligerent powers) the victorious Americans had independence. The Loyalists had nothing but the vague clauses that urged the congress to ask the states to be nice. Even if those windy words had been fulfilled in action, the Loyalists would have been in difficulty. But they were promptly forgotten. One fleeing refugee said it for most of his fellows: "The War never occasioned half the distress this peace has done to the unfortunate Loyalists."

Loyalists who attempted to return home, as under the treaty they were entitled to do, were seized, beaten and robbed. One New Yorker trying to visit his parents was tarred and feathered, had his head and eyebrows shaved and was forced to wear a hog yoke and a cowbell around his neck, along with a placard depicting Benedict Arnold and a Tory driving off a cow. New bills of attainder, in clear violation of the treaty, were brought against prominent Loyalists who were then robbed and driven from their homes.

Not all were ill-treated, of course. Many Loyalists simply waited for time the healer to patch things up. In some cases they escaped detection entirely and simply became citizens of the new republic, with their ancient loyalties discreetly concealed. In other cases, although they had been identified as Tories, they resigned that honor by signing oaths of allegiance to congress and repudiating the king. Often that was enough to win forgiveness. In still other cases they felt the lash of popular rage for a time, but were eventually accepted despite their dangerous and unneighborly views. Doctors, in particular, fell into this class; their politics were suspect, but there was nothing wrong with their physic.

Some prominent Loyalists were allowed to linger on, despite their known proclivities, because they had never made a fuss. General Thomas Gage's father-in-law, Peter Kemble, was allowed to retain his home and lands near Morristown, New Jersey, despite having been a member of the royal legislative council. There were even some instances where notorious Loyalists were rehabilitated by time. William Samuel Johnson, arrested for Toryism in 1779, kept his nose clean thereafter and was allowed to stay in Stratford, Connecticut, after the war. He became president of Columbia College in 1787. William Byrd III of Virginia and Daniel Dulany of Maryland were other prominent Tories who suffered confiscation for their royalist views, but stayed put at war's end, prospered, and sent down into history families of righteous republicanism.

Avarice and Rapine Are Great Incentives

The only stronghold of British troops left in America as 1782 drew to a close was the city of New York, where Sir Guy Carleton was given the thankless task of trying to feed, shelter and protect a swelling horde of refugees. Carleton commented in a letter to the colonial office that the persecution of the Loyalists was "Not to be attributed to politics alone—it serves as a pretence, and under that cloak they act more boldly, but avarice and a desire of rapine are great incentives."

So, of course, is a desire for revenge. Combine rapine and revenge, and you have a heady brew. Local associations sprang up with the express goal of preventing any fraternization with Loyalists and ensuring that no restitution of property was made.

The states came up with still more laws to stifle the Tories, including one that whipped through the New York legislature, declaring that anyone who had held office under the British or served in the British forces, regular or militia, or even who had left the state during the war, was guilty of "misprision of treason," which meant that if they hadn't actually committed treason, they had meant to. Under this law, if you had ever been a public servant or soldier when it was a normal and natural thing to be, you were now branded a traitor and—more to the point—your property was now up for grabs.

Loyalists were denied the vote or the right to hold public office, but they were allowed to practice law if they took a special "oath of abjuration and allegiance." New taxes were heaped on them to the point that one Loyalist complained, "Those . . . whose estates have not been confiscated are so loaded with taxes and other grievances that there is nothing to do but sell out and move into the protection of the British government."

Many Loyalists were ordered to seek that protection whether they wanted to or not. When John Cook of Nine Partners, a town in New York state, tried to return to his home after the peace was signed, the local committee informed him, "You are hereby notified to depart this county by the first day of September, as you are considered an enemy to your Country—therefore take your all, and your Family, and follow your friends to that Country that the King, your Master, has provided for those of your Character."

It was going to be hard for Cook to take his all since, aside from a wife and ten children, he had a 260-acre farm. Not for long; it was confiscated. At least he was better off than some. One of his neighbors was sent on his way only after he was "whipped 39 lashes, and a Resolution made to repeat the whipping if he remained 24 Hours in the Precinct, and to give the same Punishment to such as harboured or assisted him."

One of the prominent Loyalist families of New York were the DeLanceys—part of the DeLancey Cowboys who were either tried-and-true Tories who fought for the king or a gang of outlaws who plundered where they would, depending on your point of view. They operated out of Westchester County, New York. One of the groups they tangled with during the war was called the Honeywell gang, and at war's end the Honeywells made it their business to call on former members of DeLancey's Cowboys and pay their respects. One man named Foshay was beaten so badly he died three days later. Most of the DeLanceys had gone to England by this time to press for compensation that would allow them to settle in Canada, but Oliver DeLancey was still in Westchester County. The Honeywell gang "bullied and clubbed" him and advised him to "run to his damned King." It seemed like good advice, and he took it.

Then the Honeywells went to work on other Loyalists, beat and robbed a number and killed several. In one case the sister of a Loyalist tried to intervene, offering the gang ten pounds if they would leave him alone. They beat her, too, and took the ten pounds.

Sir Guy Carleton, whose desk in New York was beginning to overflow with the petitions of Loyalists that carried a litany of complaints of robbery, brutalization and murder, knew that something had to be done. He wrote Lord North, back in the saddle as prime minister: "It is utterly impossible to leave exposed to the rage and violence of these people men of character whose only offence has been their attachment to the King's Government."

If the Loyalists could not be protected where they were—and they could not—those who could would have to be removed. There was only one sensible place for the bulk of them to go: north, to Canada and Nova Scotia.

SECTION THREE
1783-1791

THE MOST INHOSPITABLE CLIME

"All our golden promises vanished in smoke. We were taught to believe this place was not barren and foggy as had been represented, but we find it ten times worse. We have nothing but His Majesty's rotten pork and un- baked flour to subsist on. It is the most inhospitable clime that ever mortal set foot on."

A Loyalist complaining to
the royal commission on Loyalist
claims, 1786

8
The Great Migration

"I climbed to the top of Chipman's Hill and watched the sails disappearing in the distance, and such a feeling of loneliness came over me that although I had not shed a tear through all the war, I sat down on the damp moss with my baby on my lap, and cried bitterly."

Loyalist recalling her arrival
in Saint John in May, 1783

Loyalists had been dribbling north to Nova Scotia, Quebec and Fort Niagara all through the war, and as early as 1778 camps were established to receive the refugees. Sorel, on the south shore of the St. Lawrence where the Richelieu discharges into it, guarded the northern end of the route from Quebec to the New York heartland through Lake Champlain, and was, accordingly, heavily fortified. This became the headquarters for the provincial regiments and the wintering quarters for Sir John Johnson's Royal Greens, when they weren't out raising hell along the frontier. A parallel civilian encampment sprang up on the north side of the St. Lawrence and about twenty miles farther downstream toward Quebec; it became the town of Machiche. Trois Rivières, a substantial civilian settlement another fifteen miles along the St. Lawrence, became a third main Loyalist camp that included civilians (many of them the destitute wives and offspring of missing Loyalists) and members of the provincial corps or the irregular bands of fighters who sprang up, re-formed and dissolved throughout the war.

It was confidently assumed that the families of Loyalists would remain in the tents and rough huts hastily erected in these spots only temporarily, until the unpleasantness in their native southern provinces was sorted out. Most of these people lived in miserable conditions. Food was scarce, and privacy was impossible. Twelve houses were constructed for 240 women and children at Machiche, the first civilian camp. As the confident assumptions faded, the camps became permanent and spread into small, unregulated clusters along the main north-south routes through the Lake Champlain Valley and along the St. Lawrence.

Before the war ended, there were more than 1,700 "non-military" Loyalists in the three main camps[1] and scattered in smaller groups at Chambly, Montreal, St. Johns (St. Jean), Ile aux Noix, Lachine, Yamaska, Coteau du Lac and other settlements.

Then there were those who had followed the Mohawk Valley route, moving west toward Fort Niagara and Detroit. Twenty-five Loyalist families were camped opposite Fort Niagara, raising crops to feed themselves and to sell to the garrison there. These were clusters of refugees who simply drifted in, settled down and began farming in patches torn from the fertile soil. Finally there were the Indians—Mohawks and Senecas mainly—who had been driven from their own homes and had followed the families of Butler's Rangers to cluster around Niagara and Detroit. Muster rolls of the time show four hundred people drawing army rations at these two posts. Some of these refugees spent six years squatting in temporary quarters, waiting out the war.

Many of the Well-Heeled Cleared Out

Those who could afford to, or were not bound by ties of blood or love to someone serving in one of the Loyalist regiments, cleared out. They went to England, or the West Indies, or to East or West Florida—Spanish possessions that had been seized by the British. Oliver DeLancey, the New York Tory who was beaten up by the Honeywell gang, settled in England, where he added his considerable outrage to the clamor to ease the lot of his Loyalist friends still trapped in America.

Finally there were the 1,100 Loyalists who accompanied the fleet north on the evacuation of Boston, and who scattered from Halifax to London, even, in some cases, returning to the northern United States to wait for peace.

That was the first Loyalist migration—a confused trickle. However, with the war drawing to a close, an entirely different kind of migration began. It started with the swarming of Loyalists into the British lines for protection from Charleston to Long Island. Then as the garrisons were withdrawn from city after city, the Loyalists were faced with a cruel choice: follow the British northward, move elsewhere or stay where they were and hope for the best.

A Romantic Tale. True, Too.

While many Loyalists were prevented from returning to collect their chattels, this was not always the case. In one well-known incident, a Loyalist went back into hostile territory to reclaim a fiancée. Stephen Jarvis of Danbury, Connecticut, joined the British army and served throughout the war, then came back home in 1783 to visit his parents and to marry the beautiful Amelia Glover. That was bold of him: Danbury was not far from the notorious mine-cum-jail at East Granby where many Loyalists who had been less active than Jarvis wound up moldering in the grave. In his *Journal* (ponderously called "Journal of Stephen Jarvis, Esquire, during his Service in the British Army in the American Rebellion, his Residence in the Province of New Brunswick and in the Province of Upper Canada"), Jarvis noted that "Several other people have been punished very severely, carried on a rail and mounted on horseback without a saddle with their face to the horse's tail; their coat turned and a wooden sword at their side; then drove back and forth, to the great joy and satisfaction of the spectators."

Jarvis was willing to risk this for Amelia, though it seemed for a time that he might well wind up riding backwards on a horse, or worse. Bearing a permit from the American army authorities allowing him to visit his home, Jarvis made his way to Danbury and greeted his friends, family—and Amelia. But shortly after his arrival an American officer turned up at the Jarvis place to warn Stephen that a mob was on the way. The army might have given him a permit, but the local toughs hadn't. "This gave me no small uneasiness," Jarvis wrote. I bet.

He took the fair Amelia home, then came back to face the thugs, who told him they didn't think much of his permit and warned him that if he didn't get out of town by sundown, "You must abide by the consequences." Well, that wouldn't do. Jarvis had come home to get married, and he wasn't married yet. He told the boys he would be willing to leave when the deed was done; not before.

"Be assured," he told them, "I have no wish to become an inhabitant of the States and of this place in particular." That could have been more diplomatically put, but the gang reluctantly agreed, although "The mob were not disposed to depart."

In due course the marriage of Stephen and Amelia was so-lemnized, and the local dragoons very decently provided a small guard to ensure the newlyweds an undisturbed wedding night. Then came the dawn. The dragoons withdrew, and the local sheriff arrived carrying a warrant for Jarvis' arrest. Not a shy man, the sheriff barged into the bedroom where Stephen and Amelia lay, upon which, Stephen later wrote, "I sprang from my bed and ordered him to retire or I would blow out his brains."

The sheriff was so alarmed that he fell down the stairs. He left the house, only to return with a posse, which surrounded the house and waited for the bridegroom to emerge. He declined to do so. Instead he threw a coin out the bedroom window to one of the posse, with a suggestion that he trickle on down to the local inn and bring back something with which to drink the bride's health. In due course a bottle of bitters was produced, but before the posse would drink to Amelia, they demanded that Jarvis should drink to them. So the bottle was sent up to the bedroom window by rope and bucket. Stephen and Amelia drank to the posse, the posse drank to them, and all went merry as a marriage bell.

After breakfast Jarvis slipped out the back door and took off through the woods. The befuddled posse wandered away, and Amelia went home to pack. The couple were reunited in nearby Newtown and went from there to New York, where they joined the great migration of Loyalists to Canada. They settled in Fredericton, then moved to Upper Canada, to York. Stephen Jarvis served as adjutant general of militia during the War of 1812, and in 1833 he became Gentleman Usher of the Black Rod in the provincial legislature. At last, a story with a happy ending.

The New York to which the newlyweds fled was jammed with refugees of every class and condition. The richer ones took rooms at inns, found boarding-houses or camped on relatives. The poorer ones crowded in wherever they could. The Charleston evacuation alone brought a fleet of 300 ships carrying 3,800 Loyalists and 5,000 slaves, along with the escaping army. When the refugees of a dozen other centers were added, New York's prewar population of 25,000 was almost tripled. The city was short of food and fuel, medical supplies, water and every amenity. Two major fires during the war helped to destroy the small stock of decent housing. It was not a pleasant place to be for either the refugees or their sometimes-reluctant hosts.

The task of resettling the Loyalists fell on the shoulders of three very different men: Sir Guy Carleton, commander in chief of the British forces and the man in charge at New York; Sir Frederick Haldimand, the governor of Quebec (the job Carleton had held not long before) and John Parr, the governor of Nova Scotia.

Carleton had already shown himself to be a man of energy, good sense and compassion in his term at Quebec during the war, but he was also impatient, impolitic and hampered by the military man's abiding disdain for most civilians. However, on behalf of the Loyalists, he strained every sinew and broke a few rules. It was Carleton who, when the Americans kept pressing him to take his unruly rabble and clear out of New York, delayed and delayed so that every Loyalist who wanted to leave with the fleet would have a chance to reach the city and refuge. The city's evacuation was supposed to have been complete on September 3, 1783, when the formal peace was concluded, but Carleton stalled until well into November while Loyalists beat their way into the city and safety.

Haldimand was a French Swiss soldier who, after he joined the British army in 1756, served his adopted country with tenacious pride. He was able and—unusual for his time—utterly honest. He was also proud, stubborn and narrow-minded. Because he knew himself to be honest, he tended to believe that anyone who disagreed with him must be self-seeking or disloyal—or both.

Parr wanted nothing more out of his position than a quiet posting in the few years left before his retirement from the army, with suitable homage paid to his rank by the natives and enough banquets to maintain the padding on his 250-pound frame. It was his ill fortune, and that of the Loyalists, that he became governor of Nova Scotia late in 1782, just in time to face the deluge.

Nova Scarcity Was British, Available and Near

From early in 1782, when it became obvious that a new place would have to be found for the Loyalists, Nova Scotia was considered the logical place to put most of them. Overwhelmingly, the Loyalists themselves favored Nova Scotia over Quebec, where the resident population was suspiciously French and incorrigibly Catholic. While a modern map shows Quebec to be much closer to New York than Nova Scotia, Nova Scotia was the shorter trip by sea, which was the way most people traveled.

The Nova Scotia of that time was not today's province. It included Cape Breton and New Brunswick, which were made into separate provinces in 1784 (Cape Breton was reattached in 1820). Prince Edward Island, then called the Island of St. John, had been part of Nova Scotia briefly, but was detached again in 1769 and renamed in 1799 to honor Prince Edward.

Nova Scotia was British, available and near. Not much else could be said for it. "Nova Scarcity,"[2] as the first refugees from Boston had already dubbed the place, was not the ocean playground advertised on today's license plates. Halifax, the only considerable town, was cold, squalid and unhealthy. The local dung patrol cleaned the privies out into wheelbarrows, which were trundled through the streets and emptied into the harbor. Slop pails and chamber pots were dumped into the gutters, where the frequent rains washed the refuse down towards the town pumps. Bathing the entire body was said to be dangerous, so fleas, lice and ticks tended to settle down once they called a body home. In church it was common to see an elegantly coiffed lady pull a thin skewer from her muff and chivy the insects in her hairdo with it.

Except in the summertime, when fresh fruit and vegetables were plentiful, there wasn't even enough to eat. Salt meat and fish were the staples of diet, along with potatoes and bread.

Complexions were bad, teeth few and smells rank, even at the fashionable balls that marked the winter social season. The advances Benjamin Franklin had bestowed on Philadelphia— street lamps and an efficient stove—had not penetrated this far north. In the winter most homes were heated by fireplaces, which looked cozy, but sent most of the heat up the chimney. Bitter drafts swept through the frame houses (very few were built of brick). In the summer the night air was considered to be bad for the health, so Haligonians kept their windows closed and suffocated in the summer to make up for freezing in the winter. Ladies avoided the sunshine to keep that fashionably pallid complexion and thus joined consumption to smallpox as the fashionable diseases. Smallpox was so common that ladies wore small black patches over the worst ravages and called them beauty spots.

For the men, liquor—mostly rum—was the abiding passion, and the household keg stood beside the potato bin and keg of salt herring in the better Halifax houses. The Loyalists would bring a taste for wine, but it was a long time catching on, and drunkenness on cheap rum continued to be the bane of the place.

Most of these conditions prevailed in any colonial town, but Halifax added to them a cold, wet climate and the straitened mentality of a garrison town. To add to the garrison mentality there was a constant tension betwen the Haligonians and the rural provincials, and between the neutral Yankees who had drifted north before the war and the earlier settlers, whether Acadian or those who had come directly from Britain. There were also about 1,500 "foreign Protestants"—Germans and some French—recruited from Europe and settled around Lunenburg in 1752, but they kept to themselves and did not mingle much in the quarrel.

Since the neutral Yankees made up about two-thirds of Nova Scotia's population of about 20,000 (Edmund Burke said the province was formed "by overflowings from the exuberant population of New England"),[3] their pro-American and pro-Republican proclivities aroused much comment and suspicion among the quality folk who guided colonial policy. If the province's destiny had been a mere matter of counting noses, it would probably have joined the Revolution. As historian Thomas Raddall wrote, "Had the Americans played their cards with more insight, there is little doubt that Nova Scotia would have become part of the United States."[4]

Indeed, at one time during the war, there was a sentiment in England to dump the Nova Scotians and be done with them. "Good God!" shouted Edmund Burke, "What sum the nursing of that ill-thriven, hard-visaged and ill-favoured brat has cost this wittol nation!"[5] But the British, for once, had the sense to hold onto Nova Scotia.

Congressional appeals to lure Nova Scotia to join the unrolling experiment in republicanism failed for two main reasons. The first was that government in Nova Scotia was firmly in the hands of the stiffest-necked of the garrison men from the army, the navy and the corps of merchants and traders who supplied the military. Nova Scotia was not a democracy and had no ambitions to become one. It was an autocracy, and proud of it. The newcomers often found themselves in the same kinds of battles with authority that occurred farther south, but there were no town meetings to keep the kettle boiling. While there were frequent and palpable outbreaks of discontent, they had no effective political expression.

The second encouragement to loyalty was the fact that Yankee privateers could never keep their hands off the coastal villages. The neutral Yankees, when they weren't busy fighting off British and colonial thugs who sailed in to choke off what they were sure was incipient rebellion in the small ports—and, incidentally, to press local fishermen into the navy—were busy instead fighting off raids from freelancing thugs who sailed up from Marblehead or Boston to steal everything of value. At Lockeport, a lovely village in southeast Nova Scotia, a band of local women chased off raiding privateers by dressing up in red wraps to make themselves look like regular soldiers and brandishing broom handles in a fierce manner. The would-be raiders, who had been counting on a passive populace, formed the impression that a company of British regulars was waiting to greet them, and they sheered off.[6]

Congress sent an invitation to Nova Scotia to support the boycott of British goods after the Boston Massacre, but the province made no official reply. Unofficially some of the residents formed themselves into militia on either side to await the expected incursion of a Patriot army from the south. It never came. Congress was not much concerned with Nova Scotia, preferring to strike at what was seen to be the soft underbelly of Quebec in 1775-76. When that expedition ended in bloody and expensive failure, there was little inclination to repeat the experiment farther east.

There is some irony in this. Most of the conditions congress thought would prevail in Quebec (a restless native populace, a disenchantment with the British trade laws, a natural affinity for things American) did in fact exist in Nova Scotia. A strong expedition to the north might well have swept through Nova Scotia, gaining recruits as it went and driving the British from the area. At that time there were about 300 British regulars in Halifax, a company of Royal Highland Emigrants at Windsor and about 250 Royal Fencible Americans recruited in the streets of Boston just before the British withdrawal. It was a defensive force that might easily have been routed.

But it never happened. Congress confined itself mainly to firing off letters of encouragement and petitions full of piety and promise—every form of assistance short of actual aid. Would-be local rebels, left to their own devices, mounted an abortive attack on Fort Cumberland (now Fort Beausejour) in the Chignecto Peninsula near the present town of Amherst, Nova Scotia. That was where the Royal Fencible Americans were stationed under Colonel Joseph Gorham, a neutral Yankee.

The attack was led by Johnathan Eddy and John Allen, Cumberland-area hotheads who recruited a small band of volunteers around Machias in northern Maine and marched north to liberate Nova Scotia. Arriving at Fort Cumberland, they signed up some three hundred local farmers, whose arms consisted mainly of old fowling pieces, and mounted a siege. Colonel Gorham refused to come out and fight, instead sheltering behind the earthen ramparts of the fort and waiting for help. The rebels, who had no cannon, were not in a strong position to take the place, but after three weeks of desultory action, they launched a night raid that was easily beaten back. Finally a small force of regulars were rounded up in Halifax and Windsor and dispatched by ship to the fort. They landed at night, unobserved by the sleeping rebels, and mounted an assault on the Army of Liberty's camp. Within half an hour the rebellion was over, the rebels scattered through the woods and many of them taken prisoner.[7]

They were ordered to Halifax to face trial on charges of treason, but most of them escaped along the way. There is some evidence they were allowed to. The siege on Fort Cumberland put the wind up the British officers in Halifax, but was not taken too seriously in the Chignecto Peninsula. One of the escapees was Richard John Uniacke, an energetic young man who became disenchanted with the Americans as a result of his experiences (and the non-appearance of a constantly-promised army to help out with the task of liberation). He became a Loyalist and eventually became the attorney general of Nova Scotia and the Tory of Tories. Not many provinces can boast an attorney general who was taken in arms against his native land.[8]

The Word Was Freedom, But the Goal Was Plunder

The Cumberland fiasco took some of the joy out of the American cause in Nova Scotia. So did the dawning realization that privateer raids on the Island of St. John (later Prince Edward Island) and Newfoundland were motivated by dreams of plunder, not liberty. American raiders swept into Charlottetown and rounded up many of the leading citizens as part of their spoils, to exchange for ransom. However, when General Washington heard about the raid, he denounced the perpetrators and ordered the prisoners released. Soon after this, John Paul Jones, who was to become a hero in the War of 1812, began seizing unarmed Nova Scotia fishing vessels. As privateering raids ravaged the coast, delegations of Nova Scotians descended on the committees of safety in New England ports to protest, pointing out that they were not the enemy. As it happened, many of the committeemen to whom they addressed their earnest pleas were receiving a share of the spoils, so while many shoulders were lifted in bewilderment and much sympathy was expressed, the raids went on.

Fort Howe, named for the general, was erected at the mouth of the St. John River to provide protection against the raiders, and its presence helped to convince the band of settlers there of the virtues of neutrality. And so, by one of those neat twists of history, the province that might well have become the fourteenth state became instead the main haven for those fleeing the new nation.

Plans for the move started early among the Loyalists, as well as among the military. In August, 1782, Sir Guy Carleton wrote to Sir Andrew Snape Hammond, who was the acting governor of Nova Scotia before John Parr's arrival, asking about towns and villages where demobilized soldiers and their families might be settled. At that time, Carleton apparently envisioned the transfer of about 600 families, and he asked that arrangements be made to provide them with grants of land—500 to 600 acres for each family, 300 acres for a single man.[9] He also asked that building materials and skilled tradesmen be provided to help the refugees to settle. It quickly became obvious that the aid required would be massive.

In the meantime the Loyalists, fired by Carleton's efforts on their behalf, sent exploring parties north to check out the new land and to form themselves into associations for the purposes of settlement. Late in 1782 the first large group of exiles left New York on the ship *Amphritrite* to take up land on the shores of the Annapolis Basin as "the Conway Associates." There were about three hundred of them, a mere drop in the bucket.

The main body of Loyalists left New York in three fleets in the spring, summer and fall of 1783, but in fact there was an almost constant traffic, with vessels arriving in Nova Scotia, discharging their bewildered passengers onto an unprepared shore and hurrying back to New York for more.

Carleton soon found that so many families met the qualifications for Loyalists status (those who had been behind British lines for at least a year and wanted to remain under the British flag) that they could not be shifted in naval vessels. He began to hire private ships, including many owned and operated by Patriots who were happy to take the king's gold to transfer their enemies elsewhere.

One of the best descriptions of the voyage north was written by Sara Frost of Stamford, Connecticut.[10] She and her husband, William, had fled behind British lines in July, 1781, and settled in a camp on Long Island. Later William led a raid back across Long Island Sound to Stamford, where he captured a minister and his entire congregation, and brought all forty-eight of them back as prisoners. Frost clearly could not go home again, so he obtained space for himself and his wife on the *Two Sisters*. They would sail to Fort Howe, then make their way upstream. To add poignancy to their leave-taking, the Frosts were bidding farewell to Sara's parents, who were staunch Patriots. In addition, Sara was pregnant; she would have her child five weeks after the arrival in Nova Scotia, in a tent pitched on the rocks.

The Frosts left Lloyd's Neck to board their ship in the harbor on May 25, 1783, with high expectations. Sara wrote in her diary: "We have very fair accommodation in the cabin, although it contains six families, besides our own. There are two hundred and fifty passengers on board."

"I Think Sometimes I Shall Be Crazy"

They started out well enough ("The captain drank tea with us. He appeared to be a very clever gentleman"), but struck a rock, got off, then struck another. Then they settled down at anchor in the North River waiting for the summer fleet to gather. There were parties on shore to break the monotony and then, on June 9, word came that the fleet was leaving at last. A false hope. That night, Sara wrote with some exasperation and a little snobbishness: "Our women with their children all came on board today and there is great confusion in the cabin. We bear with it pretty well through the day, but as it grows towards night one child cries in one place and one in another, whilst we are getting them to bed. I think sometimes I shall be crazy. There are so many of them, if they were as still as common, there would be a great noise among them."(That is, there were so many that even if they had behaved, which, being common, they did not, the hubbub would still be great.)

The summer fleet of eighteen ships finally departed a week later and raced north at "two miles and a half an hour." There was a lot of fog and much disputing, and then measles broke out. The food on board consisted of bread, salt pork and beef, butter, peas and oatmeal. It was adequate but unexciting, as was most of the trip, although there were games of cribbage to relieve the monotony. The fleet was out of sight of land for nine days, finally sighting Cape Sable at the southern tip of Nova Scotia on June 26. The captain told Sara it would only be another day's sail until they reached the St. John River, and she told her diary, "Oh, how I long to see the place, though a strange land."

However, the captain was wrong, as usual. It was not until Sunday, June 29, that the fleet anchored off Fort Howe at the river mouth, and the Frosts went ashore the next day. Sara's diary entry for the occasion reads a little uncertainly: "It is now afternoon and I have been ashore. It is, I think, the roughest land I ever saw. . . . This is to be the *city*, they say! We are not to settle here, but to have our land sixty miles further up the river. We are all ordered to land tomorrow, and not a shelter to go under."

Actually, the Frosts had a comparatively smooth journey. Other Loyalists suffered from seasickness, fights and crowding that included animals as well as children. Sarah Winslow reported that on her trip north there was "not an hour good weather," and that everyone was "sick and afraid" except for one old gent who was "neither sick nor afraid of anything, except that he should get victuals enough to eat."[11]

Smallpox broke out on a number of ships, but that wasn't the worst that could happen. The *Martha* sank entirely. She was part of the fall fleet and carried families and troops of Colonel William Hewlett's battalion of Maryland Loyalists and some of Oliver DeLancey's brigade. On September 25, the *Martha* struck a rock just off the mouth of the Tusket River between Cape Sable and the Bay of Fundy. The ship went down within a few hours, drowning one hundred and fifteen passengers including fifteen women, twenty-seven children and four "servants" (i.e., slaves).

The *Martha's* gallant captain bailed out early, taking the ship's jolly-boat and abandoning his passengers to their fate. After rowing about for a while, he was picked up by a small cutter traveling with the fleet. He turned loose his jolly-boat and went on with the cutter. To add insult to injury, when he caught up with the rest of the fleet, he reported the sinking of the *Martha*, but persuaded other fleet captains that there was no point going back to look for survivors, because there were none. But there were—seventy-five of them. One small group of six managed to cling to a piece of wreckage for three days. Then two of them died, while the other four drifted onto an island. For a week they lived on raspberries, snails and water trapped in the cavities of rocks, until they were "taken up by a Frenchman, that was out a fowling." Most of the other *Martha* survivors were picked up by fishing vessels, and they made life uncomfortable for their former captain at a subsequent inquiry, which held him culpable for abandoning them.[12]

In all, somewhere between 34,000 and 40,000 Loyalists poured into Nova Scotia, which had a native population of under 20,000.[13] Not all the newcomers came in the fleets, but the three large shipments lifted about 10,000 refugees out of New York. The largest groups of newcomers went to Port Roseway (Shelburne) and the St. John River, while smaller groups fanned out across the province. At Digby, 1,500 Loyalists settled in and named their new town after Admiral William Digby, the man who had brought them. That was only one of a score of new communities that blossomed under the sudden influx. Among them were Windsor and Truro north of Halifax, Dartmouth and Preston near the provincial capital, Guysborough on Chebucto Bay, Parrsboro in Cumberland County, Antigonish, Pictou, Kingston and Ramsheg.

Halifax became a jumping-off place for those Loyalists who did not ship directly to their new homes, and conditions in the capital moved quickly from the difficult to the appalling. Carleton had named Edward Winslow (who had served as mustermaster general of Loyalist troops during the war) to the post of secretary to the commander in chief of Nova Scotia, with the task of sorting out the Loyalists as they arrived. It was Sarah Winslow, Edward's wife, who had complained about the rude weather on the way north, but that was nothing compared to what awaited them. Governor Parr did almost nothing at all, and Winslow had to deal with the consequent chaos. He wrote, bitterly and unfairly, to his own deputy, Ward Chipman: "What in the world are you about? Not a packet arrived—a General without Commission or Instructions—37,000 people crying for provisions—Magazines empty—& no Provisions at Market. . . Add to this a Governor without abilities—a Council of Republicans—combating with every weapon in their reach the whole corps of Loyalists."[14] Winslow was upset, and he landed on Chipman because he couldn't get sassy with Parr.

In the end it got straightened out, and Winslow went on combating inefficiency and Republicans in a number of high offices until his death in 1815. However, there were some messes that took longer to straighten out than the chaos in Halifax.

"Poverty Keeps Me Here"

The single largest and single most disastrous Loyalist settlement was at Port Roseway, now Shelburne, along the south shore of Nova Scotia about eighty miles from Halifax. Port Roseway was actually Port Razoir, for the razor clams in the area, but the French name got corrupted. Before the Revolutionary War it was a modest fishing village and then the site of an experiment in settlement by Alexander McNutt, who brought in Scots-Irish and later some New Englanders. McNutt complained to the council of Massachusetts Bay that privateers from their area had raided his settlement, but in truth there was not much there to raid. When the Loyalists arrived, surveyed the desolate shore and asked one of the earlier settlers why he had bothered to stay, he replied, "Poverty brought me to Nova Scotia, and poverty keeps me here."[15]

The Loyalist influx to Port Roseway actually began with a Rhode Island sea captain, Joseph Durfee, who had visited the region and wrote from his temporary New York haven to the provincial secretary of Nova Scotia, asking for land for himself and a hundred heads of family. When he got an encouraging reply, he convened a meeting at Roubelet's Tavern in New York where an association was set up with Joseph Pynchon, a Connecticut farmer, as president. Sir Guy Carleton had suggested the formation of these associations, which would serve, in large part, former Loyalist soldiers and which would be run on semi-military lines. To join the association, which would exploit the opportunities of Port Roseway and surrounding area, Loyalists had to apply at Captain Durfee's New York address. The notice announcing the meeting noted that in accord with the laws of England, Jews "cannot possess any land," and they were not to be accepted as members of the association.

Indeed, looking over the early records of the Port Roseway associates, it is clear that one of the major preoccupations of the group was to exclude others. If they could get up the ladder, their first thought was to pull it up after them. The associates passed a resolution, which they thoughtfully sent on to Guy Carleton. The resolution restricted all land granted in Port Roseway, which they confidently expected to become "a capital city," to themselves alone. Carleton had no objection, but other Loyalists did. The spring fleet brought 3,000 men, women and children—along with 420 servants (slaves)—to Port Roseway on behalf of the associates. But later fleets landed many who had no connection with the association, and there was not much the first-landed could do. In the end about 10,000 people moved into Port Roseway. It was, briefly, one of the largest cities in North America.

"I Quit This Dam'd Country With Pleasure"

Just before the Loyalists pulled out of New York, there was an exchange of civilities with their former countrymen. The Massachusetts legislature passed a resolution calling all the Loyalists "ingrates" and "declared traitors to their country" who "ought never to be suffered to return." The Boston *Gazette* joined in with a declaration that the real reason the fleet was pulling out was that "Independence fever" was spreading:

"General Carleton, in order to prevent the infection from spreading, has ordered many away to New Scotland."

A Loyalist wrote in reply, "I quit this dam'd country with pleasure."[17]

Arriving was not so pleasurable. The Loyalists began to quarrel among themselves, and with the authorities, almost as soon as they landed. They fought over the size of their allotments, their locations, the shape of the town, the rations (they were entitled to six months' supply of salt meat, flour, peas and other foodstuffs) and the fact that at Port Roseway as elsewhere the association agents had dealt themselves and their friends all the choicest lands.

The newcomers insisted on taking votes on eveything, as they had been accustomed to do. They elected sixteen "captains" from among their number, on the suggestion of Carleton, who thought this would add to the illusion of military discipline. Then they spent their time criticizing the captains. One of the association leaders wrote in desperation, "This cursed republican, town meeting spirit has been the ruin of us already, and unless checked by some stricter form of government will overset the prospect which now presents itself of retrieving our affairs."[18]

In school texts, the portraits of Loyalist landings always show a group of men dressed in frock coats, with three-cornered hats, and women in long dresses suitable for attending a ball—a vision of loveliness. This vision is recreated whenever the descendants get together for Loyalist Days, but it is, as Thomas Raddall once noted, "sheer nonsense." Many of the civilian Loyalists arrived in rags and more arrived in working clothes—wool shirts, breeches and rough coats.

The Port Roseway bunch, unlike the Loyalists who went to Quebec and Niagara, were ill-equipped to face life in the wilderness. Most of them were city dwellers, for a start; short of wind, except for making speeches. They were, said William Morris, the provincial surveyor whose job it was to persuade the arrivals to carve out a new town, "Gentlemen, Barbers, Taylors, Shoemakers, Tinkers &c who have neither the fear of God nor man before them."[19]

They spent four days hacking down trees to clear a space for their houses, and then most of them decided they had had enough of trees and refused to work any more. William Morris, the beleagured surveyor, grumbled, "Not a soul in town to assist me, the third time I have been served so."

They tried repeatedly (but in vain) to have any fellow Loyalists who were not members of the association excluded from drawing lots. Then when the lot-drawings were held, those who received parcels they didn't like refused to move off the shore properties they had begun to work on when they first landed.

The newcomers had great and misplaced confidence in their ability to conquer a wilderness by jawing it down. They may not have had much energy for the crude business of chopping trees, but they had plenty for taking votes. This, as much as anything, drove the provincial authorities to distraction. Morris' deputy, Benjamin Marston, himself a Loyalist from Marblehead, Massachusetts, harrumphed, "Sir Guy Carleton did not reflect that putting sixteen illiterate men into commissions, without subjecting them to a common head, was at best contracting the mob."[20]

In due course Governor Parr rolled up to take a tour of the new town, and he promptly renamed it Shelburne. He aimed to curry favor with the new colonial secretary, but did not make a hit with the Loyalists. They blamed Shelburne for the abandonment of their claims during the peace negotiations, and some of them took to referring to their new home as "Port Roseway alias Shelburne," to indicate disapproval.

They Weren't Much for Hutting

At least some of the Loyalists believed they had done their bit for king and country merely by showing up in Shelburne. From here on it was up to the Crown to look after them. These people refused to carry the survey chains necessary to mark out their own lots unless they got paid for the work. Others, arriving late in 1783, were advised to build themselves some kind of shelter as soon as possible, but did nothing. "They don't seem on the whole to favour the idea of hutting,"[21] Benjamin Marston observed. As a result, many suffered cruelly, and many died in the severe winter of 1783-84.

The Shelburne settlement was a disaster almost from the beginning. Although the idea was that the Loyalists would settle down to raise crops to feed themselves and sell to others, there was not enough good farming land around to make that a realistic possibility. Governor Parr dwelled in the delusion that because pine, oak and spruce grew readily on the sandy, rocky soil, so would corn and wheat. Alas, it didn't work that way. But even if the land had been rich, it wasn't available. Many of the newcomers had to wait as long as two years to receive an assignment of land. In part this was because the huge influx of refugees overwhelmed the local administration, and in part it was because Parr, terrified that he would do something wrong that would offend his superiors, did very little.

Those new settlers who took matters into their own hands and threw up homes for themselves on waterfront lots, found that they had worked in vain. They were ordered off the properties, which were turned over to some of the more favored among them. One Loyalist wrote darkly, and correctly, that they were being moved "to accommodate Sons of Favour that go to Halifax with full pockets of a mettle well known in Mexico."[22]

The combination of envy, anger, fear, anxiety and unemployment blew up into a full-scale riot in Shelburne in 1784. Hundreds of blacks had been settled in Birchtown, a shantytown suburb of Shelburne. In violation of the promises made to them during the war, the blacks were denied equal access to lands, or rations, or indeed anything, and many of them scraped out a bare living by working for those whites who had managed to cling to prosperity. The other whites promptly blamed the blacks for their own miseries. They claimed they were being robbed of employment because the blacks would work for such paltry wages. On top of all their other concerns, this outburst of bigotry led to violence. On July 26, 1784, "Some thousands of People assembled with Clubbs, and Drove the Negroes out of the Town and threatened Some People."[23]

That this was not exclusively a race riot became clear when it was learned that the deputy surveyor had had to flee for his life to Halifax, and that some of the disbanded troops were taking up arms. A regiment was dispatched from the capital to restore order. Governor Parr came, too. He had finally received written instructions on how to go about the distribution of land, and he came by to establish a board of agents to oversee the work. He also dealt himself five hundred acres to build "a little house, and to go there every year for a short space of time."[24] The board of agents started in at once—giving themselves and their allies the plum parcels of land. Isaac Wilkins, president of the board, obtained a grant of ten fifty-acre lots—ten times the normal grant within Shelburne—and then got another five thousand acres on the nearby Jordan River.

Shelburne began to collapse as rapidly as it had grown. Most of the blacks who were not slaves left for Halifax, on their way to Sierra Leone. Many of the soldiers moved on, too, to settle in other parts of Nova Scotia, or in Quebec and Upper Canada. Many of those who had not taken a combat role in the United States—men like Isaac Wilkins—went back home and were accepted in their old communities. Others just drifted away.

Hundreds of homes, hastily thrown up out of the green timber cut from the clearings where they stood, were abandoned and sank gratefully back into the soil.

In time a nucleus of the settlers managed to make Shelburne into the pleasant and prosperous town it is today. Their descendants gather on the waterfront every summer to read solemn speeches around the plaque that marks the first Loyalist landing on May 4, 1783, and to say soothing and patriotic things about their bold, brave ancestors. No harm done, but the truth is that for every Loyalist who stayed, ten others found the experience in early Shelburne a brief, bitter nightmare, and nothing more.

Happily, there were other places where things went much better.

9
Struggles and Squabbles

"There was no floor laid, no windows, no chimney, no door, but we had a roof at least. A good fire was blazing and Mother had a big loaf of bread and she boiled a kettle of water and put a good piece of butter in a pewter bowl. We toasted the bread and all sat around the bowl and ate our breakfast that morning and Mother said: 'Thank God we are no longer in dread of having shots fired through our house. This is the sweetest meal I ever tasted for many a day.'"

From the Narrative of Hannah
Ingraham, Loyalist, about 1783

The fate awaiting the Loyalists in their adopted country was, like that dealt to them in the thirteen colonies, various and capricious. Many died on the way north, many found themselves in settings, like that at Shelburne, from which the only recourse was escape, and many wound up in places where hard work, tough-mindedness and persistence paid off. Finally there were those for whom most of what happened remained a puzzle.

Take the six-hundred-odd Loyalists who wound up on the Island of St. John, later Prince Edward Island. How were they to know that they partly owed their warm welcome on the island to the fact that its governor, a palpable rogue named Walter Patterson, had picked the wrong man's wife to make his mistress?[1]

Patterson was a Irishman from Donegal who joined the British army and served in the Eighth Regiment in America. In 1769 he was appointed governor-in-chief and captain general of the Island of St. John when the island was hived off from Nova Scotia and made a colony on its own. The island's population when he arrived was a meager 274, despite the rich soil, fishery and gentle climate. That was because most of the original Acadian inhabitants had been chased out by the conquering English. Other English settlers were too smart to step into what had been the subject of one of the most breathtaking bits of jobbery in the rich history of such activities in North America.

In a single day in 1763, sixty-seven favored Englishmen drew lots for each of the sixty-seven 20,000-acre parcels into which the island had been divided.[2] When Patterson took over six years later, only a handful of the parcels had been developed, although they were supposed to be settled and quit-rents paid on them. (A quit-rent was a fee paid by a freeholder in lieu of services he might otherwise be called on to perform; such rents were almost uniformly charged on Crown lands in the eighteenth century. One of the privileges of being a Loyalist was that you were usually exempted from these charges, sometimes for a period of ten years.) The absentee landlords of the Island of St. John had achieved the same happy state by simply not paying. On the other hand, they tried to collect quit-rents, not always successfully, from their own tenants. In 1770 Robert Stewart, one of the lucky lottery winners, began to settle sixty families on Lot 18. He also agitated for his fellow landlords to develop their properties rather than, as was their fixed intention, simply waiting for history to make them rich.

Governor Patterson joined in this effort and made a number of attempts to force the proprietors to pay their dues, without avail. In 1775 he went back to England to confront the absent owners in person and clear the matter up. He stayed there five years, with little progress being made, while back on the island chaos reigned. There was little settlement and less government. During the war American privateers raided Charlottetown with very little resistance. When Patterson returned to the island in 1780, he got the details of the raids and wrote a dispatch to Lord North. The success of the scoundrels in attacking his island showed, he said, that the place needed 215 miles of roads on which to move troops. Lord North replied smoothly that building roads would only make it easier for the invaders to get around the island, laying the smaller villages open to the sort of attack that had fallen on Charlottetown. The subject was dropped.[3]

Patterson was now finding that the quiescent appointed council and elected assembly through which he had ruled was becoming restive. To add to the problems, his lieutenant governor, Thomas DesBrisay, had disposed of 116 parcels of land, 58 of them to members of his own family. Patterson managed to make him disgorge the lands, and that started a feud between the two men that made government more difficult.

The Governor Went Into Land-Jobbing for Himself

Then in September, 1780, Patterson appointed his brother-in-law as receiver general of quit-rents, his private secretary as deputy receiver general, and went into the land-jobbing business for himself. He persuaded his brother-in-law to bring escheatment proceedings against the absentee landlords for failure to meet their obligations. As a result eight whole and six half-townships were marked for sale at auction. Patterson kept shifting the date of the auction until only he and his friends knew when it would take place, and in this way they managed to grab up 230,000 acres—about one-sixth of the entire island—at bargain-basement prices.

There was hell to pay. Captain John MacDonald, who had fought with the 84th Regiment early in the Revolutionary War, had had two lots snatched from him by Patterson's action. MacDonald sailed to England in 1781 to agitate against the governor, and in due course the British Parliament passed a bill ordering the lands returned. Patterson acknowledged the order but did nothing to implement it. Instead he called an election for March, 1784. If all went well, he would get the new assembly to pass legislation validating his land-grab.

Alackaday, it did not go well. John Stewart, ably abetted by his father, Peter Stewart, the chief justice, organized the campaign against Patterson. Peter had reason to carry a certain animus into the campaign; his wife had become the governor's mistress. The Stewart faction charged Patterson with lining his own pockets, helping his friends out of the public trough and "by conversation and example spreading the principles of infidelity and irreligion."[4]

That was how you referred to marital monkeyshines in those days—nothing crude. The accusation, which everyone on the island knew to be founded in fact, counted against the governor's candidates during the election and the Stewart faction walked off with a majority of the seats. John Stewart was elected speaker of the new hostile assembly. He was now being dubbed "Hellfire Jack," and did his best to live up to the name by making life miserable for the governor.

In the eighteenth century, the proper way to deal with a hostile assembly was to dissolve it, which Patterson proceeded to do. But what to do next? Patterson got the really bright idea of luring in the Loyalists, who would be duly grateful. Then he could call another election and get rid of Hellfire Jack and his cronies. So he sent his brother off to England to talk to the absentee landlords and eventually they offered to give up one-quarter of their lands to Loyalists—a total of 109,000 acres. Anticipating colonial office approval, Patterson then circulated proclamations to the Loyalists—including those at Shelburne— advertising the glories of his rich island. Hundreds flocked to his call.

The colonial office gave its approval in due course and lifted the quit-rents. Then the absentee landlords, with a few exceptions, refused to give up the land. They would allow the Loyalists to settle on it, but they steadfastly refused to produce the promised titles. Instead they demanded from the newcomers the rent that they themselves had refused to pay. When the Loyalists discovered they were to be tenants, not land-owners, many of them left, and others heading for the island turned back as tales of the land-jobbery circulated.

Nevertheless, enough Loyalists were attracted to the island for Patterson's needs, and he gave them title to some of the lands he had managed to lay hold of in 1781. They gratefully threw the Stewart fraction out of office in the 1785 election and tried to settle down. Alas, political life continued rough on the island. Patterson still refused to obey instructions to give back the properties seized in his 1781 raid. The Loyalists were now settled on this land, anyway. By this time Patterson had managed to alienate so many people at home and abroad that the absentee landlords—whom he continued to press to pay their rents and develop their properties—succeeded in having him replaced by Colonel Edmund Fanning, a former Loyalist fighter in North Carolina. Patterson refused to turn over his office to Fanning, until he was abruptly summoned home in 1786. He was investigated, disgraced and wound up in Newgate Prison for unpaid debts.

Fanning took the part of the Loyalists, but in the end wasn't much more successful against the powerful proprietors than Patterson had been. The island was renamed for Prince Edward in 1799, not that that helped much. In 1803 the assembly passed a law to escheat the neglected properties, but the legislation was somehow "lost" in the colonial office and never enforced. It was not until 1877 that the absentee landlords were stripped of their hold on the island. Long before that time, many of the Loyalists who remained through the Patterson era had settled down and, with or without clear title, gained peace and prosperity.

Such a man was William Schurman, who fled New Rochelle, New York, during the war (his brother was imprisoned as a Tory, but William escaped) and emigrated to Shelburne. He did not tarry there, but moved to a lot near Bedeque in response to

Governor Patterson's call. He had managed to sell some property before leaving New York, and sank the proceeds into a ship and a sawmill on the Dunk River. He discovered that the title to the land he thought he owned was clouded, because all the necessary papers had somehow disappeared from the records. So he ended up paying rent on land he properly owned. He was a stubborn man, however, and despite a number of setbacks (his house burned down, and one of his vessels sank with all hands, including his nineteen-year-old son) became a prosperous businessman and a magistrate. His son, Peter, who lived to the ripe old age of ninety, finally saw the family get clear title, in the 1860s, to the land they had been "granted" in 1784.[5]

The Prince Edward Island experience underlines the unhappy truth that the Loyalists, in addition to combating cold, forests and rocky soil, also often had to do battle with the vested authorities, the entrenched habits of the colonies and each other. Thus, inevitably, beside the stories of courage, strength and endurance are others of skulduggery, patronage and internecine warfare.

New Brunswick Gets Its Start

Both kinds of stories were plentiful in the founding of New Brunswick.

The hub of what was to be the new province came to be the area around Fort Howe, at the mouth of the St. John River. Governor Parr, with his usual sagacity, thought this was the wrong place to put a large band of Loyalists. "There is scarce good land enough for them already sent there," he wrote. The right place was good old Shelburne, formerly Port Roseway, Parr said—"It will in a short time become the most flourishing Town for trade of any in this part of the world, and the country will for agriculture."[6]

Even if this was the wrong place to plant Loyalists, Parr thought it would be nice if the new community were to be named Parr Town, and so it was. Or at least part of it was. The area on the north side of the river was named for Parr and divided into two sections, the Upper and Lower coves, while the south shore settlement was named Carleton, to honor Sir Guy.

The Loyalists who came ashore in the Lower Cove at Parr Town, beginning on May 18, 1783, had high hopes. The land agents who had been sent north from New York to check out the area had returned with glowing reports. Edward Winslow, one of the agents acting for the Loyalist regiments in New York, had been as far as 120 miles upriver and returned "delighted beyond expression."

Winslow was in some ways the quintessential Loyalist—proud (even haughty), shrewd and, until the Revolution came along, well-to-do. He was a direct descendant of Edward Winslow, the governor of Plymouth Colony, and he received his B.A. from Harvard in 1765. Despite his high office as muster-major general to the provincial corps and secretary to the commander in chief, he came out of the war without property. As he himself later put it, "I had no plans and my prospects were blacker than hell." But what he had, after his first visit to the St. John region, was an idea. What if, he thought, a separate province were to be carved out around the region? As he wrote his deputy, Ward Chipman, that would provide "the greatest field for Speculation that ever offered."[7]

On a less-crass note, he wrote, "Take the general map of this province, observe how detached this part is from the rest. . . . Consider the numberless inconveniences that must arise from its remoteness from the metropolis (Halifax) and the difficulty of communication. Think what multitudes have and will come here and then judge whether it must not from the nature of things immediately become a separate government and one of the most gentlemanlike on earth."

It was a good argument, and except for the crack about being gentlemanlike, would prove to stand up to the test of time. Accordingly, Winslow told Chipman to head for England to begin a campaign for partitioning Nova Scotia. At the same time, Winslow persuaded Brigadier General Henry Fox, the man who had been his immediate superior in New York, of the need for such a plan. Fox just happened to be the brother of Charles James Fox, then in alliance with Lord North at the head of the British government, so it was helpful that when the brigadier sailed home in the spring of 1784, he carried with him a parcel of maps, papers and other documents to support Winslow's case.

More support for that case was to come from Governor Parr, although he never meant it to. In fact it came chiefly because of complaints about his incompetence, some of which were undoubtedly exaggerated and inspired by Winslow, but many of which were soundly based.

The Loyalists who came to the St. John River area had formed themselves into an association while waiting in New York. This was the normal form of organization. Their particular association was called "The Bay of Fundy Adventurers," and it was composed mostly of 1,020 officers and men from Loyalist regiments, as well as their families. They were called "provincials," as a group, to distinguish them from the "refugees," who were the civilian Loyalists, and they came to the area around the mouth of the St. John River in a series of landings that lasted through the late autumn of 1783. They were expecting to find ready-made homes, cleared lots and supplies. Instead, they found tents, axes and trees. These were not people used to hacking out homes in the wilderness, and they were not, despite their military label, very well organized. They were not permanent army types. Rather, they were people drawn from every walk of life—mostly in the cities and towns of the Thirteen Colonies—who had joined the army for the war and hoped to go back to minding ships, tanning leather, keeping books or the thousand of one other occupations of prewar America.

Many of them, like those who arrived in Shelburne, expected things to be done for them. They felt they had done their bit. Thus, when a batch of army blankets was condemned as unfit for use, and an army supply officer got the bright idea of giving them to the Loyalists, they, instead of showing proper gratitude, kicked up a stink because many of the blankets had holes in them. The Loyalists didn't know the blankets were an extra. They thought they were part of the "King's Bounty" (officially "The Royal Bounty of Provisions"—the term used by government spokesmen since the formation of the first Loyalist associations in New York), and they fired off a note of protest to Guy Carleton to tell him what they thought of his shoddy merchandise. The army commissary responded by stopping the issuance of any blankets at all. That would teach them.

It didn't, though. Most of the newcomers demanded pay to unload the transport of provisions that accompanied them, nor would they build storehouses unless they were paid to do so.

Loyal Whigs vs High Tories

What they would do for free was to criticize the government. Or at least some of the would. When the Loyalists transferred themselves to Nova Scotia, they brought not one but two political parties and points of view with them. One was the reform party—Loyal Whiggism, if you like; the other the High Tory party. The High Tories had more weight, if fewer numbers. They reached for preferment and patronage as naturally as a flower turns its petals to the sun. Indeed, they turned such reaching into a virtue as well as an art. After all, what was the point of Loyalty, anyway? Surely it was to preserve the Empire and with it the sense of worth, of class, that England's autocracy imbued.

The battle between these two points of view was to mark the politics of every part of Canada the Loyalists touched. It was Edward Winslow's genius that he, one of the toffs of all time, was able to use the discontents of the reformers—the rebels, as they were inevitably called in an attempt to link the Canadian dissidents with the American revolutionaries—to establish an autocracy in the province-to-be of his dream.

It began with a petition by a group of fifty-five out of the Bay of Fundy Adventurers, who described themselves, with suitable immodesty, as "of the most respectable Characters." They wrote to Sir Guy Carleton, on July 22, 1783 (that is, while most of them were still in New York). The petition asked that each of the fifty-five be given five thousand acres of land in Nova Scotia. This was necessary, they assured Carleton, to allow them to regain their former standing in society, and it would be "highly Advantageous in diffusing and supporting a Spirit of Attachment to the British Constitution."

In short, Carleton was given the chance to create an instant autocracy, not because of the services of the fifty-five—they were mostly minor office holders, not war heroes—but simply because you needed an autocracy to get things off to the right start.

Carleton had no objection to the petition (which, after all, accorded with the normal rules of politics of his day) and was prepared to ship it off to Governor Parr. But word got back to New York, where Loyalists—including the main body of the Fundy Adventurers—were waiting for transport. They were outraged. In the first place, four of the petitioners were supposed to be acting as agents for all the Fundy Adventurers, not just the fifty-five. The leader of the petitioners was Reverend John Sayre, head of the Adventurers. He was supposed to be ensuring fair play, not working out a special deal for his cronies and himself. In the second place, if the fifty-five got away with it, the rest of the settlers, as they noted in a counter-petition to Carleton, "Must either content themselves with barren or remote Lands or submit to be Tenants to those, most of whom they consider as their superiors in nothing but deeper Art and keener Policy."

That counter-petition, signed by six hundred Loyalists after a protest meeting at Roubelet's Tavern in New York, sent Carleton scurrying for cover. He told the counter-petitioners that he doubted if the fifty-five would get their grants and promised to forward their counter-petition to Parr with the original demand of the fifty-five.

So when the Loyalists sailed into St. John harbor they bore, along with their hopes, dreams and memories, a cargo of suspicion and a sense of injury. It would be given an opportunity to grow.

Parr had been unable to get clear instructions on how much land the Loyalists were to have and was afraid to move without such orders—the same problem that plagued Shelburne. The Loyalists were expecting grants of five hundred acres per family in farming areas and generous lots in town. What many of them got instead was an ax, a spade, a hoe, a scant supply of food and the governor's best wishes.

Before land could be distributed to the first group of arrivals, a new lot landed, clamoring for space until, as a contemporary report put it, "The Lotts of those who came first had been reduced to one sixteenth." There was jobbery, too. Sarah Lester, a widow with a large family, was allotted a fine commercial location in Lower Cove, sank £34 into starting a house there, and then had it snatched from beneath her and given to a Captain Robert Murry, who stood higher in the favour of the agents and directors of the Bay of Fundy Adventurers, who were running things.

Many Loyalists spent the winter of 1783 in Parr Town, because the lands on which they were supposed to plant crops for their winter's food had not been surveyed. These lands had been escheated from the original grantees who, as on the Island of St. John, had not met the conditions of the grants. This took time and money, neither of which were readily available. John Parr's own attorney general, Richard Gibbons, represented many of the proprietors whose land was being converted to the Loyalists' use, and Parr was reluctant to offend him.

It was well into 1785 before the Loyalists were settled in any numbers on their land. They received 100 acres for the master or mistress of each family, with an additional fifty acres for each additional family member. To encourage disbanding soldiers to settle, they were given larger allotments—1,000 acres for field officers, 700 to captains, 500 to subalterns, 200 to non-commissioned officers and 100 to privates—in addition to anything they might be entitled to in respect of their families.

In Six Feet of Snow, They Lived in Tents

It was generous enough, if you could live long enough to collect. Mary Fisher, whose husband had served in the New Jersey Volunteers, went with him to St. Anne's, seventy miles upriver from Parr Town, and the family spent the bitterly cold winter of 1783-84 in a tent by the river. She wrote later that the snow was six feet deep and the tents, despite layers of spruce boughs put over them to add insulation, were frigid. "How we lived through that awful winter I hardly know. There were mothers, that had been reared in a pleasant country enjoying all the comforts of life, with helpless children in their arms. They clasped the infants to their bosoms and tried by the warmth of their own bodies to protect them from the bitter cold."[8]

Many died—no one knows exactly how many—in that first winter, of cold and hunger. The government ration for the Loyalists was supposed to be a pound of flour, half a pound of salted beef, and an "infinitesimal amount of butter " per person per day. This ration was to be cut off as soon as they were able to support themselves, but that date kept slipping farther and farther down until it stretched from six months to three years. Once a week they were entitled to a pound of oatmeal and a pound of pease, while children drew half rations. You could live on this fare, if you could get it. But all too often the rations had been sent to the wrong place, were stolen and sold, or were simply swallowed in the bureaucratic bungling that was a feature of that time, as of ours. And people died. Mary Fisher wrote, "Graves were dug with axes and shovels near the spot where our party had landed, and there in stormy winter weather our loved ones were buried. We had no minister, so we had to bury them without any religious service, besides our own prayers."[9]

Even those who had anticipated the tough conditions suffered, though no fault of their own. The King's American Dragoons were one of the first groups to arrive at the mouth of the St. John River and they began by clearing land, erecting huts and starting to put in crops, in brisk and responsible fashion. Then came word of a decision that the provincials were to be moved upriver, leaving the refugees in place at Parr Town and Carleton. The soldiers' land, except for those who had preferment, like Captain Murry, was taken from them.

For a time, it appeared they would refuse to go. Edward Winslow, for one, talked openly about defending the land on which provincial troops had already squatted, but in the end they grumbled and went, some of them beyond St. Anne's, the settlement that was to become Fredericton.

The Loyalists who survived became hardened over that first winter and gradually became adept at catching fish and shooting pigeons. They ate wild plants and turned the fiddlehead into a provincial delicacy. Some ate poisonous weeds and died; it must have been a bitter ending to escape the wrath of mobs and armies and be felled by a trail-side berry or root. Some, who had planted potatoes, dug them up again and ate them. And everyone waited for spring, when provisions would arrive. And so, for a miracle, they did. That first winter ended with many dead and many embittered, but with many others ready to forget the trials and tribulations and get on with the business of planting crops and beginning a new life.

At Parr Town houses began to go up to replace the huts, tents and bark-covered shelters in which so many had suffered the hard months. These houses were built of logs—squared logs, for those who had the time or the servants to do the work; round logs for the rest. The house was centered on a stone fireplace with an oven built at the side and iron rods sunk into the mortar to support heavy cooking pots. The logs were chinked, then plastered. Later the whole structure was sheathed in clapboard to give it a finish.

Soon fine frame houses were going up in the new settlement, with such refinements as ornate lintels and doorframes. Most houses started as a single room, sometimes with a sleeping loft. As time went by more rooms were added, and the doors, slung on crude leather straps, were properly hinged. Finally the small, precious windows were added of wavy, expensive but undeniable glass, and the interior walls were finished and festooned with rugs, shawls, even paintings. Within a few years Saint John boasted fine colonial homes alongside the shacks (Saint John was incorporated in 1785, when Parr Town and Carleton were united into one town). In most of the early houses the chimney was shaped of wood, then covered with a mortar made of clay and straw. The design was serviceable but far from fireproof, and a series of devastating fires wiped out all the early structures. They were replaced over time with fine brick structures for the well-to-do. The poor stayed in wooden homes, and kept burning.

While the newcomers were still getting settled, they began to agitate for reform and push for power in a way that would cause poor old John Parr to dismiss all Loyalists as "a pack of dogs." One lot of refugees formed themselves into a group called Company 22, and proceeded to step on official toes. The men of Company 22 were mostly once-prosperous artisans and businessmen (among the twenty-eight households were a shoe-

maker, a millwright, a surgeon, five masons and five merchants)
who brought, in most cases, "servants" with them. They were
an assertive bunch with slaves to do the hard work and a habit
of articulating demands and having them met.

They got up a series of resolutions questioning the way things
were being done. One wanted to know by what right the Bay
of Fundy Adventurers and the commander of the provincials
had been given the power to sort out land claims. Another said
that if there was to be a portion of land set aside for the Church
of England, and there was, then another should be set aside for
the Church of Scotland. A third complained about the quantity
and quality of the lots being distributed, both in town and in
the farming areas, and a fourth enumerated grievances ranging
from the non-distribution of clothing and building materials to
the fact that "The Principal Town Lots as well as the best of
the lands in this part of Nova Scotia have been and are reserved
for particular Persons." They were, too.

"The Common People Were Beginning to Indulge Themselves"

These complaints inspired a letter from Edward Winslow which
was transmitted to one of his English contacts, and thus to the
British ministry. In it Winslow described Gilfred Studholme,
commander of the Fort Howe garrison (and thus the British
military presence on the spot), as "A man accustomed to dis-
sipation and who (tho' possessed of many pleasant qualities) is
as incompetent to the performance of the task assigned as a
spider would be to regulate the great factories at Manchester."

The result, inevitably (and this was a line that got in among
the colonial office bureaucrats), was that "The common people
were beginning to indulge themselves in all manner of excesses
and (uncontrolled by the fear of punishments) they are becoming insolent and rude."

What to do? Winslow had the answer. In the short term, get
the Loyalists the land they had been promised; in the longer
term, create a new province, properly run, for the Loyalists.

Governor Parr was called upon to defend his administration
from the hammerings of Company 22 and Winslow, and chose
what has always been the time-honored defense. Most of the
Loyalists were "peaceable and quiet," he said, but they were
being manipulated by outside agitators. Parr named, in particular, Elias Hardy, a lawyer from Virginia who was one of the
agents for Company 22. Parr blamed Hardy, quite wrongly, as

the one who had "Stirred them up to the forming of a Committee"—that is, Company 22. He was, said Parr, this time with more justice, a man of "Bold and Factious disposition."

Hardy's Loyalist credentials were established by the fact that he had been seized by the mob in Virginia, but escaped before they could tar and feather him. He served in the Associated Loyalists, one of the paramilitary groups operating out of New York. At war's end, he was one of the leaders of the attack on the fifty-five and their attempted land-grab. However, he did not arrive in Saint John until November, 1783, about the month after Company 22 had circulated its hard-nosed resolutions. Never mind—he was marked by Governor Parr as the outside agitator these occasions demand, and he stepped into the role with pleasure.

The proper place to fight out these battles in colonial Canada, as in colonial America, was in petitions and in the newspapers. The *Saint John Gazette* of January 19, 1784, carried a vitriolic poem by "A Spectator," identified only as a resident of Upper Cove Parr Town, which set forth the Loyalists' plight in bitter poetry:

No recompense for service past,
The future too, an airy blast,
A piece of barren ground that's burnt,
Where one may labour, toil and grunt.

Not one of the great rhymsters, A Spectator. However, he was a better hand at vitriol and poured it out in full spate against the Reverend John Sayre, the agent of the Bay of Fundy Adventurers who had turned himself instead into an agent of the fifty-five. A Spectator described him as "the author of our woes," which was pitching it strong, considering the role George Washington et al. played in the war. Pitching it stronger still, A Spectator consigned Sayre and his pals to the grave:

May living worms his corps devour,
Him and his comrades fifty-four:
A scandal to both church and state,
The rebel's friend, the public's hate.

Not long after, on March 4, the *Gazette* published a letter from "A Soldier," which outlined all the Loyalists' complaints, took time off to libel Gilfred Studholme, the beleaguered commander of Fort Howe (he was accused of having signed up in the Fencible Americans because of "pinching want, not principle") and wound up with an invitation to outright rebellion: "No feeling men whose hearts are warm with loyalty could wish to rob you of your just rights, and those miserly wretches . . . must feel the force of a justly enraged soldiery should they succeed in their mercenary attempts."

This invitation to anarchy, obviously addressed to the provincials, brought down the wrath of constituted authority. But it was not James Eccles, a lieutenant in the Prince of Wales' American Regiment and author of the letter, who was accused. Instead, William Huggerford, who delivered the letter to the printers, and William Lewis and John Ryan, who printed it, were charged before a grand jury with "seditious and scandalous libel."

At this point Governor Parr, who had never visited the St. John region, sent Byron Finucane, Nova Scotia's chief justice, to investigate the case. Parr had ulterior motives in doing so. Under Winslow's onslaught, he was facing accusations that he had been neglectful and incompetent in settling the Loyalists. If he could show that it was instead the "gross partialities" of the Loyalist agents who were causing the unrest, much of the argument for splitting the province in two would vanish.

Finucane, a man described as "haughty and imperious," turned up in Saint John with Elias Hardy, the agitator, and proceeded to round up evidence that the agents and directors of the Bay of Fundy Adventurers had indeed been dealing themselves the best lands. Not surprisingly, Finucane's probing and his "hauteur and parade" toward the Loyalist leaders, some of whom were used to unrolling their own stock of hauteur and parade, brought howls of protest.

"For God's sake," George Leonard wrote to Edward Winslow, "let us have in our new-expected Province a Chief Justice that will not give credit to every idle report from Barbers and Grog shops, as this man has done."

If Finucane's visit was supposed to restore order, it failed. Instead it enraged the agents and directors who had nominal charge of the area and encouraged the upstarts, resulting in a number of outbreaks of violence, including "daring attempts at assassination," reported in the *Saint John Gazette*, without further explanation.

The upshot was a petition from the agents and directors for a full hearing in Halifax before the executive council of Nova Scotia. Their kind of people. That body reversed everything that Finucane had claimed, found that the agents and directors had "acquitted themselves with fairness, impartiality and propriety" and condemned Elias Hardy for "interference." The agents and directors had won a notable victory, but before they could savor it, on June 18, 1784, the area was turned into a new province. It was originally to have been called New Ireland, but instead, to honor the royal family, who came from Brunswick in Germany, it was called New Brunswick. Soon after, Parr Town and Carleton were united into a city, which was incorporated as Saint John in 1785.

The official reason for creating the new province was because of the distance the Loyalists would have to travel to Halifax to obtain recourse to the courts of justice and "for other salutary purposes." Esther Clark Wright suggested another reason—the constant din of complaints from Winslow and other Loyalists about Parr and his administration. The easiest way to still these seemed to be to carve out a new territory for the complainers.

In any event, to Parr's disgruntlement, Nova Scotia was split in two. Cape Breton was annexed to the Nova Scotia end, and the province of New Brunswick was created. Its first governor was Thomas Carleton (Sir Guy's brother), an able and honest man, but imperious. He took with him a gaggle of courtiers— Loyalists who had gone to England in 1783 to be near the font of patronage. The key post of secretary of the new province, which Winslow was expecting, went inside to Johnathan Odell. Apparently Winslow had earned the wrath of Sir Guy by some of the intemperate language of his complaints.

Odell was a doctor and clergyman who wrote satirical Loyalist poems during the Revolution and served as a captain in the New Jersey regiment. He managed to cling to the offices of provincial secretary, registrar of records and clerk of the council until 1812, when he passed on all three jobs to his son.

Winslow had to content himself with the job of surrogate general and member of the executive council. He later became a judge of the supreme court of the province he had invented. Ward Chipman, his aide, became solicitor general.

The Loyalists Took Over

Once you had an imperial appointment in New Brunswick, it tended to become a lifetime job. Governor Carleton suffered a title change in 1786. When his brother became governor general of Canada, Thomas was renamed lieutenant governor, but he held the same powers from 1784 until his death in 1817, even though he had left the province in 1803 and ruled for fourteen years through administrators. His colleagues in office were mostly officials who, like Odell, had never set foot in New Brunswick—

men like Chief Justice George Ludlow, Attorney General Jonathan Bliss, and Surveyor General George Sproule, all of them filtered Loyalists, whose appointments came to them in London after they had fled from the revolting colonies. The agents and directors who had worked so hard on the ground for preferment were largely ignored, except for non-paying jobs on the executive council. They had to go to work all over again to prove their worth, and many of them, because they had the right connections, education and conservative leanings, were able to do so. New Brunswick was to be ruled by Loyalists all right, but not exclusively by those who had suffered through the province's first eighteen tumultuous months. That was all right. There was tumult enough to come; they would get their initiation.

The new governor and council set to work to sort out the many problems of New Brunswick. St. Anne's was made the new provincial capital (it was more easily defended than a coastal city) and renamed "Frederick'stown" to honor a royal prince. Work began sorting out conflicting land claims, of which there were many, and later-arriving Loyalists were awarded lots, while the tedious business of surveying and laying out farms went on.

So did the battle between the dissidents and the administration. It came to a climax in the election of 1785. Governor Carleton held off an election as long as he could, in order, as he wrote, to curb "the American spirit of innovation." What he had in mind was "strengthening the executive powers of government" before allowing the voters a look-in, but in late 1785 the Loyalists, who had been without an elected assembly for almost ten years, were adding this delay to their list of complaints, and London became insistent.

So on October 15, electoral writs were issued in the eight counties into which the new province had been divided, for an election to select members of an assembly to meet in early 1786. These were open elections, not secret ballots. The voters met in a public place with the sheriff of the county and declared their choices. Normally only property-holders could vote, but since many of the Loyalists, even those already on the land, had not yet received title, New Brunswick's election was open to any male who had been in the province for three months. This innovation into universal suffrage made Carleton nervous, but it was unavoidable, as he explained to the colonial office, adding hopefully, "We may notwithstanding the indiscriminate privilege of Election, have an assembly composed of worthy and respectable characters."

It was going to take more than hope. The election went smoothly enough in most counties—the voting in Kings County was accompanied by the display of a huge flag, with a painting of George III crowned by Britannia and supported by Mars and Neptune (Mars had rather let him down in America, but let it pass).

However, in Saint John there was trouble. In most of the new communities, felling trees, breaking land and putting up houses kept the Loyalists too busy to worry their heads about the vote, but Saint John contained, as well as most of the dissidents, most of the unemployed. The city and county of Saint John coincided and had the right to elect six of the new assembly's twenty-six members, more than any other county. The voting was to start November 7 and continue for four hours each day until William Oliver, high sheriff of city and county, closed the poll. Six voters were allowed to vote at one time.

Ballots, Booze and Blood

As soon as the election was announced, the trouble started. There were petitions and counter-petitions, handbills and articles in the newspapers, threats and counter-threats. The city quickly became divided into two camps, the Upper Covers, centered around the Mallard House tavern in the better-groomed part of Parr Town, and the Lower Covers, who used McPherson's Coffee House for a headquarters. The Upper Covers were by and large the conservatives, and the group included the agents and directors whose unsuccessful land-grab scheme had gone awry; they naturally allied themselves with the provincial authorities. The Lower Covers included people like Elias Hardy. Upstarts and democrats.

Inevitably there was a riot—a full-scale mob-scene around the Mallard House. It broke out on November 9, when Sheriff Oliver moved the poll from McPherson's across to the Mallard House, hoping to run up a lead for the government candidates. A group of Lower Covers, "very drunk," according to one witness, descended on the place with stones and brick-bats, smashed all the windows and started in on the thirty-odd government supporters inside waiting to vote. Before it was done, the troops from Fort Howe were called in, and five rioters arrested.

The violence, so reminiscent of life in the Thirteen Colonies, brought instant official response. Governor Carleton blamed the Lower Cove's election candidates for "intoxicating the lowest class," which was one way of putting it, and Sheriff Oliver closed the poll for a week. Then he tried to arrange for the Fort Howe garrison votes to be submitted as a block for the government slate, but that plan blew up when it appeared that the ordinary soldiery might vote instead for the Lower Cove slate. When the final votes were taken on November 24, the Lower Covers had won in a walk, electing all six candidates.

There was only one thing to do—steal the election on behalf of the government. Sheriff Oliver refused to return the electoral writ from Saint John, and with Governor Carleton's support, appointed himself to the job of scrutinizing all the ballots. Then he disallowed enough Lower Cove votes to elect all the government candidates instead, and only then did he return the official writ. The Lower Covers bellowed, but in vain. The new assembly ruled that Oliver had conducted himself "legally, fairly and impartially," which was demonstrably false and gave a thumb in the eye to the upstarts.

The night the assembly's verdict was posted in McPherson's Coffee House, the Lower Cove headquarters, George Handesyde, one of the dissidents, got into an argument with Christopher Sower, a government man and, in fact, the king's printer. Sower later claimed that during this debate, Handesyde recklessly blurted out, "The House of Assembly ought to be tore limb from limb." Handesyde was forthwith summoned before the assembly, charged and convicted of contempt and "tending to excite Sedition," and ordered to ask pardon on his knees. He complied and was thereafter known as "the kneeling man."

The matter did not end there. Lewis and Ryan, the men who had printed the soldier's libel in the *Saint John Gazette*—a matter still hanging fire—printed another open letter signed "Americanus," which complained that the rights of the Loyalists as Britons, including the right of free speech, were being trampled on. They turned out to have the facts right, but it didn't do them much good. Lewis and Ryan were charged with publishing "a scandalous and seditious libel." They dissolved their partnership and folded their newspaper. They were convicted and fined, anyway, and Lewis went back to the United States.

Dissent was not going to be permitted. When a petition attacking the assembly's seating of the non-elected Upper Covers was circulated in York and Sunbury counties, Carleton drew up, and a compliant council and assembly promptly passed, a law that historian David Bell has called, "the most repressive piece of legislation ever enacted in New Brunswick." Called "An Act Against Tumults and Disorders," it effectively banned petitioning, which was at that time the most pervasive and

persuasive form of political action. Carleton and his administration took the position that any opposition to the administration was, in effect, an attack on the king. Free speech, by
one of those nice ironies of fate, had become, instead of an
Englishman's inherent right, proof of disloyalty.

"The people," says Esther Clark Wright, "had exchanged whips
for scorpions."

The effect was the creation of an oligarchy, which continued
to rule New Brunswick as a personal fiefdom for half a century,
and which only came to an end as a result of the nation-wide
struggle for self-government in the mid-nineteenth century. In
a way this development was predictable and understandable.
What the Loyalist leaders—the men of position and power,
education and wealth—feared more than anything else in their
new land was a repetition of the excesses of the old. Sheriff
Oliver was the son of Andrew Oliver, the former stamp officer
of Massachusetts whose house was destroyed by a Boston mob
in a scene that must have impressed itself mightily on his mind.
His reaction to anything that smacked of rebellion—and dissent
smacked of rebellion—was bound to be strong. Many of his
fellow Loyalists had been through similar experiences and shared
similar views. Of those who did not, most were content to get
on with the job of building new homes and to leave the messy
business of politics to someone else. They had seen what excesses political participation could produce in their former
homeland. In the circumstances it is hardly surprising that any
form of political discontent became equated with revolutionary
fervor, and that it was crushed with little regard to the niceties.

Loyalists brought with them from the Thirteen Colonies a
tendency to question authority, but they also brought the desire
for stability. In the end it was the yearning for stability that
won out.

Much the same thing happened in the remolded province of
Nova Scotia. Halifax swarmed with Loyalists and disbanded
soldiers who were used to town life and unable to cope with
the wilderness.

Coconut Head Takes a Mistress

For John Parr and his hangers-on, there were elaborate balls and
other entertainments, especially after the arrival of Prince William, George III's roistering son—the man who would later be
King William IV. He was known in the navy as "Coconut Head";
he would be known on the throne as "Silly Billy." In Halifax,

he was known as a gambler, drunk and womanizer.[10] His favorite mistress was Frances, the wife of John Wentworth, former royal governor of New Hampshire. Wentworth had gone to England during the war, but came to Nova Scotia as surveyor general of woods and forests. He didn't mind his wife's dalliance with Prince William and cleared off for a tour of the woods whenever the prince came to visit. This discretion paid off. He was later named lieutenant governor of Nova Scotia.

It was a society in which preferment was all important, family connections were crucial and politics remained in the tight control of a close-knit group of ruling families. For most Loyalists in any event, life was a matter of struggle against the elements, and that was struggle enough. Political lethargy became the hallmark of the newcomers in both Nova Scotia and New Brunswick for some time to come. Those who hurled themselves into politics in the name of reform—rather than in the more acceptable pursuit of favors, place and position—were regarded with dark suspicion. In the next generation there would be a renewal of the struggle for freedom of expression, a rekindling of political dissent. But not for now. John Howe, printer, was one of the Loyalists who settled in Halifax. It was his son, Joseph, born in 1804, who would take up the battle for responsible government. Significantly, the case that propelled Joseph into prominence was his prosecution for attacking the government—he was charged with libel. In the decades immediately following the establishment of the Loyalists in Nova Scotia, that kind of behavior had become aberrant. For most of the newcomers the natural course was to accept the ministrations of constituted authority, work hard and hope for the best. If that was not to your liking, there was only one sensible thing to do—remove yourself.

Some did, to Quebec and farther west. But of all the ricochet refugees the most unusual and most tragic group were the blacks.

10
Betrayal of the Blacks

"I think I never saw wretchedness and poverty so strongly perceptible in the garb and countenance of the human species as in these miserable outcasts."
William Dyott *describing the Loyalist blacks at Shelburne, Nova Scotia, in 1784.*

A black American was the first man killed by British troops in the Revolutionary War. His name was Crispus Attucks, and he was in the crowd that tangled with troops on guard at the Boston custom house on March 5, 1770. Captain Thomas Preston, the British commander, suggests in his account that Attucks intervened when a British soldier struck a child with his rifle butt, and he was the first to fall when the troops panicked and opened fire. Attucks was a free black, not a slave, and he chose the Patriot side.[1]

Most blacks did not have the opportunity to make a choice. Since most were slaves, the choice was made by their masters. Some simply went to war as servants when their masters enlisted. Others were shoved into uniform as substitutes. A man called up by his state could send a slave in his place, and in the northern and middle states this was frequently done. Some states required that the slave be freed when the substitution was made, but in others the slave continued to be a slave, and his pay was transferred to his master. This system was not popular in the south, where there were more black slaves than white masters; the danger was that the underlings would "when armed . . . become our masters."[2]

There were a few cases in which slaves ran away and joined the continental army, purporting to be freemen; they were generally accepted as such. In other instances black slaves fought so bravely that they were freed as a reward. A continental army payroll book shows that one Zachery Prince, a private, was rewarded in this way, but he did not live long to enjoy his freedom. He died in battle.

Blacks were used as spies by both sides. General Joseph Lafayette, the French marquis who joined the rebel army, had high praise for James Armistead, a Virginia slave who enlisted with the permission of his Patriot master and conducted a number of successful intelligence missions across the British line. The Virginia assembly bought Armistead his freedom, on Lafayette's recommendation, after the war. But for many others the end of the war simply meant a return to the plantation and slavery.[3]

No record was ever kept of how many blacks served on either side in the fighting, although they numbered in the thousands. There were at least three Black Patriot regiments, the most prominent of which, the "Bucks of America," was raised in Boston. However, there were far more blacks in Loyalist ranks than in the continental army, for obvious reasons. They were promised land, rations and, most important of all, freedom. Thomas Jefferson claimed that Virginia alone lost 30,000 blacks to this lure, and the total may have ranged as high as 100,000, or about one in every five slaves then in America.[4]

This process began when John Murray, earl of Dunmore and royal governor of Virginia, issued a proclamation on November 7, 1775, promising freedom to any "rebel" black—though not to any slave held by a Loyalist—who would join the British forces. His wording was specific, and cunning: "I do hereby further declare all indentured servants, Negroes or others, (appertaining to Rebels) free, that are able and willing to bear arms, they joining His Majesty's troops."

In response to this offer hundreds of blacks downed tools and joined the British, and the Virginia whites were enraged and worried. Patrick Henry wrote that Dunmore's proclamation was "fatal to the publick safety" and demanded "early and unremitting Attention to the Government of the Slaves."

The Virginia assembly responded with a carrot-and-stick proclamation of its own, promising death—without benefit of clergy—for "all negro or other slaves, conspiring to rebel."

Strange wording, that. What it really meant was that if slaves chose to rebel against the rebels, they would be executed. On the other hand, if they chose to surrender to "col. William Woodford, or any other commander of our troops," they would receive a full pardon. Along, of course, with instant return to slavery. There is no record that any Virginian slave took up the offer of pardon, and as Dunmore's plan was adopted in colony after colony, it became harder and harder to keep the blacks penned.

They Bolted for Freedom from the Sons of Liberty

They walked, swam, rowed and ran away. They stole horses or mules and rode away. They hid themselves in boats and wagons that crossed into British-held territory and then made a bolt for freedom. Sometimes homes and plantations were abandoned by fleeing rebels, leaving the slaves behind, and these decamped when the British retreated. George Washington, James Madison and Benjamin Harrison were three of many prominent revolutionary leaders who lost slaves to the British army.

When the Declaration of Independence made it clear that the much-vaunted rights to life, liberty and the pursuit of happiness applied only to whites, the impetus to flee was strengthened. It was strengthened again in 1779, when Sir Henry Clinton, who was then the British commander in chief, offered "to every Negro who shall desert the Rebel Standard, full security to follow . . . any occupation which he shall think proper." Before this only those who could serve as soldiers were welcomed, and many blacks hesitated to abandon wives, children and aged parents to the wrath of their masters. Now there was a place for whole families. In one case a Maryland band of twenty-two slaves, including two women and four children, broke into their owner's barn, stole his boat and literally sailed to freedom.

Many of the slaves, despite Clinton's promise, were not free to practice any line of work. They served instead as foragers, cooks and personal servants. Sir Guy Carleton had a black Loyalist valet, and almost every regiment had a black drummer or fifer. Boston King, one of the most prominent of all the black Loyalists, worked for a time as body servant to a British captain.

Black Loyalists fought in the army and royal navy, served as pilots on coastal vessels, formed their own pioneer corps to conduct engineering projects and even created a black cavalry troop. They fought bravely and well, but in many cases it didn't matter a whit. Slaves, after all, were property, and freeing them to annoy the rebels was one thing; actually turning them loose was another. It became official British policy that slaves who were seized became public property. They could be kept on confiscated rebel plantations to keep them working, or they could be sold or assigned to army units. There was even a bonus

system under which army officers or units showing conspic-
uous merit would be awarded slaves as a reward, and they might
be used or sold. In one sale in Montreal, forty-three slaves brought
an average of £33 15s on the auction block. The proceeds served
the same function as prize-money for sailors, obtained from the
sale of captured ships.

Even slaves who had gained their freedom by escaping to the
British were not safe. Guy Carleton's valet, Pomp, for example,
was not allowed to leave his master's service at war's end. The
truth is that the British, as much as the Americans, regarded
the blacks as property and, if human, certainly worth less than
any white. A group of free blacks, "The Company of Negroes,"
fled Boston with the British evacuation in 1776 and went to
Halifax with the other Loyalists. They were immediately confronted with a suggestion that they should be traded for white
Loyalist prisoners in the hands of the rebel army. Although the
suggestion was not acted on, it must have made the blacks a
trifle uneasy.

When Charleston was being evacuated in 1781, the British
promised to restore "property" to the rebels in return for their
safe-conduct, and property included slaves. Simply to hand back
the black Loyalists to their owners would violate the promises
already made to them, so a commission was set up to sort out
the conflicting claims of blacks claiming freedom and whites
claiming their slaves. The commission bogged down in hope-
less arguments, and in the end the army sailed away, taking
thousands of slaves and ex-slaves with it, but leaving many
more behind—including those who had been promised freedom.

The evacuation of New York at the war's end brought more
problems and more terror. Sir Guy Carleton argued that anyone,
black or white, who had been behind the British lines for at
least twelve months was, by definition, a Loyalist. He did not
include British slaves in this line of reasoning—they were still
just slaves—but he did include escaped slaves. They were to be
treated like other Loyalists. The Americans responded that, on
the contrary, since the peace treaty required the restoration of
all property, and since the slaves were plainly property, they
must be given back. While the fine points of debate were being
bandied back and forth, a number of Patriot slave-owners took
matters into their own hands and grabbed the blacks. Boston
King wrote in anguish, "We saw our old masters coming from
Virginia, North Carolina and other parts, and seizing upon their
slaves in the streets of New York, or even dragging them out
of their beds."[5]

Finally Carleton met with General Washington at Orange-town, New Jersey, on May 6, 1783, to sort the matter out. Washington insisted that all slaves must be returned. Carleton replied that even if he wanted to comply with that demand, he could not. Many slaves had already been evacuated. However, he said, he had compiled a record of their numbers, so that compensation could be paid to their owners. Washington was angry and upset, but there wasn't much he could do except to insist that a commission be set up to examine all departing blacks and determine if they had the right to leave.

So that was done. Brigadier General Samuel Birch, the British army chief, issued a permit—instantly dubbed "The General Birch Certificate"—to any black who could prove that he had been behind the British lines for twelve months and was not a British slave. These were free to board the transports for Nova Scotia. From the certificates was drawn up a "Book of Negroes" containing the name and status of every qualified black. Whites who wanted to contest the right of anyone in the Book of Negroes to leave New York were required to appear before a joint board composed of British and American officers. Few bothered, and a great many blacks escaped by virtue of a piece of General Birch's paper.

In total, 3,000 blacks were entered in the Book of Negroes. They sailed from New York while others made their own ways north along with the whites. In addition, at least 3,360 black "servants"—slaves—left with Loyalists, although it appears there was some duplication between the lists, and a number of blacks appeared on both. In any event, at least ten percent and perhaps as many as twenty percent of all the Loyalists who went to Nova Scotia in the great migration were blacks. Many of them would come to wonder why they bothered to make the trip.

They endured the same rough sea voyage as many of the whites and the same crowded conditions. But at journey's end they found themselves even more bereft than their white neighbors, who counted themselves lucky if they could, as one Annapolis newcomer recounted, find room in "a single apartment built with sods, where men, women, children, pigs, fleas, bugs, mosquitoes and other domestic insects, mingle in society."

There was to be no mingling in society for the blacks; that much at least was clear. They were not even allowed the same meager rations as the whites. At Halifax, arriving whites were to have "Codfish, molasses and hard biscuit," with occasional additions from "a very limited supply of meat." Not the blacks. They were to make do on "meal and molasses," although there was no question of their escaping the hard physical labor that awaited the newcomers. Whites might insist on being paid to unload ships or build housing; the blacks were handed tools and put to work with no discussion of the matter on either side.

When they arrived in the midst of the chaos created by the vast influx of Loyalists in Nova Scotia, their claims were lost in the clamor of their white companions. Although they had been promised treatment equal to every other refugee, it was not forthcoming. Their land claims were met even more slowly than those of the whites. They almost never received the full allotments promised, and they were fobbed off on the worst town lots and the scrubbiest, rockiest farmland.

By far the largest concentration of blacks was at Shelburne, where a separate community for them was set up and named for General Birch, the man whose certificates wafted them out of New York. Almost at once, whites tried to grab the land at Birchtown, but they were blocked by the quick action of Benjamin Marston, the deputy surveyor, who managed to ensure that Birchtown remained open to black settlement. This did not mean that the blacks got their land—far from it. In November, 1786, when all the white loyalists who remained in the Shelburne area were at last in legal possession of their properties, the Birchtown Loyalists were still squatters. None had been issued with a title. While farms for the whites in the area averaged seventy-four acres, fewer than one in three of the blacks who qualified for farmland ever got any. For those who did get legal possession when the deeds were finally completed in 1788, the average farm size was thirty-four acres, less than half the white man's allotment.

Most of the blacks had acquired marketable skills during their years of slavery, and they were pressed into work at low or no wages to construct Shelburne's public buildings. When that was done they went to work for individual white masters and promptly ran into more trouble. Because they were willing to work for such low wages, they were seen as a threat to their white neighbors. This was one of the causes of the riot in Shelburne in 1784. During that fracas the few blacks who had managed to move into the main town area were driven out, and at least twenty of their homes were destroyed.

For most blacks, accustomed to the warmer climate of the south, Nova Scotia winters in the drafty shacks that comprised most of Birchtown's housing stock became contests of endurance. Many lost the contest and died of cold, disease, starvation and despair. Boston King, a preacher and a man of education (he could read and write, which was rare among blacks), was able to find work one summer as a fisherman, which delighted him because he was paid £15 and two barrels of fish. He wrote in his memoirs, "I was enabled to clothe my wife and myself; and my winter's store consisted of one barrel of flour, three bushels of corn, nine gallons of treacle, twenty bushels of potatoes which my wife had set in my absence, and the two barrels of fish; so that this was the best winter I ever saw in Birchtown."

He was lucky. By his own account many of his neighbors, after they had sold everything (including their clothes and blankets) to obtain food, ran out of things to trade and starved to death, while "Some killed and ate their dogs and cats; and poverty and distress prevailed on every side."

The white Loyalists suffered from the incompetence and corruption of Governor Parr's administrators, but the blacks suffered more. The lot of slaves and indentured servants, whose masters had run out of funds, was particularly hard. As the whites fell on hard times, they drew the rations allotted to their servants, but they kept most for themselves and turned the unfortunate blacks out to survive however they could. Thomas London, a cooper, was given only two-and-a-half-months' worth of the year's provisions his master drew in his name. Robert Turnbull drew a year's rations for his slave, Betsey Rogers, but refused to give her any of them. Cyril Williams, a barber indentured to Alphea Palmer, was charged twelve shillings a week— a considerable sum at the time— for provisions that his master had drawn free in his name.

Blacks who rebelled or disobeyed were harshly treated. William Young turned on his master and was administered a public whipping of thirty-nine lashes and sentenced to two months' hard labor with a whipping at the end of each month. Slaves or servants could be shackled or whipped "in case of being stubborn or idle," and their food could be withheld. They could be hired out to other masters, and the money earned kept by their own. Slaves could be sold, even away from their families, or willed to new owners on the death of the old, and they had no more protection in law than any other piece of property.

Mary Was Sold for One Hundred Bushels of Potatoes

Mary Postell was a slave who escaped to the British lines at Charleston and worked on the fortifications for the army alongside other freed slaves. When Charleston was evacuated, her husband persuaded her to go to St. Augustine to work for a man named Jesse Gray. Gray promptly claimed her as a slave and sold her, along with her two daughters, to his brother Samuel. At war's end, St. Augustine was ceded to the Spanish along with the rest of East Florida, so the Gray brothers fled north and wound up in Shelburne. There Jesse brought Mary and her children back from his brother, but she managed to get away and applied to the Shelburne magistrates—the font of all local law—to claim the freedom repeatedly promised in the British proclamations during the war. Two black Loyalists, Scipio and Dinah Wearing, came forward to testify that Mary had been freed and did not belong to either of the Gray brothers. However, the local whites did not take kindly to uppity blacks appearing in court. While the Wearings were away, their home was burned to the ground, and one of their children was killed. The magistrates refused to accept the evidence of any of the blacks, and Mary was deemed to be the property of Jesse Gray. He sold her for one hundred bushels of potatoes, kept one of her daughters and sold the other.

In another case dealt with by the Shelburne magistrates, James Singletory, his wife and son, were all awarded by the court to a white Loyalist, Samuel Anderson, although Anderson was unable to produce a shred of proof that they were his or anyone else's slaves. He said he had paid £50 for the trio, but had lost the bill of sale. It was normal in law to take the word of any white man over that of any black, but this case seemed so blatant that the magistrates thought they might adopt a compromise. They said Anderson should return to them within a year with some other proof that the blacks belonged to him. But in the meantime, they were his to do with what he would. The record doesn't show what happened in the end. Apparently Anderson moved from Shelburne and took his slaves—as they now unquestionably were—with him.

Life for the free blacks in Shelburne was better, but only marginally so. Most of them were poor, and starvation drove them to theft. Then they were brutally punished for lawbreaking. One man was hung for stealing; another was sentenced to twelve lashes and two months' hard labor for the theft of two pieces of pork; a third was given a month's hard labor and thirty-nine lashes for taking a pair of shoes. Whites convicted of the same crimes were fined.

The black Loyalists of Shelburne and Birchtown were not the only ones who received short shrift. The treatment of blacks throughout the province was much the same. A group of Black Pioneers who had worked as military engineers during the war landed at Digby and found themselves in the midst of a series of scandals surrounding land distribution. The corruption eventually led to rioting, and the rioting brought about an investigation that uncovered a system of graft operated by a handful of government land agents. Some of the whites were able to make good on their land claims once the investigation had been concluded, but most of the blacks were just out of luck.

The Digby blacks also ran into problems getting their allotted rations of food. Consignments of flour and pork were delivered to Digby for their use, but went instead to the Reverend Edward Brudenell, "a particular friend" of Governor Parr. Brudenell, who was also involved in the land scandals, was damned if he would waste the food destined for the blacks by giving it to them. Instead of distributing it, as he was ordered to do, he stored it and doled it out in small quantities in return for free work on the township roads. Even when protests led to some distribution of the king's bounty, Brudenell moved in his own mysterious way. Blacks who were supposed to get a supply for three years instead got it for three months.

Because they had neither food nor coin nor land, many blacks were reduced to tenant farming, despite the early promises that they would be able to support themselves. They became sharecroppers on the land of whites—allowed to keep one-half the crop while the landlord took the rest. The first Anglican bishop of Nova Scotia, Charles Inglis, benefited from the services of a sharecropper named John Brown, who proved to be a superior farmer. Brown cleared and cultivated eight acres of the bishop's land in a way that man of God described as "in better order, neater and more flourishing than any of the others." The bishop knew what to do about that. He moved Brown off the good land and made him start all over again on a new and untouched plot.

When blacks found work, they were paid less than whites as a matter of course, and they were lucky if they were able to collect even that. Simeon Perkins, a white Loyalist, wrote in his diary, "It is a Common Custom in this Country to promise a Black so much money per day and in the Evening, when his work is almost finished, the White man quarrels with him and takes him to a Justice of the Peace who gives an order to mulct him of his wages."

Some blacks in their distress sold their own children into terms of indenture—a sort of apprenticeship for a certain period of time. Then the child could be claimed by the master as a slave. After all, in a court where the matter might come to dispute, it was his word against that of a black. In other cases indentured servants were charged board, so they could never get free again, since there was always a debt to work off. Since most of the blacks (as well as most of the whites) were illiterate, indenture agreements were avenues to fraud. Lydia Jackson, a freed black living in Manchester, Nova Scotia, thought she had agreed to a one-year term of indenture with Henry Hedley, but the indenture certificate on which she made her mark was for thirty-nine years. When she realized she had been swindled, Hedley sold her to a doctor in Lunenburg, whose wife beat her with fire tongs and, although she was in an advanced state of pregnancy, kicked her in the stomach. Jackson managed to get before the town magistrates in Shelburne, but they refused to accept any of her testimony, and she remained in bondage.

Blacks were denied the basic right of trial by jury in both Nova Scotia and New Brunswick. New Brunswick governor Thomas Carleton explained, "Having come within the British lines with no other View than to escape from the service of their American master, [they] cannot be considered as entitled to claim anything further than personal protection and freedom from servitude." No one pointed out to Carleton that that was not the way matters had been put in the proclamations that had led many blacks across the British lines. The blacks were also, as a matter of course, denied the right to vote.

Negro Frolicks Were Against the Law

The 1780s were a tough decade for all Nova Scotians. Trade was down, crops poor, prospects worse, and, in the winter of 1788-89, there was a famine. Not surprisingly, the reaction of many whites was once again to blame the blacks—for undermining wages, for working, for not working, for being alive. Shelburne passed laws "forbidding Negro dances and Negro Frolicks in this Town," and any blacks who danced or frolicked were charged with "riotous behaviour."

It became too much. The blacks could not flee back to the United States, as did many of Shelburne's disgruntled whites; that way lay certain slavery. One man who was determined to find another solution was Thomas Peters, a freed black who had served as a sergeant in the Black Pioneers and was a leader in the black community at Digby. He was a remarkable man— patient, intelligent, educated and not at all overwhelmed by the notion that he ought to accept whatever fate the whites chose to mete out. His dogged persistence in the teeth of repeated rebuffs finally paid off, but it was a long struggle.

At Digby, blacks who had managed to establish themselves were ordered to move so whites could have their property. They grumbled, but they went and re-established themselves. Then they were told to move again. This time Peters was determined to find a permanent solution, so he crossed the Bay of Fundy and went to call on New Brunswick governor Thomas Carleton, who was anxious for settlers with the skills many of the Black Pioneers possessed. Peters extracted a promise from Carleton that if he would bring his followers to New Brunswick, they would receive the same treatment as whites.

Soon after, Peters applied for a block of land near the new provincial capital of Fredericton (formerly St. Anne's). Carleton rejected the request and gave the land to a group of whites instead. Peters held his temper and went to call on Carleton once again. This time he discovered that blacks who had applied for town lots in Saint John were finally awarded plots in a ghetto outside the built-up area. It was clear that the administration preferred the blacks to stay in hovels downtown and work as laborers.

Peters began to circulate among all the black communities of Nova Scotia and New Brunswick, gathering information, support and petitions along with powers of attorney allowing him to act on behalf of the blacks in laying their grievances before the colonial office in England. It took him months to get together a small fund and to make his way to Halifax. But he got there and boarded ship for England. He landed in London late in 1790, stony broke and with no clear idea of what to do, except that he thought somebody ought to do something about the plight of the black Loyalists.

He got in touch with a London-based group known as "the Black Poor." They were a strange bunch, the beneficiaries of a 1772 court judgment in the case of a black slave who had been returned to the West Indies and had claimed the right to freedom in England. The case had resulted in a ruling from England's chief justice, William Murray, earl of Mansfield, that "The state of slavery is of such a nature that it is incapable of being introduced on any reasons, moral or political, but only by positive law."[6] In the absence of any law specifically permitting slavery, he ruled, slaves in England could no longer be held in servitude. The case freed several hundred blacks in London. These men and women were not, however, given a means of livelihood. Most of them became beggars and formed themselves into a sort of paupers' collective under the sponsorship of Granville Sharp, a reformer, educator and abolitionist, and, most important, the man who had brought to court the landmark case decided by Chief Justice Mansfield.

When Peters explained to the Poor Blacks that he wanted to lay a petition before the government, but had neither the means nor the patronage even to begin an approach, they took him to Granville Sharp. Sharp, who had already heard something of the plight of the black Loyalists, immediately embraced Peters' cause, arranged for him to present his case to the secretary of state, Henry Dundas, and introduced him to the directors of the Sierra Leone Company.

This was a company formed to start a colony in Africa where blacks could live free forever from the threat of slavery. Granville Sharp was one of its most enthusiastic backers. On May 14, 1787, 330 settlers from the black ex-slave community of England, along with thirty white prostitutes, were deposited on the coast of West Africa on a piece of land purchased from a local chief identified as "King Tom," and a colony began. It ran into many of the same difficulties the Loyalists encountered in Nova Scotia—lack of organization, lack of cleared land, lack of everything except causes of dissension. By the time Peters arrived in London, Sierra Leone was badly in need of an influx of new settlers, especially if they carried many of artisan skills common among the black Loyalists.

Birchtown Opts for Sierra Leone

The upshot was a decision by the Sierra Leone Company to offer land and goods to permit the Nova Scotia blacks to join the African venture. The British government, once Peters had laid his dossiers before the administration, agreed to provide transport. All that remained was to let the Nova Scotians in on it. Lieutenant John Clarkson of the British navy, a brother of one of the directors of the Sierra Leone Company, was dispatched to Halifax and then to Shelburne to lay the proposal before the black Loyalists.

This development came as something of a shock to the whites of Shelburne, especially to those who were used to regarding the blacks as a pool of cheap labor. There was also the worry that the best and hardest-working blacks would be the ones to depart, leaving the old, feeble and lazy behind.

Lieutenant Clarkson called an open meeting in Birchtown at the black meetinghouse, and with great care he laid three alternatives before the blacks to relieve their obvious distress. The chastened local authorities were now willing to offer new and more generous terms to the blacks, and they could resettle elsewhere in Nova Scotia on these terms. They could enlist in the British army for service in the West Indies. Or, those who could show themselves to be "honest, sober and industrious" could emigrate to Sierra Leone.

The Birchtown meeting opted, to a man, for Sierra Leone (although some later changed their minds).

Clarkson was touched and appalled by some of the stories he heard in Birchtown. One man, a slave who belonged irrevocably to a Loyalist, begged Clarkson to take his wife and children to West Africa, although he knew that he himself could never go. At least for the rest of his life he could "cheer himself with the pleasing reflection that his wife and children were happy."

Clarkson offered to buy the man's freedom so he could go, too, but he was told that it could not be done, due to "the intricacies of the law."

Another man was asked by Clarkson if he was sure he understood the nature of the proposal, and what it would mean to go to Africa. The man replied, according to Clarkson's notes, "Mr. Massa, me no hear, nor no mind, me work like slave, cannot do worse, Massa."

Within a few days Lieutenant Clarkson had a list of six hundred blacks who wanted transport to Africa—far more than he expected. He curtailed visits to other areas of the province. He was afraid the threat of a black exodus might arouse anger.

So it did, as Thomas Peters discovered when he returned from England to press the provincial governments for aid in transferring the blacks. In Halifax Governor Parr refused to help in any way. In Saint John, New Brunswick officials harassed and threatened Peters. In Digby, he was physically attacked by an outraged white. However, the expedition had the official British stamp of approval on it, thanks to Granville Sharp's influence, and if Governor Parr could refuse to deal with Peters, he couldn't ignore Clarkson. What he could do, though, was delay and temporize. Parr sent orders to Shelburne canceling the enlistment of all the emigrants signed up there; then he had to countermand that order.

Individual whites, anxious to keep their labor pool, went farther. False debts were concocted to keep blacks from leaving. Employers withheld salaries. Local white dignitaries refused the testimonials of honesty, industry and sobriety demanded by the Sierra Leone Company, and rumors were circulated that what the company really had in mind was to sell the blacks back into slavery.

However, the blacks had some allies on their side, including Nova Scotia's attorney general, Sampson S. Blowers, a dedicated abolitionist, and a group of influential Quakers.

In the end, with all the complaints, threats and delays, the thing was done. On January 15, 1792, 1,190 blacks shipped out of Halifax for Africa on fifteen British transports, leaving behind a country "whose inhabitants had treated them with such barbarity," as Clarkson's biographer wrote. Of the nearly 1,200 blacks who fled, 544 were from Shelburne, a town from which another 2,500 blacks had departed over the bleak years. Where did they go? Again, the record is unclear. Presumably not back to the United States. Some drifted to other towns, some wound up in Halifax, and some probably did not survive the punishing Maritime winters long enough to leave a mark. Only fifty black families were left of all those who had originally come to Shelburne, and the locals felt aggrieved. Stephen Skinner lamented the loss of "Upwards of Five hundred good and efficient Citizens . . . labouring People and servants who have been flattered by imaginary prospects of happiness to leave a comfortable and decent maintenance."

Not many of the black Loyalists would have chosen the words "comfortable" and "decent" to describe their lives in Nova Scotia and New Brunswick. About one in every three went to Sierra Leone, and, but for the obstacles put in their way (not the least of which was Lieutenant Clarkson's constant series of reminders to them of how difficult life might be in Africa), many more might have gone. The British government was so startled by the numbers and the expense of transport that the Nova Scotia administration was authorized to offer other blacks land in the West Indies, on the grounds that it would be cheaper to ship them there than to West Africa, although few went.

Nova Scotia's new governor, John Wentworth, made an interesting point in a letter he wrote to King George III in 1792. He said it seemed strange to spend so much money removing the blacks to Sierra Leone when they might have been fairly treated in Nova Scotia for one eighth the cost. He found it strange "for government to spend so much to remove labourious people and will spend nothing to help those who remain."

The blacks who followed Thomas Peters and John Clarkson to Sierra Leone faced years of hardship, deprivation and poverty before that country gained even a modest affluence. What they did not ever face again, however, was the threat of slavery, or the litany of cruelties, small and large, that had been the lot of so many of them in the ranks of the Loyalists.

11
Refugees Into Settlers

*"At first they all had to experience great privations,
but being possessed of indomitable courage and love
for the British Constitution, they soon set to work
with the materials they brought with them and
erected a log House . . . and thus got a shelter from
the storms and winds of Heaven."*

From the testimonial of Roger
Bates, District of Newcastle

Most of the Loyalists who fled to Canada came in the great
migrations of 1783, but there were others who had been drifting
northward throughout the war by canoe and cart, on foot and
on horseback. Many of these, especially those who lived away
from the seacoast, made their way to the sprawling province
of Quebec. Large bodies of refugees came north with Sir John
Johnson and Colonel John Butler. More came as Butler, Johnson
and Joseph Brant unleashed their raids on the border area, and
still more when General Sullivan's avenging regiments smashed
through the same region, destroying Indian and Tory strong-
holds. As early as June 2, 1774, a British army officer wrote to
Quebec announcing the arrival of Loyalists at St. Johns on the
Richelieu River and complaining of "their unreasonable expectations."

Unreasonable or not, the Loyalists who came to Quebec were
treated with much greater care and compassion than the Nova
Scotia arrivals. Frederick Haldimand, the Swiss-born soldier
who was named governor of Quebec in 1777, arranged for the
establishment of a camp at Machiche, on the St. Lawrence near
Trois Rivières, early in 1778. Militia captains in the area were
ordered to help build huts and barracks, while food and other
supplies were shipped in from Trois Rivières. Later, Haldimand
bought the seigneury of Sorel at the junction of the Richelieu
and the St. Lawrence, which became a Loyalist reserve. By the

end of 1778, there were upwards of a thousand refugees in these camps, along with another two thousand provincials and their families.[1]

Conditions in the camps were crude. The Loyalists lived in crowded quarters on scanty provisions. But despite some comlaints they bore up well. This was, after all, temporary. They would be going back to their homes when the war was won.

When it became clear that the war was not going to be won, Haldimand, a man of meticulous organization as well as considerable compassion (despite a somewhat haughty exterior) moved quickly to accommodate the thousands who began to trek, paddle and sail north. The 12,000 or so Loyalists who arrived in Quebec at war's end came in four groups. The largest consisted of the so-called "incorporated Loyalists." While still in New York City, they had been organized by Sir Guy Carleton into associations under quasi-military rule, although not all the men were military. They probably made up half the newcomers. Then there were disbanded soldiers and their families who had not been in New York. Some were provincials, some German mercenaries and a few British soldiers who decided to remain in North America at war's end. There were perhaps 2,000 of these, including their families. The third group were the "unincorporated Loyalists"—refugees who arrived in batches, in families, or even alone. There had been 1,000 of these in the camps earlier. Now there were perhaps three times that many. Finally there were the Indians, who numbered about 2,000. They are not generally counted among the Loyalists, so the Quebec figure is usually given as somewhere around 9,500 or 10,000.

Haldimand was not particularly happy to see any of them. He was already having problems with the battle between the English merchants of Quebec and Montreal and the "French party," which represented the great majority and the vested interests of his territory. Just the same, Haldimand did his best—ignoring or deliberately overriding colonial office rules, spending money for which he had no legal authority and which he might have been called upon to pay out of his own pocket, and straining the sinews of his meager administration to settle the newcomers.

He hoped they would go to Cape Breton. "The unconceded lands in this country are unfortunately of little value," he wrote, whereas Cape Breton had "a great quantity of improvable land" as well as the prospect of rich fisheries.[2] Actually, Haldimand was mainly concerned to keep Quebec in the hands of French Canadians to avoid the constant and escalating strife he already faced whenever the two main language groups met. Cape Breton seemed a reasonable alternative. Or, he was willing to ship the newcomers to the fort at Detroit until the peace treaty gave that area away to the Americans. The refugees were welcome anywhere, he might have said—anywhere but here.

They Could Form a Loyal Barrier. But They Didn't.

They were not welcome in the most obvious place to put them—southern Quebec between the St. Lawrence and the borders of Vermont and New York—the area that would become the Eastern Townships. The land was rich, comparatively open and available in plentiful supply close to settlement. It was such an obvious choice that Lord North wrote to Haldimand directing him to put Loyalists there. They could form a barrier against the Americans and help to convince the people of Vermont, who had remained largely neutral during the war, of the advantages of life under the Crown. But Haldimand would not have the Loyalists in this sector, and when some squatted there anyway—a natural thing for them to do on their way north—he cut off the king's bounty of provisions and threatened to burn their huts down around them.[3]

Haldimand didn't want the Loyalists trucking and trading with the Yankees, on the one hand, and he suspected that smuggling was more on the minds of those who applied for border-area grants than farming. On the other hand, if they weren't too friendly with their late foes, he feared, they might be too hostile and start another conflict. Finally there was his concern for the French Canadians, whose pursuit of a policy of "revanche de berceau" was filling cradles at an alarming rate. French Catholics would make a better buffer with the Americans—with whom they shared neither language nor religion—than the Loyalists. So Haldimand tried to palm the Loyalists off on the scrubby hills of Cape Breton. He was sure they would like it there. They begged to differ.

In the summer of 1783, Abraham Cuyler, the former mayor of Albany, (who had ambitions to become a power in the new settlements) visited many of the Loyalists. He convinced himself that he had persuaded three thousand of them to ship to Cape Breton. With Haldimand's blessing and a strong letter of support, Cuyler sailed to England to ask Lord North for a land grant. He got it, too, but only about three hundred Loyalists went with him and his wife to the area around what is now

Sydney. The trees and rocks of Cape Breton have always been more attractive to tourists than to permanent residents.

Back in Quebec, an attempt was also made to start Loyalist havens on the Bay of Chaleur and around the Bay of Gaspé, which were away from the main French settlements and which, again, held little allure for the newcomers. In 1785 about five hundred Loyalists had taken up homes in these two places, and about the same number had been absorbed into the old colony, split among the towns of Montreal and Quebec and the seigneury of Sorel.

Haldimand was beginning to wonder what do do with the rest of his new charges, who were so unamenable to his suggestions, when an alternative was proposed. Sir Guy Carleton, before he left New York for England, met a German-born saddler and harness-maker named Michael Grass, who had once been held prisoner by the French at Frontenac on the St. Lawrence near the present site of Kingston. Grass was convinced that this would make a fine place to settle the Loyalists, and saw himself as a kind of buckskin Moses leading them there. Carleton was impressed enough to give Grass a militia commission and, with six hastily organized companies of incorporated Loyalists, bundle him off to the area around the old fort at Frontenac, where the principal settlement was now Cataraqui. It would later become Kingston.[4]

The St. Lawrence Solution

Haldimand had considered and rejected this area because he wanted to reserve it for the Indian Loyalists. He was horrified that the peace treaty had done nothing whatever to provide for all the Indians who had fought on the side of the king. He was determined to provide these dispossessed Mohawks, Senecas and Cayugas with a new home to replace the one torn from them. The obvious place was in the hunting territory along the St. Lawrence west of the main settlements. Whites would have to be kept out, especially since the fur trade, which would sustain the Indians, was likely to be far more valuable than farming to the colony. However, the Indians were anxious to settle alongside whites and welcomed the possibility of sharing land along the St. Lawrence. The Mississaugas who then held the land were also pleased. Haldimand's problem was solved. The Quebec Loyalists would have a home, although, as it turned out, it would not long be Quebec.

The man who bought land from the Mississaugas for Indians and whites alike—as usual, he effectively stole it with presents and promises—was Sir John Johnson. He was living in Montreal in 1783 and wrote to Haldimand to ask that his regiment be awarded the lands along the St. Lawrence westward from Longueil, the last seigneury in the province. Haldimand replied that he could move half his men—the first battalion— into the new country, but his second was to remain on garrison duty for the time. Johnson's men would be flanked by those of Edward Jessup, former commander of the Loyal Rangers.

Through the Ice to New Homes

Over the winter of 1783, a working party at Lachine, where the St. Lawrence rapids began, built a fleet of the thirty-foot, shallow-draft boats called "bateaux," suitable for river travel. In the spring all Loyalists who wished to obtain land around Cataraqui and Oswegatchie (Kingston and Prescott) were instructed to assemble at Quebec, Sorel or Lachine for the voyage upriver. Those who assembled at Sorel and Quebec had a slow, cold trip of it because of heavy ice in the river, and many of them arrived at Lachine exhausted from a winter in camp and the long journey. But at least they were on their way, and they were soon assigned to the brigades of bateaux assembled for their use.

A single bateau would hold four or five families, and eighteen bateaux made up a battalion, under a pilot whose job it was to see the awkward but sturdy craft paddled, poled or dragged up the river. The trip often lasted ten days before the huts of Cataraqui came in sight. The flotilla that pulled out of Lachine must have been a strange sight, with the men, women and children bundled into the boats with their precious belongings piled around them—shouting, jabbering and shivering in the brisk spring breeze.

These Loyalists were quite a different breed from the city dwellers who had been deposited so abruptly at Shelburne, Halifax and Saint John. Most of them had been farmers and backwoodsmen (that is, before they had gone into the army) from what is now upper New York state, with a scattering from the interior of Vermont, New Jersey and Pennsylvania. Few of them could write. They signed their documents with a mark, or had someone copy out their name, and traced it. Many names got changed this way, through errors on the muster lists. There were few professional men among them—a study of six hundred of this group turned up only two doctors and no lawyers—and they had little of the pleasure in public debate and argument that marked the town-meeting sophisticates of the seaboard.

What they did have was the ability to use an ax and a hoe, and the willingness to do so. Thanks to Haldimand's fore-thought, they were soon put to work. The survey of the land west from Longueil had begun in the winter of 1783 and con-tinued in the spring. By the end of the summer fourteen town-ships were laid out along the St. Lawrence and the Bay of Quinte. The nine St. Lawrence townships were called the Royal Town-ships and numbered Royal Township 1 through 14, while the five Quinte townships were Cataraqui 1 through 5.

All very efficient. The ex-soldiers were sorted out, at their request and with Haldimand's approval, according to race and religion. Johnson's first battalion, which consisted of Catholic Highlanders, got Royal Township 1, then came Scots Presby-terians in Royal Township 2 (this grew up around New Johns-town, the site selected by Johnson and later named Cornwall). Above the Scots were the German Calvinists mustered out of the British army. Next to them were more Germans, but this time Lutherans. Then came three townships of Anglicans and then Jessup's corps. While these groups were called soldiers and formed into battalions, only some of them ever saw service. Because the Crown tended to be more generous in lands and provisions toward the military, and because custom then al-lowed babies to be registered as officers, there was a certain amount of fakery involved. Thomas Gummersall Anderson wrote in his *Reminiscences* that he was born in camp at Sorel in 1779, enlisted in his father's company at birth and discharged on half-pay in 1783, when he was four.[5]

Babes in Arms However You Look at It

"It is true I was too young to do much service, even in devouring the King's pork, but in those days it was not unusual for the nursery-maid to say to her mistress, 'Ma'am, the major won't take his pap this morning', and this may account for my having been an infant soldier." One of Anderson's brothers enjoyed the half-pay allowance of a lieutenant for sixty-eight years.

Michael Grass and his pilgrims drew the first Cataraqui town-ship (today's Kingston), while Johnson's second battalion drew townships 3 and 4, which came to be Fredericksburg and Adol-phustown.

There were inevitable problems in land distribution, but Haldimand solved one of the major headaches by sticking to his decision to muster, move and settle the Loyalists in their military units, which provided them with known neighbors and gave a semblance of discipline even after the units were disbanded.

The townships were divided into equal lots between parallel concessions roads, and every man, whatever his rank had been, drew for a lot on a random basis. When Sir John Johnson and Major Samuel Holland, the surveyor general, allowed ex-officers a preference, Haldimand sent a blistering reprimand up the river. Although the location of farms was set by lot, the size allotted was determined by the recipient's rank. Civilians received fifty acres, if single; one hundred if the head of a family. Privates got the same allotment, while non-commissioned officers received two hundred acres, and so up the scale to field officers—colonel and above—who got one thousand acres.

That kind of discrimination was standard for the time and occasioned no problems, although attempts by some officers to make their choices before anyone else did lead to complaints. Some of them got away with it, despite the complaints.

The land grants were later increased when it became clear how much land there was. There was room enough for everyone—more land available, in most cases, than anyone could cope with. The Loyalists did not get clear title to their lands; this was Quebec, after all, and land was still held under the feudal system. In theory they were all tenants on seigneuries. There were no seigneurs for these seigneuries, of course, but that was the only way to hold land in Quebec at this time. In law, the governor of Quebec was their seigneur, and the land was held by way of a location-ticket which the settler drew in a lottery. In fact, for the time being, the land was treated as their own. Location-tickets were exchanged or sold—sometimes for a quart of rum[6]—with the seller writing his name on the back to surrender his land. Endless confusion resulted from the multiple transfer of many blocks of land, eventually requiring the establishment of land boards to sort out the mess.

By July 10, 1784, Sir John Johnson was able to report to Haldimand that 3,776 Loyalists were settled on crown lands from Lake St. Francis to the Bay of Quinte. They were also clamoring for supplies. The Loyalists, never shy by nature, had drawn up a list of their requirements that started with "Boards, Nails and Shingls," ranged through "One Grind stone allowed for every Three Families," and included such exotics as "Fifteen Iron Harrow Teeth," "Three Iron Wedges" and "Leather for Horse

Collers" for each family.[7] The entire list was dismissed as "extravagant," but Haldimand did undertake to provide each man with an ax and a hoe, as well as whatever building tools and other materials, including clothing and blankets, could be rounded up.

He began distributing food without, as one of his subordinates wrote, "having the least Sanction for it in his Instructions from Home."[8] The standard food ration was one pound of flour and twelve ounces of pork (or a pound of the less popular beef) per adult per week, with half-rations for children. The imperial government wanted these rations cut to two-thirds in 1785 and one-third in 1786, arguing that the Loyalists should be self-supporting by that time, but Haldimand ignored the demand for cuts. Some of the Loyalists without farming experience claimed rations for their slaves because these were the "only means" they had of cultivating the land. This was not well received.

Government buyers went into the Mohawk Valley, so lately the scene of battle, with orders to buy seed-wheat along with seeds for turnips, carrots, cabbage and onions (the Loyalists were expected to bring corn with them, and many did so). The settlers had asked for cattle, but Haldimand demurred, fearing that London would consider he had gone too far. It was up to the Loyalists to buy or trade for their own cattle, and they did.

Lumps of Stalking Pride Came Later

In many families there were usually only two meals a day consisting of "sup-on" and milk. Sup-on was ground and boiled Indian corn mixed with butter or the all-purpose sweetener— maple sugar. It was wholesome, nourishing and cheap. Later, the struggles of the Loyalists became wrapped in a haze of romanticism, as early times often do. Thomas Gummersall Anderson, writing early in the eighteenth century, noted that things had gone to the dogs since he was a lad: "The first generation born in Upper Canada were without book learning, but they laboured like slaves to render their children more fortunate. The result is, that we see the young of the present day wallowing in wealth, yes, the hard-earned wealth of their forefathers, and have become such lumps of stalking pride and arrogance that to remind them of old times . . . is to bring upon your head every evil their weak minds can invent or command."[9]

Anderson felt that the tough times of his youth were worth it, because "People were honest, kind, accommodating and friendly to each other." That is, of course, except when they were shooting at each other.

Lumps of stalking pride and arrogance have not entirely vanished from the world, but whether we want to go back to life in a hut covered over with bark shingles and spend the day chopping trees before coming home to a hearty bowl of sup-on may be open to question. What a reader of the early Loyalist narratives is struck by is the incredible toughness of these people. They bitched, certainly, first, last and foremost, but they put up with conditions that must have been truly appalling. In the winter, keeping warm was a full-time occupation for those who were lucky enough to get a shelter of some sort erected before the snows came. For the rest it was not a matter of keeping warm, but trying to keep alive. In the spring, the work of clearing began—hacking down giant trees with small hand-axes (with the larger trees, it was necessary to girdle the tree one year and chop down the corpse the next), then burning, digging or, later, when oxen became available, hauling out the stumps. Then the ground had to be broken, then raked, then seeded between the still-standing stumps. And then you hoped cold or drought or damp or disease didn't wipe out the whole crop before you could eat it. In the meantime there were bites of salt pork and good old sup-on to lift the spirit. The work was often performed to the accompaniment of a plentiful supply of flies and mosquitoes, which must have added to the fun.

Because it took time and money to build a grist mill, some settlers made their own mortars for grinding corn. This was accomplished by digging a six-foot length of hardwood, about two feet in diameter, four feet into the ground. Then a cavity was burned in the two-foot section that projected, and this was scraped and cleaned. A six-inch piece of ironwood formed the pestle, suitable for pounding corn. It would not do for wheat, however, and that meant a week-long trip for many of the Loyalists down to the grist mill at Cataraqui, provided by the government. At first two wooden canoes were lashed together to provide transport. Later when horses became common in the settlements, carts were used and, in winter, when transport became swift on the frozen river, sleds.

Weddings provided holidays for the early settlers, according to a chronicler of the time, Roger Bates,[10] although there were no fancy dresses. "The Ladies had no white dresses to spoil, or fancy Bonnets—with deerskin petticoats, homespun gowns, and perhaps a Squirrel skin bonnet, they looked charming in the eyes of their lovers, who were rigged out in similar materials."

There wasn't much jewelry around, either, and Bates records one wedding at which a magistrate, joining a ringless couple who had walked twenty miles through the woods to his place, found a ring attached to "a pair of old English skates" and put the job across with that. The ring remained in the family for generations.

A magistrate, stray missionary or even an adjutant or surgeon from one of the regiments might perform the marriage, which left some of the ceremonies open to legal doubt. Later a law was passed legalizing all the backwoods marriages and legitimizing the offspring.

Feudalism Would Not Do

As the land was cleared, crops put in, mills established, towns built and roads begun, it became clear that something would have to be done about the political situation of the Loyalists. They were beginning to sort themselves out; they were even showing some signs of prosperity. A return from Matilda Township shows that in three short years of settlement one family of four had managed to clear twenty of their hundred acres and that year harvested 240 bushels of wheat. They were the proud owners of a horse, two oxen, a cow, a heifer and eighteen hogs. Not exactly wallowing in wealth, but not doing badly, either.[11]

But they were still feudal tenants. Haldimand's instructions, with which he thoroughly agreed, did not allow him to make freehold grants. As the Loyalists began to get more settled, this struck them as more and more undesirable, especially when they knew that their counterparts in Nova Scotia and New Brunswick had their own assembly, courts and freehold tenure. In late 1784, once he had seen his people settled, Sir John Johnson sailed to England. There in April, 1785, he laid a petition before the government, signed by himself and other prominent Loyalists, protesting in a humble and polite way against the "rigorous Rules, Homages and Reservations and Restrictions of the French Laws and Customs which are so different from the mild Tenures to which they had even been accustomed, and which continue to be enjoyed by the rest of Your Majesty's Subjects."[12]

He suggested that "One District distinct from the Province of Quebec" but responsible through Quebec be created in the newly settled lands, starting at Point Baudet on Lake St. Francis and running "from thence westward." This district would have its own lieutenant governor and (appointed) council, but would be under the direction of the governor and council at Quebec.

It was a shrewd argument. Who better deserved the blessings of British institutions than the Loyalists? Besides, as Johnson argued, the creation of such a district close to the Americans would undoubtedly draw new settlers from below the border, helping to open the land and, coincidentally, underlining the advantages of British rule over the direction of that rabble in congress.

Just the same, there were problems. Haldimand had grave doubts as to whether it was possible to mingle the French and English under his rule into one people. Giving some of them English laws, English courts and the English electoral practices that were certain to follow, was bound to lead to difficulties. He inherited Sir Guy Carleton's hope that the way to rule Quebec was to work through the priests and seigneurs, and the more he saw of the fractious, ambitious, grabby English merchants of Quebec and Montreal, the more inclined he was to stick with French law, French customs and that nice sense of hierarchy that went with feudalism.

Haldimand's objections were buttressed by those of George Chalmers, chief clerk of the privy council, who had lived in America and knew that "A free and common socage [socage refers to land held in performance of services or for rent paid] necessarily produces independence of mind, independence of action, and independence of government."[13] Johnson's petition was put on hold.

It couldn't stay there, though—not for the long run. British subjects who found themselves before courts run by the appointed magistrates from the French population were complaining bitterly in the older part of the province. There was no trial by jury in civil suits, and the judgments rendered were capricious and quite often legally indefensible. In one famous case, an English settler rented a horse, which was stolen when he stopped at an inn. The horse's owner brought a suit against the inn for negligence, and the horse-renter turned up at court to see how it came out. The French judge spotted him in the courtroom and fixed responsibility and all costs on him, although he had never been part of the lawsuit. The judge who did this was something of a drunk, and the key question on any of his judgments was "Was it a morning or an afternoon judgment?"[14]

The Law Was Indeed an Ass

The French habitants, who didn't spend much time in litigation anyway, were quite tolerant of their courts, where judgments might be rendered according to the custom of Paris, royal edicts from the French reign, Roman law or "the custom of the country." It was notoriously possible to obtain a favorable result by using any lawyer known to be friendly with Adam Mabane, the dominant judge in the province and a confidant of Haldimand's. (He was a Scot, but the leader of "the French party.") The English, used to more regularity in their law, objected, but when James Monk, the English attorney general, attacked the "inconsistent, arbitary and ignorant" judges of the common pleas in a speech before the legislature, he was dismissed and replaced by Mabane himself.[15]

The fact was that the French were the key to power in the province, not the English. No one felt that more strongly than Sir Guy Carleton, who (translated for his services during the war to Lord Dorchester) had returned to Canada in 1786 after Haldimand departed. Actually, Haldimand left in late 1784, but it took almost two years to lure Carleton out of retirement and return him to Quebec. However, the passage of time could not alter the fact that he had been the architect of the Quebec Act and was not about to vary its emphasis on French rights.

"A considerable degree of attention is due to the prejudice and habits of the French inhabitants who compose so large a proportion of the community," he wrote, "and every degree of caution should be used to continue to them the enjoyment of those civil and religious rights which were secured to them by the capitulation of the province."[16]

Those rights included not only French civil law with all its peculiarities, but feudal land tenure. Not that Dorchester wasn't aware of the problems. He had brought back to Canada with him William Smith, the Loyalist former chief justice of New York, and had made Smith chief justice of Quebec. Smith, who was half French and bilingual, wanted to assimilate the French by setting up schools at which the habitants would be taught English. This system would be paid for out of the revenues of the Jesuit estates, seized at the time of the conquest. The notion did not go down well with the Catholic bishop of Quebec, the Anglican bishop of Nova Scotia (who had charge of Anglican souls in Quebec; his objection was not against the scheme's Englishness, but Smith's proposal to top it off with a secular university free of any church influence) or, despite his high regard for Smith, with Lord Dorchester.

Smith briefly wrestled control of the legislative council from Mabane, but Dorchester refused to back his ambitious plan and instead kicked it back to England for determination. There the obvious solution was to take Sir John Johnson's petition, which had been gathering dust, push it one step further by creating a separate province instead of merely a distinct district, and make that province the recipient of the blessings of British rule. It would have an appointed council but an elected assembly. English law was established in four judicial districts that had been created in 1788. They were all given German names to impress the king (actually, George III was a thorough anglophile, but he kept getting German shoved at him): Luneberg, Meckleburg, Nassau and Hesse, reading from east to west.

In the end a new province was created by the Constitution Act of 1791 because it was the line of least resistance, although there was another factor. Canada was costing Britain about £100,000 a year, and Britain had given up the right to levy taxes in its colonies in 1778. (That was a vain attempt to appease the revolting colonies.) To raise money in Canada there would have to be a legislature and the British Parliament would not sanction one that did not provide the vote to British subjects. But a single assembly for the province would be marked by "Dissensions and animosities" based on race, and the vast stretch of territory—almost 1,100 miles—would create an administrative nightmare.[17] It kept coming back to the same solution— two provinces, with the new English-speaking settlers hived off to the west and the old French-speaking element left in control of Quebec.

William Smith waded into the debate about the new arrangements with a proposal to link all the British North American provinces in a single federal union (his original dream for all the colonies before the war), and Dorchester agreed that this was a good idea. But London was not interested, and the idea was never widely discussed.

What we got, instead, was a division into Lower and Upper Canada, with each province given an appointed legislative council and elected assembly. Land in Upper Canada was to be freehold. Voters in the towns were to be those who held property worth five pounds or paid rent of at least ten pounds, and those in the country who possesed a freehold worth at least forty shillings annually. There were no property qualifications for a seat in the assembly, but clergymen, in accord with the British parliamentary customs of that time, were not allowed to run. (One has to draw the line somewhere.)

If there had been any justice, the lieutenant governor of the bold new province of Upper Canada would have been Sir John Johnson, whose idea, in a way, it was. Lord Dorchester recommended Johnson, but his name was scratched because he owned so much land by now that the London authorities were afraid he might act in his own interest (the normal rule was to use the office to accumulate property; Johnson already had the property, so his case must have confused the authorities). Instead, a non-Loyalist was given the job, and he made a mess of it.

John Graves Simcoe was his name, and he had a dream.

12
Simcoe's Dream

*"A thousand details crowd upon my mind that could
be productive of the most salutary consequences."*
John Graves Simcoe to Henry
Dundas, secretary of state,
November 16, 1796

The year 1789 was remarkable in Canada for two major events.
The first was Lord Dorchester's wish, translated into action by
the executive council of Quebec on November 9, 1789, "to put
a mark of honour upon the families who had adhered to the
Unity of the Empire, and joined the Royal Standard in America
before the Treaty of Separation in the Year 1783."

The "mark" was to be the inclusion of the Loyalists—"not
only the sons . . . but the Daughters, also"—in a list called the
"Old Loyalist List." The land boards of the judicial districts
were ordered to draw up official rolls of all the Loyalists in their
jurisdiction who were entitled to the honor, signaled by the
letters "U.E." to be inscribed after their names.

The list was catnip to the Loyalists and has been ever since.
It gave them a distinction and separated forever the proper, true
and recorded United Empire Loyalists, who had repaired to the
flag while the fighting was still going on, from those who snuck
up later merely (for all we know) to take advantage of the free
land. These were the "late Loyalists"—mere pretenders, the
unwashed. In point of fact, many of the so-called late Loyalists
were just as loyal as those on the list. The land boards did not
do much of a job of compiling. They included many who did
not merit the distinction and left out many more who did,
which, in the primitive conditions that then prevailed in the
colony, was inevitable.

Of 5,400 names scratched out in fine copperplate writing on heavy rag paper on two documents—the original list and a supplemental—hundreds had no right to be there at all. There were four hundred British regular soldiers inscribed, who fought for the king because the alternative was a court-martial. German mercenaries got on the lists for the same reason. Many names appeared more than once, because those involved had moved from one district to another during the compilation of the lists and became recorded in both. The list even included a batch of Scottish immigrants who came straight over the sea to Upper Canada with never a whiff of the Thirteen Colonies. They got in by sheer accident.[1] And, of course, the 5,400 who did become documented represented only a fraction of the Loyalists.

Just the same, the list was a document—the Canadian equivalent of certified membership in the Daughters of the American Revolution—and it has sponsored more debate among enthusiasts than sex education. To this day it is possible to start an argument among the descendants of "proper" and "late" Loyalists just by mentioning the subject. (It was a near fistfight at a historical display at the fair in Brome, Quebec, in 1968 that first aroused my interest in the Loyalists. One gent was displaying his family tree and calling himself a Loyalist. The man in the neighboring booth said he was a fraud, a mere "late Loyalist." This was heatedly denied and offers to punch each other on the nose were exchanged. As the air quivered with outrage and anger, I got out of there, but I couldn't help wondering what could have happened two centuries ago to get people so exercised at a tranquil county fair. Now I know.)

The other big event of that year was a famine. In 1788 the wheat crop was light all across North America, probably because of an outbreak of wheat smut.[2] But in their anxiety to promote trade for the budding colony, the colonial officials permitted a heavy export. Ten thousand barrels of flour, five thousand of biscuit and more than 200,000 bushels of wheat left Canada. By late summer, when it was clear that crops had failed in much of old Quebec and around Niagara, it was obvious that the colonists were in for a hungry winter. The king's bounty extended by Haldimand had now finished, and there was little money to buy food with—even if there had been food to buy. One farmer with a large family sent all his savings to Quebec City to buy flour. The money came back to him; there was no flour to buy. The abundant game that was such a common feature of the area disappeared, apparently because of extreme heat in the summer of 1788 and over-hunting in the areas around the settlements.

The Hungry Year

The year 1789 became known as the "Hungry Year." Beef bones were boiled with wheat bran to provide nourishment, then fished out of the pot and passed on to a neighboring house where the process was repeated. Roots were dug up and eaten—and some people died from poisonous concoctions made this way. (The more experienced backwoodsmen would only eat weeds and roots that their pigs found fit for consumption; of course, not everyone had a pig.) Instead of planting seed potatoes, the Loyalists dug out the eyes of the potato, planted these and ate the rest of the vegetable. Buds and weeds were cooked and eaten. In the absence of grain it had been common for Loyalists to feed their cattle on browse from bushes and small trees. Now they began to compete with the animals for this stuff. Sometimes animals were bled, and the blood made into a thin broth to provide nourishment. When a field of early grain sprouted on a sunny hillside in Cataraqui Township 4, neighbors gathered and, with the permission of the field's owner, cut off the heads of individual stalks as soon as they were full, boiled them and ate them. Animals that died of age or disease were devoured. Family pets went into the pot.

At Niagara the *Quebec Herald* reported, "cats, etc." had been substituted for "beef, etc.,"[3] while the price of a bushel of wheat shot up to one pound York currency, if it could be got. At Kingston a bushel of potatoes sold for a guinea, many times its normal value. One boy hired out to work was provided with his breakfast as part of his pay. He "carried his little sister two miles on his back, to let her eat his breakfast, and they gave him none till dinner."[4].

The same report notes, "They came to an allowance of one spoonful of meal per day, for one person—eat strawberry leaves, flax seed dried, and ground in a coffee mill—catched the blood of a little pig—bled the almost famished cow and oxen."

Another account records the eating of the family dog and speculates on a story that a marooned sailor once ate a raw owl, "To him it was a savoury dinner".[5]

The crisis eased with a good crop the next year, but not until many had starved to death, and the entire colony had been presented with stark evidence of the narrow line between survival and extinction in a pioneer community.

Enter John Graves Simcoe. He was the son of a British navy captain, John Simcoe, who had been present at the siege of Louisbourg. Young John followed his father into the forces, joining the army as a subaltern in 1770 when he was eighteen.

He was posted to Boston with his regiment. He was an active and energetic soldier, a gifted leader and a man who readily inspired confidence and loyalty in his men. Invalided home in 1781, he lived the life of a country gentleman on his estate at Wolford, until in 1790 he was returned as an MP for St. Mawe's, Cornwall.

From that vantage point he was able to maneuver successfully for appointment to the lieutenant governor's post in Upper Canada. It was a post for which he was singularly ill-equipped. Although it was customary to put military men into these governing posts, what was most often required were the very qualities—flexibility, tact, discretion, empathy—so often purged by military training. Simcoe was a splendid soldier; that did not make him a splendid governor.

Lord Dorchester was now promoted to a new rank, governor general, with overall direction of the British North American possessions under their various lieutenants governor. There was confusion and contradiction in the appointments, since the provincial governors reported both to Dorchester and to the colonial office. Supposedly they reported through him, but this was not always possible, and a division of command responsibility followed. This led to endless difficulties with Simcoe, who saw Canada in quite a different light than did Dorchester. The governor general didn't want Simcoe in the post in the first place, and that didn't help. Dorchester wanted Sir John Johnson for the job. In this, as in many other things, he was wiser than his London masters.

When Johnson was turned down, Simcoe became the obvious choice. He had influence, a distinguished record and experience in North America. He also had bold, broad ideas on what should be done there and was soon inundating his new masters with schemes and dreams. He thought it would be a terrific idea, for example, to name eighteen "Lords Lieutenant" for Upper Canada's projected counties. These men would be loyal to him— and to Britain, of course—and they would be the foundation blocks for an aristocracy to rule the colony. Simcoe also wanted to make the appointed posts in his legislative council hereditary, but the notion of a packet of bush-league barons running around the Upper Canadian outposts was too much for the colonial office. Simcoe managed to get his hereditary notions written into the Constitution Act, but Henry Dundas, the secretary of state, pronounced the scheme "very unfit to be encouraged by a Parent State in an dependant Colony," and nothing ever came of it.[6]

A Few Words About Simcoe: He Was a Fathead

Mark you, Dundas wasn't worried that the establishment of an aristocracy would offend democratic sensibilities. *Au contraire*; his worry was that the lieutenant governor might allow some of his accumulated power to "fritter down" to the locals. But if Simcoe lost on that suggestion, he won many others.

Simcoe was a bold dreamer. Unfortunately he was also, both literally and figuratively, a fathead. The Simcoe portrait in the Metropolitan Toronto Library, which is the one usually reporoduced, catches him to a nicety with the full lips, blank eyes and air of ineffable superiority. He was the best and worst possible choice as a Loyalist ruler. Best because he embodied and believed in all the principles the Loyalists admired—unswerving loyalty to king and country, unbridled enthusiasm for the British constitution and unshakable faith in the privileges of rank. Although he was personally charming and often showed great concern for the welfare of his subjects, he was the snob of snobs, far more so than Lord Dorchester or Frederick Haldimand. It was enormously reassuring to the Loyalists to see this pompous, self-important man strut his stuff. George III wasn't in it with Simcoe for haughtiness, and there was comfort in that.

But Simcoe was also the worst choice because he lacked common sense, proportion and flexibility—all of which were vital to the new colony. His instructions forced him to accept the presence of an elected assembly, but no one could make him like it. He noted that voters had a distressing tendency to plump for candidates "of a Lower Order, who kept but one Table, that is, who dined in Common with their Servants."[7] It was true, too. When the family gathered around the pot in the winter of 1789 to share a few strawberry leaves and a haunch from old Fido, they quite often forgot to send the servants to the other room—if they had another room.

The Loyalists needed a man like Simcoe because his kind of high Toryism was in a way their own writ large, but his four short years of pomposity and posturing left a dangerous legacy which might have been avoided with Sir John Johnson. Sir John could cock a snook with the best of them, but he knew his people and their needs far better than Simcoe did.

During his war service Simcoe got it fixed into his head that the Revolution was the act of a minority of radicals (which was true at the beginning), and that given the chance the majority would see the light and return to the blessings of Crown control and the British constitution. He would run his new province in a way that would knock the spots off congress and make the American public sit up and take notice. With a "Superior, more happy and more polished form of Government," he would lure the awestruck Americans over the border to take up lands in Upper Canada. It would be necessary, of course, to pound into the colony "British Customs, Manners and Principles in the most trivial, as well as serious matters," and this would turn Upper Canada into a showpiece. It would "become the means of preserving all the transatlantic Dominions of Great Britain by exemplifying the Felicities of its Laws and Government."[8]

Then the Americans would desert George Washington and sign up once more with George III. To make this dream reality, Simcoe saw three great needs. One was the establishment and dominance of the Church of England as the state church of Upper Canada; a second was the creation of an aristocracy to lead and mold the hoi polloi; the third was a population to fill in and clear out the land. What was not needed was a lot of argy-bargy from elected politicians. "The Levelling Spirit" was to be discouraged. If we had to have voting in the emerging towns, councils should be chosen "in such a manner as to render the Elections as little popular as possible, meaning such Corporations to tend to the support of the Aristocracy of the Country."[9]

This kind of approach in Boston, Philadelphia or New York prior to 1770 would have earned Sincoe a horselaugh from most of the populace. Certainly, it would never have been accepted without question. But the Loyalists had been through much, seen much, suffered much. For laying out a line that, even in his time, was reactionary to the point of absurdity, Simcoe earned almost universal praise, much of which clings to his name to this day.

And yet the three main points in his approach led to endless grief.

The establishment of the Anglican Church was called for in his instructions, but only a rigid and uncompromising man would have gone at the task with Simcoe's enthusiasm. The majority of his subjects were not Anglicans, but when he was petitioned by Presbyterians and Baptists to allow the ministers of other faiths to perform marriage ceremonies, Simcoe dismissed such petitions as "wicked and disloyal." He pressed the home government for the immediate appointment of a bishop to curb "enthusiastic and fanatic Teachers"—i.e., non-Anglican—and he tried to impress London with the need to provide for "the education of the superior classes." Otherwise the

Gentlemen of Upper Canada would go to university in the United States, where their British Principles would be "totally undermined and subverted." (Like many people of strong views, Simcoe apparently believed that he alone stood steadfast; allow the youngsters off the leash in a republican setting and bang would go their British principles.) There should be a schoolmaster at Kingston, another at Niagara and a university at the capital—all of them to be Anglican. The British government declined to provide the funds for this, but did approve Simcoe's plan to establish a checkerboard pattern of clergy reserves to support the Anglican Church.

The Clergy Reserves—With Reservations

Like the state church, Simcoe was given official instructions to set up the reserves when he took office. Again it was his improvement on the ill-conceived basic idea that turned an error into a disaster. One-seventh of all allotted land was to be devoted to the Crown. That would provide support for the imperial officials, avoiding some of the problems of New York and Massachusetts (where Crown officials had been dependent on local funding, and had therefore been open to coercion). Another one-seventh was to be allotted to the Anglican Church. In Lower Canada officials favored lumping all the reserves in each township into one block, but Simcoe and his acting surveyor general, D.W. Smith, had a better idea. The reserves would be scattered in 200-acre blocks throughout each township. In the normal township of 336 200-acre lots, two out of every seven lots would be held for the crown and clergy. Since that left a fraction, it was decided to increase the reserves' share to seven in every concession of twenty-four lots. This produced a checkerboard in every township, with almost one-quarter of the lots undeveloped, with no one to work on the roads—when there came to be roads—to cut weeds, build fences, stem erosion or indeed do anything to improve the land. The clergy reserves would roil the waters of Upper Canadian politics for decades.

Once it became clear that the colonial office would not willingly kiss any of Simcoe's backwoods frogs into princes, he decided to create the aristocracy of his dreams, by means of land giveaways. Land was wealth, so if you gave enough of it to the right people, a band of the worthy would be planted in the wilderness, ready to furnish that touch of noblesse without which no really well-ordered colony can survive. The land giveaways would also meet his third condition for felicity; they would encourage an influx of immigrants from America.

Even before he arrived in the province, Simcoe issued a proclamation from Montreal on February 7, 1792, addressed to "such as are desirous to settle on the Lands of the Crown in the Province of Upper Canada."[10] This set forth the land-granting system which provided for grants of 200 acres—with more available at the discretion of the authorities—to petitioners who would undertake to cultivate and improve their acres and swear an oath of loyalty to the king. The proclamation was widely circulated in the northern United States, and Simcoe sent a long letter to the British consul in Philadelphia singing the praises of Upper Canada. That would fetch the Americans in. And so, of course, it did. Americans were already streaming west in search of new farmland, but problems with the Indians made that seem a less friendly place to go than Upper Canada, where the soil was rich and free, and all you had to do was swear an oath.

A French émigré who traveled through Upper Canada, the Duc de la Rochefoucauld, met, regrettably, many settlers "who profess an attachment to the British monarch and curse the Government of the Union for the mere purpose of getting possession of the lands."[11] Loyalist Richard Cartwright, writing from Kingston in 1799, complained, "It has so happened that a great portion of the population of that part of the province which extends from the Bay of Kenty [Quinte] upwards is composed of persons who have evidently no claim to the appelation of Loyalists."[12]

Huge blocks of land were given to absentee landlords, to "friends of government," to men who promised to bring in legions of loyal subjects, to people Simcoe thought worthy of a place in his aristocracy, to speculators. In fact, one of those who turned up to swear allegiance and apply for a land grant was the rebel who had been in charge of the party that had hanged Major John André, the British spy who had signed up Benedict Arnold.[13] Whatever this man was, he wasn't an adherent of the British Crown. But he was about to get a passel of land anyway, until he was recognized by a Loyalist in the crowd and "whipped from the colony." How many other Patriots went unrecognized and claimed land intended for Loyalists and sympathizers, God only knows.

Land Grabbing Was Never Better

To add to the problem, Simcoe abolished the land boards that had been established in 1788, which provided a minimal screening process. The result, wrote the Loyalist historian, Stewart Wallace, was that "Never at any other time perhaps have conditions been so favourable in Canada for land-grabbing and land-speculation as they were then.[14]

The Loyalists, except for those favored by Simcoe, were not in on this. The single largest land-grab recorded by a speculator involved Sir William Pullency, an Englishman, who bought 1,500,000 acres for a shilling an acre and sold 700,000 of them back again for an average of eight shillings an acre.[15] He cleared £205,000, an immense fortune, and still owned 800,000 acres free and clear. And he didn't even qualify for Simcoe's aristocracy, because he never left England.

The *Imperial Blue Books Relating To Affairs In Canada* record a series of transactions through which two judges, the solicitor general and several members of Simcoe's legislative and executive councils picked up large blocks of land of from 20,000 to 100,000 acres for a pittance. Several members of the house of assembly were "very large purchasors."[16] Simcoe was going to get his aristocracy by hook or, as it turned out, by crook.

God, George and the Anglican Church All Approved

If you couldn't give extras to favorites, what was the point of an aristocracy? Historian Arthur Lower has maintained that the most significant thing about the Loyalist movement was that "it withdrew a class concept of life from the South, moved it up North and gave it a second chance."[17] It could be argued that quite a lot of the class concept survived the Revolution and gave America an aristocracy of its own under a different name, but it did not have the official blessing of authority there. In Upper Canada things were quite different. Favoritism and patronage were not things to be ashamed of—they were marks of approbation, even of loyalty. God, George III and the Anglican Church all approved; who but a rebel could disapprove? So the land grabs, far from being a matter of scandal, were the natural outgrowth of a frame of mind that Simcoe embodied as well as any man—and he did not, mark you, grab any land for himself.

However, the huge land assemblies and the intrusion of the Crown and clergy reserves played havoc with the development of the budding colony. The reserves became blocks of undeveloped land scattered all across the countryside in such a way as to discourage the growth of population centers and interfere with the natural process of growth.

At first there was surprisingly little objection to this. The Loyalists were not by definition the ones most likely to protest this kind of jobbery, for one thing. For another, they were busy trying to push back the wilderness and build their homes. Politics was not of much interest to them. "In Upper Canada," wrote Arthur Lower, "the Loyalists had a clear field. There was no one to push aside, neither previous English nor previous French. Just the trees."[18]

That is a more palatable explanation than one given by the radical reformer, Donald M'Leod, who argued in *A Brief Review of The Settlement of Upper Canada*, "The world did not and never did and never can exhibit so grovelling a class of freemen as the Tories of Canada."

It cannot be shown that the Loyalists, in fact, spent much time groveling, but what is clear is that Simcoe was in favor of those marks of respect—groveling would do nicely— that he felt were due to his station.

He was sworn in as lieutenant governor at Kingston (as Cataraqui was renamed to suit its Loyalist flavor). It was the largest settlement in the colony when he arrived, with fifty houses. He swore in his executive council (his cabinet) and members of the appointed legislative council (his House of Lords). He proclaimed elections to be held for sixteen representatives to the legislative assembly and set sail for Fort Niagara where he took up residence at Navy Hall. He renamed Niagara Newark, after Newark, New Jersey, where he had been stationed for part of the war (Simcoe was a bear for renaming) and it was here that he met the legislature. There were nineteen counties in the end, rather than the eighteen first envisioned, extending from Glengarry in the east to Essex in the west. However, there were only sixteen assembly members chosen from electoral districts based on population. There were also three executive councillors and seven legislative councillors, all appointed, to help Simcoe keep the elected rabble in line.

The legislative opening on September 17, 1792, was surrounded with military pomp. In his welcoming speech Simcoe told the two houses that with the great British constitution behind them, joined to the "natural advantages" of the province, the generosity of the home government and their own "fostering care," Upper Canada would soon blossom with "a numerous and Agricultural people." This went down well with his audience, and the session got off to an enthusiastic start.[19]

Slavery Was Abolished. Sort Of.

Its main work was to set up courts, rename the districts (Eastern, Midland, Home and Western, instead of Luneberg, Meckleberg, Nassau and Hesse), adopt the English system of weights and measures and strike out applications of the Quebec Act, such as the preeminence of French and French civil law. All that went through without a hitch. Slavery was abolished, but with a grandfather clause. Slaves already in the province remained slaves, but it was illegal to bring in new ones. That allowed the Reverend John Stuart, Kingston's first Anglican missionary, to keep his slaves. So could Peter Van Alstyne, who had at least nine slaves on his Bay of Quinte property. The grandfather clause, in fact, prevented what might have been a considerable political problem. In the District of Niagara alone, early records show that there were at least three hundred slaves.

Because of the cooperative mood in that first legislative session, Simcoe did not have to use his veto. The legislative council, he was happy to note, was well able to keep the elected assembly from doing anything untoward. There was one tight moment when some Loyalist house members, harkening back to the town meetings of their home colonies, proposed the same for Upper Canada, but Simcoe quashed the notion. It smacked of the "Elective principle" which had led to all that trouble. It was quietly dumped.

Simcoe dismissed the legislators after a month's work with instructions that they were to explain to their neighbors that "This province is singularly blessed . . . with a Constitution which . . . is the very image and transcript of that of Great Britain."[20] This applesauce was received with huzzahs, although in fact the resemblance between the constitution of Upper Canada and that of Great Britain was not striking. The sixteen-member assembly, curbed by two appointed bodies and subject to Simcoe's veto, with limited taxing powers and virtually no power to deal with any but strictly local matters, had little in common with Parliament. Never mind, it was the spirit of the thing that mattered, and Simcoe was the very spirit of the British bulldog.

He was also a man of great energy, and he charged about the province on long trips—visiting his subjects, inspecting his troops (he had brought many of the Queen's Rangers, his wartime outfit, back with him to work on engineering projects and serve garrison duty), laying out roads and renaming things. He visited the La Tranche River looking for a new capital to replace the exposed position at Newark, renamed the river the Thames and fixed on a site, which he called New London, for his new capital. Lord Dorchester vetoed that, however, and told Simcoe to set up shop instead at the end of the Toronto portage. Sighing, Simcoe went, renamed the place York to honor a royal prince and laid out a road from York clear across to New London. He visited Lake des Clais, renamed it Lake Simcoe (after his father, not himself) and sketched out the road that became Yonge Street.

He quarrelled with two of the more prominent businessmen in the colony, Robert Hamilton and Richard Cartwright, who were members of his legislative council but not as quiescent as his other appointees. They objected to a number of Simcoe's proposals and, in general, to his high-handedness. The lieutenant governor called Hamilton "an avowed republican" and accused Cartwright of "vanity and sordidness."[21] (Cartwright had been secretary to Colonel John Butler during the war; he prospered despite Simcoe's hostility, and during the War of 1812 was military commander in the Midland district. Hamilton also did well; he moved to Niagara and became rich. His son, George, bought a huge block of land not far away and it turned into a city, named for him.) To mark his displeasure, Simcoe tried to ensure that the partnership of Cartwright and Hamilton got no army business, which was most of the business there was. This, alas, was beyond his power. The army remained under the command of Lord Dorchester in Quebec. And Simcoe and Dorchester did not get along. Simcoe was constantly demanding more troops for garrison duty, in case the Americans kicked up. Dorchester declined.

Simcoe also quarrelled with Joseph Brant, the Mohawk leader. Britain had held onto a series of forts in the unsettled western regions starting at Detroit, which were supposed to be turned over to the Americans. Simcoe wanted to press the boundary west to the Ohio, keeping these forts, but the Indians were divided. Many of the western Indians agreed with Simcoe, but Brant and the Six Nations wanted peace with the United States and counseled surrender of much of the land north of the Ohio. Tactically Simcoe had a good idea. The problem was that the fighting, if it came to that, was likely to fall on the Indians who had lost their enthusiasm for battle with the Yankees.

The Quarrel with Dorchester

Finally Simcoe quarrelled again, and fatally, with Dorchester. It is interesting that the lieutenant governor, who made so much of loyalty and obedience, gave Dorchester little of either. Simcoe, a voluminous dispatch writer, seemed to forget that he was supposed to report to Dorchester and was constantly writing long letters, complaints and demands home, to Dorchester's intense irritation. Dorchester could get on his high horse, too, and he liked to point out that it was a lack of central authority that had started the unpleasantness in the Thirteen Colonies. He had a high opinion of Simcoe's military skills, but not much faith in his capacity as an administrator. In their correspondence the two men were full of veiled contempt for each other. They also disagreed profoundly about what should be done.

Simcoe wanted to plant military bastions all over the province, an idea proudly pinched from the Roman *coloniae*. Instead of the camps of Romans along the Rhine, we would have the Queen's Rangers slung across the Upper Canadian peninsula, and—this would improve the scheme—they would carry the additional advantage of their Britishness, their Church of England, and a newly furnished aristocracy. Towns would form around these garrisons, and prosperity would follow. So the soldiers would serve two functions—to keep the Americans at bay and to prop up and propagate the Almost Perfect State.

Dorchester didn't see it that way. His immediate concern was the defense of the colony, which meant all the colony—not just Upper Canada. He only had about 2,300 troops in all, and he wanted to keep most of them in Lower Canada. That was where he believed the trouble would come from if the rambunctious Americans decided to kick up their heels. After all, that was where the invasion had come in 1776.

So he wrote Simcoe to reject his demands for more men. In fact, as soon as a treaty sorting out the problems of the western forts and disputes over the Great Lakes was concluded (Jay's Treaty), Dorchester would be withdrawing troops from Upper Canada to Lower Canada, where the danger lay. Simcoe fired off a screed to the secretary of state, Henry Dundas, to lay his case before the imperial government, neglecting to inform Dorchester what he was doing. Dorchester was furious and proffered his resignation. He had no difficulty with the other lieutenant governor, he pointed out—only with Simcoe, whose actions meant that "All command, civil and military" was "disorganized and without remedy."[22]

Dorchester was old, sick and tired after thirty years of wearing service. Otherwise what was really a petty dispute probably would not have gone so far. But Simcoe resigned in a huff, and so did Dorchester. Simcoe left the colony on July 20, 1796, to take up a new post as governor of San Domingo. He had been in Upper Canada for just over four years, but he had certainly left his stamp on the place. His attempts to erect an aristocracy laid the goundwork for the formation of the Family Compact, which would finally provoke a rebellion in 1837. His efforts on behalf of the Anglican Church exacerbated the matter of the clergy reserves, which would add bile to that rebellion. His immigration policies would help to fill up the country, but would also lead to the land-jobbery that underlay most of the difficulties to come.

Simcoe's Place in History

How he came to be the lodestar and hero of the Loyalists is, like his proposal to plant a bush-league House of Lords on Upper Canada, one of those mysteries that passeth understanding. It can only be that he seemed to represent what he said he represented—the British way—and that the Loyalists believed that he had indeed given them a province that was the "soul and transcript" of Britain. He had not, of course; but he had created an illusion and set a goal. He had also begun a road system that would prove of far more value—though he created it mostly as a way to move troops around—than his moist economiums about the dangers of electing "one-table" representatives to the legislature.

It was left to history to make Simcoe into a great man; his contemporaries did not see him so. Dorchester, who had contributed far more to Canada, found him not only disloyal but dead wrong. "The impolicy of placing so many troops out of the way, and the enormous abuses in the public expenditure for twenty years are not the only objections to this method of encouraging settlements," he wrote. "The principle itself is erroneous."[23]

Nor did those who worked closely with Simcoe fall under his spell. John White wrote to Peter Russell, the administrator of Upper Canada, "The officers of Government seem to have been considered by Gen. Simcoe only as footballs: to be kick't about at his pleasure. It has always appeared to me as if that Gentlemen thought the Government had been established as a thing whereon he might exercise the sportiveness of his Fancy."[24]

White hit the important point. Simcoe was abubble with enthusiasm, but it was the enthusiasm of a magpie. He would become entranced with one glittering idea, carry it about for a while and drop it to go on with something else. The fact that Upper Canada did flourish in time has led to the notion that Simcoe must have got it off to the right start, but there is little evidence to support the idea. Certainly his dream of planting a British aristocracy in the bush failed miserably, as it was bound to do. In his letters, Simcoe wrote what might have been his essential credo: "Nothing is more essential than to possess Correct Opinions, unless to possess a Correct Acquaintance."[25] Actually, for most of the people over whom he ruled, nothing was more essential than to possess supper, unless it was to possess breakfast.

After his Upper Canadian experience, Simcoe's three-year spell of duty in San Domingo went with greater tranquility. It was easier to rule a smaller nation used to military overlords. In 1806 after more behind-the-scenes maneuvering and a change of government, he got himself named commander in chief in India, but died before he could take up the post. Pity; he'd have given the Raj-to-come a mark to shoot at.

He was a man whose energy overmatched his judgment. One of his bright ideas was to make rum out of turnips and use that to supply the Indians.[26] He imposed a martinet's discipline over his own troops. He kept a cat-o'-nine-tails swinging in his barrack yards, had deserters hunted down by Indians and had some of them shot even though it was a time of peace. One soldier, set to watch some boats at Fort Erie, left his post. For this he was taken down to Fort Niagara and shot kneeling on his own coffin.

Discipline, loyalty, subservience to authority—except his own to Dorchester, of course—were the keys to his creed at a time when what the newly emerging society needed was tolerance, flexibility and self-reliance. E.M. Gundy, in a 1925 article called "The Romance of Pioneer Life in Ontario," commented, "There was to be one Church, one university to guard the Constitution. . . . There at every street corner was to be a sentry, there the very stones were to sing, 'God Save the King'." The difficulty was that of the 7,500 Upper Canadian Loyalists whose backgrounds have been analyzed only eight percent were English, and there were more Methodists than Anglicans. Simcoe didn't care. His views were not to be embraced, they were to be imposed.

Historian Thomas Raddall, in *The Path of Destiny*, summarizes Simcoe's contribution this way: "What Simcoe planted in Ontario was an English feudal mentality as objectionable as the French one in Quebec. A future generation of Upper Canadians called it a Family Compact and got rid of it."[27]

Simcoe will always be saluted as the first lieutenant governor of Ontario and the idol of the Loyalists. The truth is that the Loyalists, or at least the one-table ones, made progress in spite of his ministrations rather than because of them.

SECTION FOUR
1791-

THE EX-
PRIVILEGED

"A majority of the leading families in all the colonies were Loyalists, and impartial history informs us that the greater portion of the brains and wealth of the colonies was on the side of the Mother Country. This is admitted by all American writers."

E.A. Owen, *Pioneer Sketches of Long Point Settlement, 1898*

13
Settling In

"On our Arrival here, it gave me inexpressible Pleasure to think of myself at a happy Distance from those Scenes of Outrage, Tumult and Oppression, which I had long beheld with fruitless Indignation, and to find myself secure from those petty Tyrants, who had involved my once happy Country in every Species of Distress."

From the Narrative of Richard
Cartwright, Loyalist

The Loyalist migration into Upper Canada was not neat; it moved in fits and starts. There were the wartime stragglers and escapees who came up the river systems to Lake Ontario and crossed by boat from Oswego. There were those who followed the Richelieu to St. Johns (St. Jean) and Sorel, and those who fled through the Mohawk Valley to Fort Niagara. Then at war's end thousands more came in the fleets from New York and by private vessel, foot, canoe and horse across the wilderness. Still more—the right sort—came from England once the fighting was done, and it was clear they could no longer go back to the United States (although some did that, too, quietly). These were the officials like William Smith, who came with Lord Dorchester, and the former officers of the Queen's Rangers who came across with Simcoe.

These surges were augmented by the immigration propelled by Simcoe's land policies, which brought both the sturdily loyal and the steadfastly land-hungry across the line to British territory. Some came with republican principles intact but tongues tied: others were as anxious as Simcoe wished them to be to live in the shadow of a benevolent Crown. Finally, there were hundreds more who had first settled in Nova Scotia or New Brunswick or the older part of Quebec, who pulled up stakes and moved on to Upper Canada in response to Simcoe's invitation and in response to stories—true stories—of the huge supply of rich land to be had in the new province.

It was a migration through time as well as space—a movement that began in the early 1770s in the southern colonies and swept north, then west, following the river valleys, until well into the first decade of the 1800s. Those who arrived and found the place to their liking brought in friends, relatives and former neighbors to help fill the empty land, until the original surge of some 10,000 or 12,000 Loyalists swelled to perhaps 30,000 by 1791 (the year when Upper Canada separated as a province, and an informal census was taken). By 1806 the population of the province was about 80,000,[1] but there is some confusion as to how many of these could truly be called Loyalists, and how many were merely immigrants. You had to have "joined the Royal Standard"—in the USA or Canada—before the peace treaty was signed in 1783 to use the initials "U.E." after your name. However, special land grants were available to "late Loyalists"—any Loyalist who had become a resident in the province and signed an oath by July 28, 1798, on the presumption that he was a Loyalist. Of course, there were many professed Loyalists who said they couldn't get across the border in time, and the title of late Loyalist continued to be claimed right up to the outbreak of the War of 1812. In numbering the late Loyalists at about 20,000, I have simply quoted a figure that is often used and taken 1791 as a reasonable cutoff date, but that is based more on a desire to establish some sort of order than on a conviction that no Loyalists entered after that date. Some probably did. In any event, the 80,000 people who lived in the province in 1806 were made up of Loyalists, their families (children born to this first group always called themselves Loyalists) and other immigrants.

They all found themselves in a province that seemed to promise much. Thomas Merritt, one of the prominent Niagara Loyalists, wrote his brother in New Brunswick: "This is one of the finest Countrys in the world for a Farmer that will be Industrious. You would be astonished to see the people from all Parts of the States, by land and by water, 250 Waggons at a time, with their families on the road, like an Army on the Move; the Goodness of the Land is beyond all Description."[2]

Some of the most elevated of the Loyalists landed in Upper Canada via New Brunswick, at Simcoe's behest. One of these was Samuel Ryerse (whose real name was Ryerson, until it got misspelled in an army muster-book—it became easier to switch than fight the bureaucracy). Ryerse had served under Simcoe during the Revolutionary War and accepted his personal invitation to rejoin him by moving to the province now opening up. He was one of the first settlers in the group that spread along the north shore of Lake Erie from Niagara toward Windsor.

Samuel's brother, Joseph, who clung to the old name, Ryerson, joined him five years later at Charlotteville in time to sire Egerton Ryerson, the Methodist hell-raiser and educator who organized the Ontario educational system.

Samuel Ryerse had a daughter, Amelia, whose memories were bundled into Egerton Ryerson's *Loyalists Of America And Their Times* in 1880, and which provide a fascinating glimpse into life in the new province. Amelia notes that her father called on Simcoe at Niagara in 1794 and was promised 3,000 acres of land in his own name, as an army captain, and another 1,200 as a settler. Then his wife was entitled to 1,200, each of his two sons 1,200 and his daughter another 600—a total of 8,400 acres of prime land. Simcoe suggested he look around the county of Norfolk on Lake Erie, which had already been surveyed, and Samuel set out with his servants, wife and family, by bateau from Queenston.

They paddled for twelve days and covered 100 miles before they came "within the Bay formed by Long Point" and discovered a small creek curving into the woods.

"Here I Will Be Buried"

"My Father had not been long on shore before he decided that that should be his home. In wandering about he came to a small eminence which would (when the trees were felled) command a view of the Harbour. He gazed around him for a few minutes and said, 'Here I will be buried'." So he was, too, eighteen years later in 1812. That was the beginning of Port Ryerse and the Long Point settlement.

Ryerse was well-to-do; not for him the hacking and hewing. "He had a log house built and made himself comfortable," Amelia writes. "Half a dozen active men will build a very comfortable primitive Log House in 10 or 12 days, that is cut and lay up the Logs and chink them, put on a Bark Roof, cut holes for the Windows and Door and build a chimney of mud and sticks, sawing boards by hand for floor and doors." The land grant was conditional—Ryerse had to put up a grist mill, which he did. That led to "a constant influx of settlers" to add to the four inhabitants in the area. (When he first arrived, Ryerse's nearest neighbor was six miles away by land, three by water.)

The land was cleared with hired help, and corn, potatoes and other vegetables were planted for the next year. Ryerse had brought along enough salt pork and flour to last a season, when combined with the readily available deer, wild turkeys, partridge and ducks ("He need scarcely leave his own Door to shoot Ducks."). There were also bears and wolves who set up a "most melancholy howl," so that the cow was tied to the kitchen door every night for safety. Fruit trees were planted, maples tapped, timber cut, ashes collected (potash for soap and a hundred other uses provided a major cash crop for the settlers) and neighbors welcomed. Well, mostly welcomed. The Quakers and Tunkers who came up from the United States seeking land were peaceable and industrious, but not so the "idle, discontented, dissipated, vicious and worthless of the United States" who came to Simcoe's land-call. Sigh.

The hired hands—who were sometimes Loyalists and sometimes mere vagabonds—apparently lived on corn cakes. "Each man ground his own allowance . . . The meal was made in johnny cakes eaten hot for breakfast, cold for dinner and the remainder in mush with milk for supper, and upon this fare they enjoyed perfect health, were always cheerful and apparently happy." Uh-huh. At least Ryerse, disgracing himself in Simcoe's eyes, sat down with the help "to show that He was not too proud to eat with them." Ryerse was a magistrate and colonel of militia, but not a snob.

Hard Work Paid Off

Compared to other immigrant groups that came before and after, the Loyalists were comparatively well off in the sense that they received provisions and some tools from the king's bounty. In *Democracy in the Canadas*, Hugh Gillis writes, "If their situation is compared with what faced other immigrant groups, the Scottish Highlanders who landed at Pictou, for example, it is evident that the founders of Upper Canada started with incomparable advantages."[3]

Just the same, it was not an easy life. Days started early and ended late, and consisted mostly of hard work. First there was the clearing of the land and the planting of crops, often around the irremovable stumps. "You might swing the axe here all day," one Loyalist later wrote, "and not let in the light of the sun."[4] Once a clearing was made, turnips, corn and potatoes went in to provide staple food. There was the house to build— with help, when neighbors were near, or alone. This was a monumental task for many of the newcomers who had never done manual labor before, and the house thus built was usually crude, cold, smoky and uncomfortable. Roger Bates, whose grandfather came from Vermont to Hamilton Township in the district of Newcastle, wrote, "At first they all had to experience great privations, but being possessed of indomitable courage and love for the British Constitution, they soon set to work with the materials they brought with them and erected a log House, after clearing a few trees and thus got a shelter from the storms and winds of Heaven. From over-exertion and exposure my grandfather had a very severe attack of ague."[5]

For some there was not even the comfort of a log house; they lived in tents. Jacob Dittrick, who had settled in the Mohawk Valley, fought with Butler's Rangers and hoped "to sit down after the war, once more under his own Vine and figtree." Instead he found himself transported to Canada with a land grant in Grantham Township near Queenston. His son, James (who was born in Canada in 1785, but certainly considered himself a Loyalist), recalled that "The whole country was a forest, a wilderness which had to be subdued by axe and toil. For a time we led a regular Robinson Crusoe life and with a few poles and brushwood, formed our tents on the Indian plan."

Living in a tent in a clearing, the Dittricks survived with scanty food and few clothes. "We none of us had any shoes or stockings, winter or summer, as those we brought with us were soon worn out." They were able to grow some flax and later, sheep, which provided wool and cloth for garments which were made by James' mother. "She had not any thread, so my father stripped off the Bass Wood Bark, saturated it in water, and obtained a fine, strong and useful thread. Necessity has no law."[6] There were also roads to be built, or else how could the crops get to market, how could the settlers move around? That involved more chopping, digging, heaving and hauling.

Loneliness was a burden almost as great as that of toil. Roger Bates remembered, "My grandfather often remarked that for six months he never saw a white man, their only visitors were Indians'"[7]

Where there were enough settlers to build a town, that helped the problem of loneliness, but not of work, since only by mutual aid could such things as schools and churches be constructed. The need for helping hands was so great that a shrewd jury at Niagara, finding a man guilty of stealing pork, sentenced him to "cut down One hundred Logs for the purpose of building a Gaol'"[8]

Towns began to grow—first in small clumps along the waterfront, later reaching back into the forests. Stores were built— usually in the front of someone's house at first. Where the population couldn't support a store, there was "the Pedlar's pack," carried by horseback through the bush. It carried needles, pots, ax blades and other manufactured goods. Peddlers didn't sell much clothing. The Loyalists learned to tan leather for their own boots, while flax provided linen, and almost every house soon had a loom. When there were sheep, wool was used, or a combination of linen and wool—linsey-woolsey—that is still used. Buckskin was used for pants, shirts, and even skirts and blouses, along with other animal skins.

Tight Pants and Tricorne Hats

As in everything else, there were sharp class distinctions in clothing, although these tended to disappear in the bush and were not much in evidence in Upper Canada until settlement was well advanced. Gentlemen wore ruffled shirts, white silk stockings, stocks at the neck and buckled shoes. They did not wear wigs, but often wore cravats. They wore waistcoats and skin-tight breeches. "If I can get into 'em, I won't pay for them" was supposed to be the rule of thumb. The hats were tricorne, cocked or beaver. The men were quite as fancily dressed as the women—and meant to be.

Ladies wore a chemise, petticoats, stays (a long corset) and a dress, usually cut low so that many of the less daring wore a piece of lace, called a modesty, across the strategic zone. An alernative was the stomacher, to fill the front of the bodice and flatten the stomach. Hats were worn and changed constantly in style. Shoes were light—slippers, really. The accessories included such exotics as panniers (false hips), buffonts (a fine linen kerchief stuffed cunningly down the bosom to create a false impression), fans and fichus (squares or triangles of very fine material worn around the neck).

You couldn't hoe corn, chop trees or hammer flax in these costumes, so the farmers and working classes wore simpler clothes. The men wore sleeves without ruffles, plain breeches of deerskin, linsey-woolsey or towcloth (a cheap, strong fabric made from the short fibres of the flax) and shorter, plainer waistcoats, usually of dark material. The coats themselves were also plainer and shorter than those worn by the nobs. The hats were wide-brimmed and deep-crowned, the shoes were clogs or knee-high boots, and the stockings dark and made of worsted. The shirt was usually worn open. For women a shift served in place of the chemise, and it had a square neckline, since nothing was going to be revealed anyway. Petticoats were worn, but they were less elaborate than those of the upper crust and were usually made of cotton. The everyday dress was a "sacque" or short gown with a low neck covered by a fichu. In the country thorns were sometimes used to fasten the bodice. Mobcaps—plain cloth caps—covered the head, and the women wore clogs or "stuff" shoes made of cloth, not leather.

Money was scarce throughout the Canadas, and much trade was carried out by way of barter. When money was in circulation, it was hard to keep track of. It came in Halifax dollars, York dollars, English pounds and a dozen other currencies. Much business was carried on by way of notes promising to pay—the pioneer equivalent of the cheque, but much more complicated, since such a note might be denominated to be paid at Halifax, or York, or Kingston at a given date in a given amount of a given currency, and it was often hard to work out what it meant or who would honor it.

Food was plain in the back country of Upper Canada, at least. Pork was the dominant meat, and it was usually salted to preserve it. One recipe begins, "For 200 lb. meat, take 14 lbs. salt, 1/2 lb. beer; mix with enough water to dissolve the salt. Bring mixture to the boil. Remove scum . . ." It took eight weeks to mature.

Never mind, there were other comforts. Love blossomed in the bush. Samuel Ryerse's daughter Amelia recorded that her mother had a live-in servant, Jenny Decow, who had been bound to a relative.

"At the age of eighteen she received her Bed, her Cow and two or three suits of clothing." This was her stake at the end of her indenture, and she was free to take a paying job. She did and moved in with the Ryerses, as a maid-of-all-work. She had not been there long when a young man named Daniel McCall turned up in response to an urge even older than fealty to the Crown.

"At that time," writes Amelia, "when a young man wanted a wife he looked out for some young Girl whom he thought would be a good helpmate and, watching his opportunity, with an awkward Bow and Blush, he would ask her to give him her company the ensuing Sunday evening. Her refusal was called 'giving the mitten', and great was the laugh against any young man if it was known that he had 'got the mitten'."

Young McCall did not get the mitten; he got the hand, after Amelia's father asked him why he didn't get on with it and cease to "wear out his shoes" coming to call. An hour later they were married by Ryerse himself—"he in his buckskin trowsers and she in her homespun. She tied up her bundle of clothes, received her wages and away they walked to their Log house in the woods."

In time McCall grew rich and became a colonel of militia in the War of 1812. "Some of their descendants," reports Amelia, "are worth thousands."

Jenny Decow went from indentured servant to wealthy matron in a few years, and that was common enough for the hardworking, the intelligent and the lucky in the new province. But there were tough times for rich and poor alike. In 1795 there was another partial crop failure, and many of the settlers at Long Point had to buy flour from the Indians who, to their astonishment, failed to raise the price, even though they could easily have done so with the supply so scarce.

The Neighbors Were Owls, Bears and Wildcats

In a rambling, discursive and often inaccurate collection of stories from the Lake Erie shore, published in 1898 and called *Pioneer Sketches of Long Point Settlement*, E.A. Owen included a fascinating account by an old woman, unnamed, of her first year in the bush. "The only neighbour we had was screech-owls, wolves and bears and yowling wildcats,"[9] she remembered. "Our nearest human neighbour was four miles from us, and it was nine miles to the settlement where mother lived—father was killed by a tree falling on him about a year before we were married."

The year before the wedding, her husband "chopped on" or cleared a section of land and put up a log shanty. After the marriage the young couple set out with a yoke of steer the husband had been given by his father and a borrowed sled, with the blushing bride perched on top of all their possessions on the sled while her husband led the steers. Later they graduated to a "crotch" for travel—a metal yoke curled up at the end to haul logs on. "My old man had a seat fixed on the crotch, and when we went through mud-holes I would have to hold up my feet to keep them out of the mud." Her husband walked with his pants rolled up and his boots laced together around his neck. When they got to town, he rolled down his trousers and put on his boots.

"We planted a little corn along the stumps and that fall we had some cornstalks of our own raising. I shall never forget to my dying day how proud I felt of them cornstalks. How happy I was when we went out to mother's that fall with a bundle of cornstalks on the crotch for a cushion for my feet. It was our first crop, and that bundle of stalks was the most precious cushion I ever owned."

The speed at which the Loyalists transformed the country and themselves was truly astonishing. Consider the transformation of Mary Sitts. She was the daughter of a pioneer in the Mohawk Valley in upper New York. During the Revolutionary War, when she was a girl of seven, a band of Indians—either working on the Patriot side or merely freelancing (the record is not clear)—came storming through the settlement. Mary tried to escape from the house, but was run down and captured, while her sister was slain. Mary was taken as a captive to the Grand River Valley, in what was then western Canada, and raised as a Mohawk.[10]

In 1787 a British captain—she remembered him as "Major Nelles"—was visiting the Grand River and came upon the white captive, so he bought her from the tribe. She was fifteen and had been living as a Mohawk for eight years. She returned to the pioneer white world in a settlement along the forest trail between Niagara and Detroit. It was here that she met and, in 1796, married a man named George Cunningham, who took her to a new town, Boston (not the Massachusetts one—a Loyalist, Upper Canadian Boston in the Long Point area). Cunningham was killed in an accident, and Mary remarried a man named Johnson and settled down to a more sedentary and less eventful life. She lived into her eighties in a prosperous and well-equipped home with oil lamps, modern stoves and the finest furniture. None of her neighbors would ever suspect that the gray-haired, little old lady with the fine home and elegant manners had spent much of her childhood in an Indian lodge. In her old age the only mark of her early life that she carried was a silver plate that protected the top of her head, and was hidden under her hair. It covered the ravages of a scalping knife from a different century in a different place. Mary Sitts went from bushland babe to grande dame in her lifetime, not so much by moving herself, as by the country growing up around her.

What had been rough forest land with a few paths and a handful of huts became, in the space of a generation, an agricultural community on the first rung up the ladder to industrial urbanization. Joseph Hadfield, who traveled through the area in 1795 and again in 1828, described the change. In 1795 he remembered, "Thousands in the midst of forests that had never been cleared from the Creation, cutting the trees, constructing wigwams for shelter . . ." Thirty-three years later he wrote, "You

can travel from Montreal to Ontario and Erie, through cultivated farms and good roads . . . the wilderness has been converted into a paradise of plenty."[11]

Well, perhaps not a paradise; but the rich soil, estimated at
about thirty inches of good loam across much of the new province, did provide bountiful crops. The Upper Canadians were
soon in possession of churches, roads, fancy clothes, dress balls,
schools, taxes, policies and all the other wonders of civilization.
Some of them went from handsome mansions on a hillside to
a log hut with a blanket across the door; some went from a log
house in Pennsylvania with a blanket across the door to a log
house in Canada with a blanket across the door. But before long
they were all housed in better quarters and contemplating a
future that seemed, for a time, without boundaries.

But there was always, in the end, a return to politics. Once
the Loyalists got their feet under them, they began to look
around and to agitate for some of the independence and local
control that had been a mixed blessing in the southern colonies
which gave birth to many of them. In a study of the development of democracy in the Canadas, Hugh Gillis says that "After
their arrival in the north the Loyalists proved, on the whole, a
surprisingly querulous lot."[12] They were querulous once they
had the leisure to be so, but they had much to be querulous
about.

Simcoe's dream notwithstanding, the Loyalists did not on
the whole share a vision of British life that stopped with obe-
dient submission to the state. They inherited a strong dash of
British truculence, combined with a habit of questioning and
debating picked up in the south. They were British by citizen-
ship but American by experience. While the community leaders
(who tended to fare rather better under the hierarchy than the
rest) were content to depend on preferment, many of the others
were not. Arthur Lower called the high Tory Loyalists "the ex-
privileged,"[13] but many of them were not ex-privileged for long.
They scrambled into power from Halifax to York with the ease
of long practice. They held that power, too, for quite some time,
but the struggle was not a pushover.

Loyalists in the Bay of Quinte area began to dun the government with petitions even before the land was cleared. They
wanted better courts, schools and roads; they wanted to import
cattle and farming implements from the United States; they
wanted to elect township officers, and they wanted depots built
where they could store their grain. They agitated for more equality
in the land grants, for the end of seigneurial tenure, for the
abolition of quit-rents. By petition and complaint, they won all

these things by the turn of the century. They objected to a rule that all mills were to be erected by government, so that was changed to a rule that mills could be privately built, but would become government property after fifteen years. They raised such a stink over the obvious inequity of private property being confiscated that the entire provision was dropped.[14]

Public agitation took the form of direct action, as it had in the southern colonies. In the St. Lawrence townships a handful of officers decided that the best way to keep the rabble under control was to hang onto the rations distributed by the government—the king's bounty. They refused to let the Loyalists for whom these provisions were aimed know what they were entitled to. The newcomers kicked up such a fuss that at Lancaster one of the captains resigned his commission and gave up the struggle. A magistrate who had been in on the racket was invited to explain his actions to a public meeting, but he took one look at the tough eggs who were going to ask the questions and departed for parts unknown.[15]

Leveling Principles Raised Their Ugly Heads

But these were isolated incidents. For the most part the Loyalists were satisfied to get on with the business of opening up the country and leave the running of it to their betters. The upper crust resumed its position. Not only did people like Sir John Johnson automatically gravitate to power (he lived until 1830 and died at Mount Johnson near Montreal at the age of eighty-eight); so did the Robinsons and the Winslows and the DeLanceys. Equality was for Americans—vulgar and dangerous. When Colonel Thomas Dundas visited parts of Nova Scotia where the Loyalists were kicking up their heels at local authority, he noted with a sniff, "We had no reason to form a good opinion of the loyal Principles of the Inhabitants of this part of Nova Scotia, and the loyal Refugees complain of the treatment they have experienced, and we saw many instances of their leveling Principles."[16]

Leveling principles, egad, where would it end? Simcoe knew: in one-table households.

Out of their experience, it was inevitable that the Loyalists, querulous or not, would move only slowly toward a more open and democratic society. But there were minimums. They would not put up with seigneurial tenure nor the application of French civil law. Their arrival in Canada effectively abolished the more autocratic provisions of the old Quebec Act and brought an elected assembly to both the Canadas.

But that, at least for a time, was as far as it went. They exhibited an astounding patience with land-jobbery, preference, class distinctions and the pre-eminent position of a church that was not the church of the majority. When the Constitution Act was weaving its way through the British House of Commons, Charles James Fox, leading the opposition, suggested that it would make more sense, if the authorities wanted a state church in Canada, to implant there the Church of Scotland or the Roman Catholic Church, which had more adherents. But of course it wasn't the number of the Anglican adherents that counted; it was their quality. During the windup to the Revolution, the Patriots claimed that the British Parliament wanted to erect a state church in the colonies. This was heatedly denied, and the project was never attempted. But it was put across in Canada and largely accepted as just and proper.

Religion played a key role in the lives of most Loyalists. The day often started with morning prayers and ended with evening worship, led by the head of the family. God was a real presence, not some vague first principle, and heated debates took place about why—since the Loyalists were obviously acting on His side, and the king's—they had been allowed to lose the war. No satisfactory answer was forthcoming—only the usual mumbo-jumbo about the inscrutability of God's will. Just the same, the orthodox religion, which was Anglicanism, had at this time as one of its central tenets the notion of submitting to higher authority. The Loyalist leaders not only believed in this principle, they found it helpful in reinforcing the notion of hierarchy which they had brought with them from their former homes.

Religion, at least in its orthodox version, reinforced politics and, for some, replaced or overruled politics. Politics, after all, brought pain; religion brought comfort. Politics persuaded people to throw off their rulers and molest their neighbors; religion taught the opposite and helped many of the newcomers—bewildered, hurt, impoverished and despairing—by giving them a sense that life was worth living, that the future would be better than the past and that their sacrifices would reap a just reward in heaven if not on earth.

Michael Grass, the Kingston pioneer, wrote in a letter to the *Kingston Gazette* on December 10, 1811, "How many of the seats of my old associates are now vacant! ...Yet I will not repine—they are gone, I trust, to another and better world where HE who causeth the wilderness to smile and blossom like a rose hath assigned to them a distinguished place as a reward for their humble imitation of his labours."[17] A bit corny perhaps for today's reader, but an understandable sentiment.

At first preachers were few and far between, and the Anglicans, so strong in the eyes of the law and govenment, were not in the forefront. They tended to hang about in the settlements. "But the Methodists," wrote Susan Burnham Greeley, a Loyalist in Northumberland County, "came as soon as there were people to preach to and their system was especially well adapted to a new and thinly settled country—a more heroically selfdenying and useful class of men history does not tell of."[18]

The "system" referred to here was the Methodist habit of sending horseback preachers through the wilderness. They were one of the many "dissenting" groups (the other main ones were the Presbyterians, the Baptists, the Lutherans, the Quakers and the Mennonites) who shared religious duties with the "official" Anglicans.

The official and orthodox view of all these sects was that they were droll as long as they confined themselves to ranting in the country, but a threat if they tried to indulge their enthusiasms in town. When the other religions finally won the right to perform marriage ceremonies in 1792, they were licensed only for their home areas.[19] When a Baptist elder, Reuben Crandall, violated this law by sanctifying a marriage outside his license, he brought down on his head the full wrath of John Beverly Robinson, scion of the noble Loyalist family and later chief justice. Crandall was sentenced to fourteen years' banishment, although the sentence was later, after much difficulty, commuted.[20]

The Reverend John Langhorne of Ernestown (now Bath) near Kingston announced flatly that all marriages conducted by other than Anglican clergy were illegal, so the partners were free to marry others.[21] Two sets of Lutherans appeared before him with a demand that he marry them, but with switched partners. He declined. Arthur Lower harrumphed, "No body of men could have conducted themselves in a way more calculated to defeat their own ends than did the Anglicans, more especially the Anglican clergy."[22]

Despite all the problems, the pains, the hungers, the irritations, the dearth of medical and educational facilities, the Loyalists remained a pretty optimistic bunch. After what they had seen and been through, the travails of the bush, the slogging labor of the farm and the snobbery of the church and drawing-room were not that difficult to bear, as long as the land was rich.

They had a country to build, and they built it. Between 1785 and 1800, Lower Canada underwent a population explosion (more French than Loyalist, but they did their bit); and in Upper Canada, settlement flowed up the Ottawa River from the St. Lawrence to the Rideau, along the Bay of Quinte, across the foreshores of Lake Ontario to York, and northward toward Lake Simcoe up the new Yonge Street. Farms appeared on the shores of the Thames and Grand rivers, across the south shore of Lake St. Clair and along the Niagara peninsula and the Detroit River. The Long Point settlement stretched out into Norfolk County, with towns and hamlets appearing almost overnight. These pinpoints of population would soon fill in—not unlike joining the dots on a child's coloring book—to form the picture of a strong and growing province. Incidentally and almost unconsciously, the original Indian inhabitants were brushed back into the bush.

Not all the newcomers were Loyalists, but many were, and it was the Loyalists, early and late, who dominated politics, culture, church and school. They set the agenda based on their own past. They had the positions, the pride and most of the power. Some of them also had money wrested, after much effort, from the British government through the longest-running royal commission on record. The transcripts of that commission provide an insight into the lives of the Loyalists, with some glimpses of impressive courage and some of equally impressive skulduggery.

14
Settling Up

"The Loss your Memorialist sustained amounts to £1000 Province Currency valuing the Goods at Prime Cost, such a severe Blow at his first setting out in the World affected him very sensibly, especially as a great part of his cargo was bought upon Credit."

From the claim of Alexander
Chisholm, Quebec, November 3, 1783

It must have been a weird scene. The setting was Lincoln's Inn Fields in the heart of London where, in a set of rooms seconded for the purpose, hearings were being held into claims of some of the Loyalists for losses suffered during the Revolutionary War. One of the first to appear was Thomas Skelton, whose file was dated October 6, 1783. He submitted his claim, neatly bound and written out in the proper form, for property confiscated in New Jersey because of his loyalty to the Crown. He had been involved in a business partnership, Skelton told the commissioners, and that was now destroyed. He could not return to business in New Jersey because he had carried a message from his father-in-law to General Courtland Skinner and was thus branded a Loyalist. He had retired behind the British lines in 1780 and now here he was asking £3,710 to make good his loss.[1]

Skelton was examined by himself in a small room while two commissioners asked grave questions and scribbled notes. He became confused. He was unable to explain how he had arrived at his losses, or what message he had carried or, as he was pressed, to whom. He was even more vague about where he was presently doing business. He was dismissed, and his place taken by a surprise witness, a Captain Laird of the British navy, who proceeded to fire a broadside into Skelton.

Skelton was never worth £3,710 when he knew him in America, Laird said. In fact he was worth "not much." He hadn't lost by the war; "He has gained considerably . . . And he ought to be ashamed of making any claim for compensation." Skelton could return to America at any time, and in fact his partner was shipping off a cargo very shortly.

Oh, dear. Skelton, confronted, explained that it was all a mistake. He "expects nothing from this Board and . . . he wishes that he had never applied." However, he got something from the board after all—a citation for fraud. The board was not to be trifled with.

The board was properly called "The Commission for enquiring into the Losses, Services and Claims of the American Loyalists." It is now usually called "The Loyalist Claims Commission." It was established by the British government in July, 1783, when it became clear that the states were not going to pay the slightest attention to entreaties that they should compensate the Loyalists for property taken from them during the war. The commission's official task was to conduct "a diligent and impartial enquiry . . . into the losses and services of all such persons who have suffered in their rights, properties and professions during the late unhappy dissensions in America, in consequence of their loyalty to His Majesty and attachment to the British Government."

The commission was appointed for two years. From where the British government sat, that was plenty of time. The officers of the disbanding regiments would round up petitions from all those Loyalists who couldn't make it to England to put in their claims, and that would be that. It was not that simple. Most of the Loyalists could neither read nor write. Even if they knew about the commission, which most did not, they had no way of putting in a claim. Even those who could read and write and knew about the commission could not, in most cases, submit a claim at London by the original cutoff date, March 25, 1784. They were too busy fighting for survival in the wilderness. In the end the commission was extended, and extended, and extended again, until it lasted seven years. One of the original commissioners died and had to be replaced.

Two commissioners—Colonel Thomas Dundas and Jeremy Pemberton—were dispatched to America when it became clear that many of the Loyalists had no means of getting their claims to London. Hearings were set up in Halifax and Montreal, and Thomas Dundas traveled widely through Nova Scotia and Quebec with one eye out for claims and another for subversion and "levelling Principles." The North American hearings at Halifax, Saint John, Quebec and Montreal processed 1,401 claims. Another 834 submitted were never heard because time ran out in 1789.

The commissioners took their work seriously, demanding proof that was in many cases unobtainable, before they would part with any of Parliament's precious money. Their parsimony stands in stark contrast to most royal and parliamentary commissions since. Late claims were accepted only grudgingly, and only if the petitioner had a good explanation as to why he hadn't heard about the commission or submitted a claim between July, 1783, and March, 1784. The commissioners had no notion of how difficult it was to get around in colonial America. When they sent an investigator to the United States to check up on land prices and track down other details, he took a four-horse carriage with him, complete with servants to ride as postilions, and a new marvel—headlights. The carriage had to be abandoned, and for the short time it was in use the headlights couldn't be lit. They "drew a large Concourse of People round us and in order to get rid of them we were obliged to put the lamps out and ride in the dark to the Hazard of being turned over every Step."[2]

There Were Those with Larceny in Their Hearts

There were reasons for caution and parsimony. After all, the Loyalists were being supported on the king's bounty (even if it didn't always get through to them) and many of them were given the half-pay of retired military officers—far more than had served in any military capacity. (Governor Haldimand complained that "There is no end to it if every man that comes in is to be considered and paid as an officer."[3]) A study of the claims concluded in 1904 that "Probably $4,000,000 was spent in surveys, official salaries, clothing, food, tools and stock before the Loyalists in Upper and Lower Canada were established on a self-supporting basis." The figures were much higher, apparently, for Nova Scotia and New Brunswick, where the bulk of the newcomers went.

There were also, alas, those with larceny in their hearts. Of all the Loyalist claims recorded, my personal favorite appears in the *Notes of Mr. Daniel Parker Coke, M.P.*, one of the original commissioners. It concerns the claim of John Ferdinand Dalziel Smith, a fascinating rogue. Smith claimed, among other things, that he was the great-grandson of Charles II. He had gone to America from Scotland in 1763 and settled in New Kent County,

Virginia. He traveled extensively in America and wrote a book, a copy of which he submitted in support of his claim.

During the war Smith raised a corps of 185 men called the "Royal Hunters," but his military career was not a glorious one. He became involved in a quarrel with Colonel John Graves Simcoe, which was not hard to do, but Smith went too far, preferring a charge against Simcoe of improper conduct. A board of inquiry found the charge groundless and Smith was dismissed from the army in 1779. He came to England "because of his health" in 1780 and stayed there until the commission was set up, when he appeared to claim for the loss of a business in Maryland and an estate in Virginia. He was not asking for much— £971 5s.

A long string of witnesses appeared to contradict Smith's story. He hadn't owned the business in Maryland; he had rented it for £11 a year. He wasn't a real Loyalist, anyway. "This Gentleman is a subject of the American State," one witness claimed. As for his estate in Bute County, Virginia, well, he hadn't owned that, either. It was to have been a wedding gift from his mother-in-law, Jane Appens. But the marriage never took place. Shortly before the event-to-be, Smith's fiancée wrote him to say, "She heard he was connected with her mother." Smith wrote back to express his surprise "that she would make such a charge." The only person he had been connected with, he said, was the daughter herself. Smith was so proud of this letter that he showed it around, the cad. "Connected with" means just what it sounds as if it means, and at that time when virginity was highly prized in a bride, Smith had committed a libel. His fiancée took him to court, and the judge awarded her £2,500 in heart balm. The estate Smith was claiming for was later confiscated by the rebels, all right, but that was no loss to him, since he wasn't ever going to get it, anyway.

In fact, said a final witness who had known Smith for a long time in America, the only thing the man owned was "a horse named Smiling Tom," who was "old and decrepit." The board voiced the unanimous opinion that Smith "had committed gross and wilfull perjury," but the record doesn't show if he was charged and convicted.

To guard against people like Smith, the board demanded strict proof—which is one reason no more than a tiny fraction of the Loyalists applied for aid. The proof was back in their American homes, effecively out of reach. There were also a number of ground rules. Losses could only be for specific items with a monetary value. The fact that you lost a wife, three children, a horse, a cow, and "my best nigger, a carpenter," might elicit sympathy, but only the slave attracted an award from the board. Only property lost through loyalty was eligible. If someone merely abandoned a home out of fear, that was not enough; it had to have been seized by the Patriots. Loyalists could claim for the loss of income from offices held under the Crown or for loss of professional income—by a doctor, for example, driven out of town—but not for any land bought or improved during the war, nor for uncultivated lands, mortgaged property (where the mortgage was almost as much as the property was worth), nor for any damage done by British troops or forage taken by them.

John Anstey's Joyless Journey

Some idea of the difficulty in establishing the claims appears in the correspondence between the board of commissioners and John Anstey, a well-known poet and sometime politician who landed the job of traveling to the United States to check particulars. He left England in February, 1786, and returned in September, 1788, after visiting every state in the new union.[4] Wherever he went, Loyalists who had no money to go to England to press their claims, or even to go to Canada, tried to get him to take up their cases. He gave them all the same answer: the deadline had passed; he was there to investigate claims already filed, not to file new ones; and there was nothing he could do for them.

In fact, to his chagrin, Anstey sometimes found that his visits did more harm than good. Despite the provision in the peace treaty that no more reprisals should take place, some states still had confiscation boards in operation. When Anstey started inquiries about the value of land or other property claimed by a Loyalist, if it had not already been seized, the boards swung into action, and took everything of value left. When he went to Albany, the local commissioners of forfeiture were as anxious to quiz him as he to quiz them. In Pennsylvania, claimants who wrote from London for documents to prove their losses sometimes, Anstey found, were merely tipping off the locals to property that had been missed through oversight, and it was promptly taken.[5]

Anstey began his task with a strong suspicion that the Loyalists had exaggerated both their claims and the persecution they had suffered. But he quickly concluded from the evidence he gathered that they had indeed suffered much. He also discovered that in many cases the losses claimed didn't correspond with state records simply because the state officials in charge of the confiscations had embezzled most of the proceeds.

He had great difficulty even discovering what laws applied to the Loyalists in the various states. He had naively expected congress to have a central record. No such luck. In fact, when John Jay heard that Anstey was going south, he asked the Englishman to collect the laws for him. So he spent much of his time tracking down local officials, borrowing copies of proclamations or, in the case of Massachusetts, looking up accounts produced in local newspapers. When he went to New Bern, North Carolina, he was told the comptroller general lived in the bush one hundred miles away. Doggedly, Anstey went there only to discover the comptroller had moved another two hundred miles inland. Ansley was blocked by "overswelling of swamps" and was kicked by a horse. What with one thing and another, he didn't have much fun.

Nor did he have much luck in arriving at fair prices for land. Property values went up and down throughout and after the war and were expressed in a wide range of currencies from English pounds to continental notes of various states and various merits, which also tended to ebb and flow. "Red money," one of the state currencies, depreciated one hundred percent within three months of its issue in 1781, but came back to par in 1785. What was the value of an estate seized in 1782 and valued by the confiscation board at £500? Nobody knew. The commissioners finally set up a sliding scale of their own. In the claim of Frederick Philipse of Westchester County (who was in fact a pretty reluctant Loyalist), the commissioners reckoned his claims, submitted in New York currency, at the rate of £1.72 New York being worth one pound sterling. (Philipse was dead by the time his claim was finished; his heirs got £53,000 sterling and his widow, living in London, a pension of £200 sterling.)

The Loyalists put in claims for everything they could think of—hoes, axes, barns, cattle, clothing, businesses, merchandise (even it it hadn't yet been paid for, like that mentioned in the quote at the top of this chapter) and "Negroes." Philipse's list of personal property taken by the American army included the following items (valued in New York currency):

20 horses at £12 each
133 sheep at £1.10 each
4 large stall fed oxen at £50 each
Wagons, carts and farming utensils, £80
40 Hogs at £5 each
14 milch cows at £7 each

3 young Negroes at £70 each and
4 pipes of old Madeira wine at £80 each.

In valuing his slaves at close to the value of a pipe of Madeira, Philipse may have been stretching it a little. His son-in-law, Beverly Robinson, submitted a table of values to the commissioners for their guidance, which notes, "A good Negro before the War began was worth £50 Sterling." He thought they were "about £40 a Head" after the war.

The commission heard 5,072 claims in England and Canada (which represented perhaps one out of twenty of the Loyalists), and 954 of these were withdrawn or disallowed. The claims totaled £8,026,045 sterling, of which about one-third— £3,292,452—was allowed. In addition, 303 of the exiles received pensions for life; these were nearly all widows. Before it was through the British government spent about £7,500,000 losing the war. It was a little late to point out that it might have been cheaper to forget about taxing the colonies.

Some Got Rich, Some Got Nothing

Inevitably, the claims produced some anomalies. At first the commissioners decided to award forty percent of proven claims to soldiers and thirty percent to civilians. But when it became clear that not everyone who represented himself as a soldier had served as such, this distinction was scrapped. Some of the most aggressive soldiers did well. Sir John Johnson got £103,162 sterling, although he also received his officer's half-pay and his salary as superintendent of Indians. Common soldiers got £10, no half-pay and no salaries. Colonel David Fanning, who had created havoc in South Carolina, claimed £1,635 but only got £60. The commissioners did not say why. William Franklin, the royal governor of New Jersey, got £800 a year.

The only Loyalist who fared better than Sir John Johnson was Oliver DeLancey, who got £108,957, mostly for land. Philip Skene, whom we met at Skenesborough, was blamed by Gentleman Johnny Burgoyne for having added to his troubles at Saratoga. Burgoyne claimed that Skene had manipulated a military road through his property which should have gone elsewhere so he could have use of the road. Undeterred, Skene put in for the loss of 56,350 acres, a stable, a barn, 2,000 sawlogs, eight slaves and twenty cows, for which he was awarded £22,000.

Benedict Arnold also put in a claim, for £16,125, but withdrew it because "I have in a great measure received by the hands of Sir Henry Clinton a Compensation for the Loss of my Personal Estate." (Arnold was an extraordinary man. He had an ego the size of Carpenter's Hall, but he was also a first-rate soldier. He went to England at the war's end but moved to Saint John in 1787 and lived there for four years before returning to London in 1792. The following year he fought a duel with a nobleman who charged him, correctly, but not very tactfully, with being a traitor. He fired one shot and missed. His opponent did not fire back. He lost much of his money in various stock swindles and died in modest circumsances in 1801, leaving behind a wife, a mistress, five legitimate children and two bastards, who stayed in Canada.[6])

Reading the notes on the proceedings of the Loyalist commission provides a glimpse into a whole series of shattered lives from two centuries ago. Here is Peter Dean, who lived at Charleston, South Carolina, and helped to restore the city's cannon when rebels spiked them so that they couldn't be fired on the king's birthday. He was hauled before a committee of safety, refused to sign a loyalty oath, and was banished in October, 1777. He was allowed to sell half his property. The other half was kept "as a security that he should not bear arms against" the Rebels. But he did, and was declared guilty of high treason in a bill of attainder, and the rest of his property was seized. He fought in the siege of Savannah and stayed there after the British victory until the 1782 evacuation. He went back to Georgia after the peace, but was refused admission. A series of character witnesses appeared to bolster his story, and he had documents to prove the value of his property. The board found "That the claimant is a Loyalist," and awarded him £816 15s.

Here is Mrs. Anne Gibbes, whose husband died, but who didn't know whether he took any part in the war or not, or whether their place was confiscated or not. She only knew she had nothing. Her house burned down, but that apparently was an accident, and her claim for £700 was disallowed.

Here is Samuel Hake, who said he served in the army carrying messages, but whom the commissioners appeared to suspect may have carried messages for the rebels, not the British. "The Board are of the Opinion that the Claimant has grossly prevaricated in his Examination and that he deserves no Credit. And, of course, disallow the whole of the Claim."

The Claimant Is a Liar

The Board was outspoken. It believed in letting its Yay be its Yay and its Nay, its Nay. "The Board are of the Opinion that

William Morehead is a Loyalist." Or, "Mr. Lyon Marten is an active and zealous Loyalist and . . . he bore Arms." That was high praise indeed. On the other hand, James McKim was "a Drunken Irishman, very little to be allowed." "Claimant is a good man," "a fine man," "a very fair witness," or "Claimant is a liar," "a prevaricator," "not to be taken at his word." One man put in a claim because he had been driven into bankruptcy by a fall-off of business during the war. It turned out that he had been bankrupt before the war. He was cited for fraud.

Most of the claims were quite small. Although the average was over £1,500 sterling, most were for less than £500. It was the presence of a few huge claims that dragged the average up. The petitioners described the "Low Sercumstances" and the miserable life in "the Deserts of Nova Scotia" where "secresy is observed." They wrote in banal prose of threats and escapes and tortures, of stealing away "on a very dark night," of living "in Great Poverty and Distress," of suffering "Every species of Barbarity which could be invented." They tried to put it all into claims, for "six sheep well-fatted," carpenter's tools, "86 boxes of soap" and, mysteriously, "Numbers of Other articles I shall hereafter Make Known."

There was nothing uniform about the claims. Although many more Loyalists wound up in New Brunswick than in Upper Canada, fewer than five hundred claims came from New Brunswick—they represented only eight percent of the Loyalists listed on the muster rolls. In Quebec there were more than five times as many claims and three out of every ten Loyalists there put in for money. This was undoubtedly because the claims were easier to organize and support in the clustered military-style settlements of Upper Canada than among the scattered and fractious denizens of New Brunswick.

Even when the process was finally done, the money was slow coming. It was paid in instalments that in most cases came dribbling back to the claimants after 1790. According to a tract circulated in London in 1788, the delay produced "the most melancholy and shocking events. A number of sufferers have been driven into insanity and become their own destroyers, leaving behind them their helpless widows and orphans to subsist on the cold charity of strangers."[7]

All very true, no doubt, and very sad. But the money when it came as hard currency into a money-starved economy, was more than welcome and put to good use. And at least the Loyalists had prospects that grew brighter with every passing day opening before them. The same could not be said for their comrades-in-arms in the recent struggle—the Indian Loyalists.

15
Peculiar Attention

"I am a Native of this Nation & of rank in it. At the commencement of the American Rebellion, I entered into the British Service & after a long Contest of faithful Services we have at the Close been most Shamefully deserted."

Alexander McGillivray,
Indian leader, March 28, 1784

On five separate occasions during the American Revolutionary War, Loyalist Indians were promised that at war's end they would be restored "to the condition they were in before the contest began."[1] The assurances were given by Sir Guy Carleton as governor of Quebec, Sir Frederick Haldimand when he succeeded Carleton, Colonel Guy Johnson as superintendent general of Indian affairs, and King George III. These were not vague promises, but specific undertakings. Carleton said, "Assist the King now, and you will find it to your advantage. Go now and fight for your possessions, and whatever you lose of your property during the war, the King will make up to you when peace returns."[2]

Joseph Brant, the Mohawk leader, traveled to England to see the king specifically because he was worried about what might happen to his people if they fought on the British side, and Britain lost. The king gave him a gold watch, a silver gorget, a commission as captain in the British army, and a clear promise: "The losses [to the Indians] certified by the Superintendent-General shall be made good."[3]

Just kidding. The purpose of all these promises was to keep the Indians fighting the Patriots. When the peace negotiations began, the Indians were simply dumped. The Americans took the position that the Indians had entered the war on their own behalf, had lost and had therefore ceded all right to their lands.

The point was made with brutal clarity: "You are a subdued people; you have been overcome in a war which you entered into with us, not only without provocation, but in violation of most sacred obligations."[4]

That was all banana oil. The Americans had been violating sacred obligations at a rapid rate since about 1760, but it is not truth that matters in these affairs, it's power, and the Americans had the power. Many Indian villages had been destroyed and the inhabitants scattered. At war's end they were huddled in tents and huts around Fort Niagara, living mostly on the king's bounty. The Iroquois confederacy was smashed. The Senecas and Cayugas, the two most populous tribes, had been broken and their villages ruined. Most of the remaining Mohawks had gone north with Brant, and other tribes were split by the new boundaries provided in the peace treaty. In fact, the Senecas were the only tribe of those who had fought against the Americans who remained as a whole tribe within American territory, and they were in no shape to put up a fight.

There was another factor as well. The west beyond the Ohio was still closed to the restless thrust of American pioneers. The most western secure enviroment was at Fort Stanwix on the Mohawk, where the city of Rome, New York, stands today. West of that point the forts were still in British hands, and the British stalled the business of turning them over to the victors until London was satisfied that all conditions of the peace treaty would be met. (They never would be, but the forts were eventually surrendered under the terms of Jay's Treaty in 1796.) There was every reason, in other words, for the Americans to argue that the Indians who had sided with the British (virtually all the Iroquois league except the Oneidas) had lost sovereignty over most of their own lands, and that is the position American spokesmen took early and late.

A Gross Mistake Becomes British Policy

The British position was that the Indians were subjects of the king, and their land was his to dispose of as he saw fit. This was never explained to the Indians nor understood by them. Sir William Johnson had explained to the British government as early as 1765 that the Indians would never accept such a proposition, and it was best not to tell them about it. As General Thomas Gage wrote to Johnson in 1772, "As for the Six Nations having acknowledged themselves Subjects of the English, that I conclude must be a very gross Mistake and am well satisfied that were they told so, they would not be well pleased."[5] Yet that "gross Mistake" became the British justification for abandoning the Indians and alienating their land.

Under the American thesis, the Indians had forfeited their land by conquest. Under the British thesis, it could be given away, and it was. The line drawn by the peace treaty delivered to the Americans millions of acres of land belonging to the Indians who had fought and died on behalf of the king.

In the south, this meant that the Creeks and Choctaws in particular—the only tribes really active on the Loyalist side—were simply out of luck. Their lands in East Florida were dealt to the Spanish. They considered leaving America entirely, and some of them asked for transportation to the Bahamas with other Loyalists, although if many went, no record exists. Some others worked their way north and wound up with the Mohawks and their allies of the Iroquois confederacy in Upper Canada.

In the north this meant that the British had a rather ticklish situation on their hands. As soon as a rumor about the abandonment of the Indians crossed the ocean, the Mohawks in particular were outraged. Molly Brant, staying at Fort Niagara, was approached by Colonel Fraser, military commandant at the fort. In her role as head of the Society of Six Nations Matrons, she was asked to speak to the Indians. Fraser was afraid they might say it with tomahawks when they found that their worst fears were well based. Molly refused. Why should she ask her people to remain peaceful in the teeth of this betrayal?[6]

But in the end both Molly and Joseph, her brother, spoke many times, urging the Indians to accept the peace treaty. The Brants knew they had been betrayed, all right, but they also understood that there was very little they could do about it, except to try to use that betrayal to get some kind of settlement from the whites.

Governor Frederick Haldimand of Quebec, whose charge the Indians were at this time, was concerned that the Indians' outrage might express itself in violence. He sent Sir John Johnson to Fort Niagara to assure the Mohawks who had gathered there in flight from their despoiled valley that "The King still considers you his Allies, as his children, and will continue to promote your happiness by his protection."[7]

Actually, Johnson's word was not that weighty in the minds of the Indians, but the Brants remained steadfast in their counsels of patience. Haldimand also urged the British government to make amends for the peace treaty's betrayal and drew from Lord North the acknowledgment that "These People are justly entitled to Our peculiar Attention, and it would be far from either generous or just in Us, after our Cession of their Territories and Hunting Grounds, to forsake them."[8] Accordingly, Haldimand was authorized to purchase land "within the Province of Quebec" for their use. Lord North hoped that these refugees would be allowed to travel back and forth to the United States without impediment, to carry on the business of trapping furs so that "This Country may enjoy the advantage of their trade."

This was a vain hope in view of the guerrilla war that had wracked the area. In New York, Tryon County alone numbered 300 widows and 2,000 orphans in June, 1783. The Americans were determined that they would never again be exposed to the threat of Indian raids. They were equally determined that what had once been the hunting lands of the natives would become available for settlement. There was a body of opinion in the new republic that wanted to massacre the Indians without further ado. In the end, protection was offered to those natives who chose to stay in the area only on condition that they should give up all claims to any disputed land, surrender all prisoners still in their hands and provide six hostages as secruity against any future unrest. The Indians had no choice but to comply. One of the hostages was Aaron Hill, a close friend of Joseph Brant.[9]

Why Brant Rejected the Bay of Quinte

Haldimand wanted the displaced Indians to settle around the Bay of Quinte, so he arranged for a land-purchase in that area, and many of them moved there. However, Joseph Brant favored land along the Grand River—land that he had hunted over many times, and knew to be good for agriculture. Brant argued that the Bay of Quinte site was too far from the other Iroquois tribes. He nurtured a dream of reviving the confederacy and refused to live anywhere more than a day's travel from the Senecas, the westernmost of the Iroquois, whom he hoped to use as a linchpin for his plan.

He asked for land "for the use of Mohawks and such of the Six Nations as are inclined to join them in that settlement,"[10] as the eventual proclamation would put it, making it clear that he spoke on behalf of all the Six Nations. He also asked for £16,000 in New York money for losses to his people and for provisions while they were being settled.

Haldimand felt he could advance no more than £1,500 and provisions, but he agreed to provide the land Brant wanted, arranging for the purchase of a tract of land stretching for six miles on either side of the Grand River "beginning at Lake Erie and extending in that Proportion [i.e., six miles] to its Head."[11] The exact boundaries were the subject of endless confusion. The land was purchased from the Mississaugas for £1,180 7s 4d.

The land was part of what Brant was after, but he also felt the Indians were entitled to the same kind of compensation white Loyalists were getting. Late in 1785 he journeyed once more to England to ask the king to make good on his earlier promise. He was lionized by society matrons, had his picture painted, attended a fancy-dress ball, received a gold snuffbox from Charles James Fox and hobnobbed with the leading lights of the day, including the Prince of Wales, Edmund Burke and Richard Sheridan.[12] Once more the king promised compensation, but it was compensation for Brant, personally, not the Six Nations. In fact the only New York Indians who actually received cash compensation, apparently, were the Brants. Molly got a pension of £100 a year, and Brant got his half-pay as an army captain, although both of these payments were for war services. Then in May, 1786, Brant received £1,449 14s 9d for war losses.[13] He also received land at the mouth of Burlington Bay, where he built a home modeled on Johnson Hall, which is a museum today.

When Brant decided to go to the Grand River, most of the Iroquois went with him, although a group of about three hundred of them, led by Brant's cousin, John Deseronto, one of those who had moved to the Bay of Quinte area, stayed there around the present town of Deseronto.

Once the Grand River site had been approved, the Mohawks and their allies began to move to their new homes during the winter of 1784 and the spring of 1785. Most of them were moving north and east from the Mohawk Valley and Fort Niagara about the same time the white Loyalists were moving south and west from the camps along the St. Lawrence.

Some trekked, some went by canoe or in transport provided by the army. In all, the Haldimand papers show that 1,843 Six Nation Indians—a fraction of a once-great nation—moved to the area around a new town called Brant's Ford. There were 448 Mohawks, 198 Upper Cayugas, 183 Lower Cayugas, 129 Tuscaroras, 47 Senecas, 20 Onondagas and scatterings of other tribes. There were even 53 Creeks and Cherokees from the southern United States.[14]

Molly Brant settled in Kingston to be near her family and her minister, John Stuart. She visited Brant's Ford but never lived there. On her last visit in 1794 she stayed too long awaiting her brother's return from a trip to the west and found that the only ship available to return her home had been commandeered by John Graves Simcoe to move his family back from Niagara to Kingston. So she went to Mrs. Simcoe, who was proud to welcome her as a guest on board, and found her to be a "very sensible old woman."[15] Mrs. Simcoe seemed surprised that Molly spoke English so well; she had been doing so for longer than Mrs. Simcoe had been alive.

Brant automatically assumed the leadership of the Loyalist Indians on the sound grounds that he "is fittest to be their Chief because he alone knows the value of Land." So he did, and that knowledge would lead to much wealth and to endless trouble.

Latin, Greek and Scalping

Brant was another of those nineteenth-century figures who spanned two worlds—an Indian chief with a hand on the scalping knife who also had studied Latin and Greek. He had moved in court circles in London and along bushland trails from the Carolinas to Lake Huron. His dinner table sparkled with silver, shone with candles and glistened with fine wines. Visitors were attended by slaves in livery with silver buckles on their shoes; on occasion he wore a breech-clout and war paint and danced around a council fire, full of rum and rhetoric. He once startled a ballroom full of London's upper crust by uttering an unearthly Mohawk war whoop, and he once got the better of a former schoolteacher in elegant English. (That had happened in 1776 when Dr. Eleazar Wheelock, who had run Moor Charity School, wrote Brant a letter begging him to join the Patriot cause and implored him to remember the lessons learned at the dear old alma mater. Brant replied that he remembered them very well. In particular, he remembered that he had been taught "to fear God and to honour the King." He added, "If this was not what you said, perhaps you would write to me again and tell me what it is you did say.[16]")

Brant could also utter a veiled threat, and would do so more than once over the land question.

That question became endlessly complex, but it was in reality quite simple. Could the Indians or could they not dispose of their land? Brant knew that the small colony of dispirited Ir-

oquois he brought with him to the Grand could never occupy
the 570,000 acres of land they had been ceded. He also knew
that a life as hunters and trappers was not a long-term solution
in the expanding province. So he proposed to sell land to whites,
who would settle beside the Iroquois and from whom the Indians could acquire the agricultural skills that would make use
of the rolling, fertile land. In their beloved Mohawk Valley the
tribal agriculturalists had been mostly women; that would have
to change.

Brant's sophisticated approach flew in the face of white myths
about the Indians. The systematic despoliation of the Indians
on both sides of the border was based on a rationale developed
in the seventeenth century to justify the seizure of Virginia
from its friendly natives. Samuel Purchas, in his four-volume
treatise *Hakluytus Posthumus*, published in 1625, wrote that
the Indians were "not worthy of the name of a Nation, being
wilde and savage." God had given them a rich land, but not for
their use; rather, "God in wisdome having enriched the Savage
Countries, that those riches might be attractive for Christian
suters, which there may sowe spirituals and reape temporals."

It was the clear duty of whites to take the land away from
the Indians, for the benefit of both, because the Indians "having
not the Law, were a law unto themselves." They were "wilde
men" who roamed the woods and had no system of government.
Purchas, incidentally, didn't believe a word of this. He knew
full well that the Virginia Indians lived in villages, cultivated
the land and had a sophisticated government of chiefs and councils governed by precedents as rigorously enforced as English
common law.[17] He was making an argument to justify the de-
pradations of the Virginia Company to its rapacious but religious backers, and he hit on the useful idea of the Hick Savage.
The myth he created has lasted to this day.

For the Indian Loyalists it meant that they were seen as the
"children"—albeit the occasionally murderous children—of the
Crown, incapable of handling their own affairs and therefore
to be protected from rapacious white land-grabbers by a rapacious white land-grabbing government. Although Haldimand's
proclamation of the land-grants along the Grand appeared to
give the Indians outright possession (it says "to take Possession
of "), the British government later argued that the Indians didn't
own the land; they were merely entitled to live there. Thus the
land could not be sold. Some Indians shared this view, which
accorded with the custom that land could not be alienated, but
Brant did not. "Unhappily for us," he wrote, "we have been
acquainted too late with the intention of the Ministry, that is,

that they never intended us to have it in our power to alienate any part of the lands . . . they seemingly intended to forbid us any other use of the lands than that of sitting down or walking on them."[18]

He argued that the land deal struck between Haldimand and the tribes after the war had been one between nations—the British and the Iroquois. Therefore the territory purchased for the Iroquois was for the Indians to dispose of as they would.

He set out his position on a number of occasions, and perhaps most clearly in a letter to Sir John Johnson in which he said, "Our design was to be on the same footing with Respect to our Lands as we were before the War on the Mohawk River, that is to have the free and indisputable Right to them, and remain a free people . . ." Had the Indians known that the British would not keep their end of the bargain, Brant suggested, they might have taken a different approach while "we still had an opening left to seek out an Independent situation." That is, they might have made a separate peace with the Americans early in the war.

A Breach of Faith, and Cruel, Too

But now "it is too late, for we are now become so attached to this place that it would be too hard for us to quit it." He rebuked Johnson forcefully, but in vain: "Dear Sir, I cannot avoid remarking that it is not only a Breach of faith but it is also cruel treatment."[19]

Other Indian leaders made the same point again and again. Alexander McGillivray, one of the Creek leaders, wrote, "If the British Nation has been Compell'd to Withdraw its protection from us, She has no right to give up a country she could never call her own." And the Six Nations Council declared in so many words that "The Indians were a free People Subject to no Power on Earth, that they were the faithful Allies of the King of England but not his Subjects— that he had no right whatever to grant away to the States of America, their Rights or properties."[20]

It was all wasted. The Indian confederacy had been smashed, and their rights or lack thereof would now be determined by the whites who had concocted the theory, never once laid before the Indians, that they were subjects not merely in the way other Loyalists were subjects—for no other Loyalists were barred from selling their lands—but in an inferior way. For their own good.

That was what Lord North meant, no doubt, by "our Peculiar Attention."

The intended executor of this policy was John Graves Simcoe. After Haldimand's withdrawal from the colony, Simcoe made it a policy, from which he never deviated, that no lands could be sold by the Indians. Brant paid no attention. In fact, he had already sold deeds for large blocks of land to a number of whites (and, according to some reports, insisted on being paid a hefty personal commission before he passed the money on to the Six Nations). These sales sparked a dispute that smoldered for a decade.

Brant was also busy. The American Indians quickly found that the land left to them on their side of the border by the peace treaty was being overrun with white settlers pushing farther and farther west. Brant made several trips into the United States to attempt to convince the Indians there that the only way to meet this encroachment was to revive the Iroquois confederacy. He received a cool reception, although he did manage to get the tribes to put together a conciliatory proposal for the American government.

The problem was that the Americans had little interest in conciliation. The Indians had been whipped; they should stay whipped. The way to do this was to keep them divided. It was, too; Brant saw that. In 1784 a treaty was drawn up at Fort Stanwix, under which the Indians agreed to give up land in the Ohio Valley and in Pennsylvania in return for undisturbed possession of their lands in western New York. The ink was scarcely dry on the documents when whites began to pour over the negotiated line and into Indian territory. Still, the Indians refused to form a common front.

The Indians Could Be Set at Deadly Variance

In 1789 General Arthur St. Clair made two separate treaties with five of the six Iroquois nations (leaving out the Mohawks) and with a group of the western Indian nations. He told congress, "I am persuaded their general confederacy is entirely broken. Indeed, it would not be very difficult to set them at deadly variance."[21] Unfortunately, the Indians believed—what Brant knew from experience not to be the case—that they could beat the whites in war. Under the leadership of Chief Little Turtle of the Miamis, warriors from the Shawnee, Miami and Wabush tribes rejected a new boundary treaty offered by President Washington and took up the tomahawk.

They won two quick victories against small expeditions sent out to crush them. General St. Clair led one of these expeditions in 1791, marching to the Wabash River where the Shawnees and Miamis killed eight hundred eager frontiersmen and sent hundreds more flying for their lives.

This defeat gave the congress pause. The Americans began to believe that Brant had in fact succeeded in uniting the western tribes, and they invited him to Philadelphia along with the western Indian leaders to try once more to get a permanent deal. "I can assure you," wrote the secretary of state to Brant, "that the President of the United States will be highly gratified by receiving and conversing with a chief as eminent as you are."[22]

Brant went, traveling mostly on horseback, in a long trip that took him through his old home in the Mohawk Valley and landed him in Philadelphia in June, 1792. There he was offered money to bring about a peace. "This I rejected," he said, although he made sure the British knew that the bribe had been offered. He was also offered land if he would settle in the upper New York area. The authorities had a shrewd idea that if Brant and his sister Molly were to move back to that area, where there were still about one thousand Indians, peace would be ensured. Both Brants refused, although Molly accepted money in payment for her lost possessions.

Joseph would take nothing, but he did undertake to speak to the western Indians and urge them to keep the peace. He traveled west once more in the summer of 1793 to ask the tribes to meet with a group of American commissioners. The Indians refused. They no longer believed that the whites would abide by any treaty (in which they were probably right), and they believed that their victory over St. Clair showed that they could whip the whites anyway (in which they were dead wrong).

Brant was now suspect because he had visited the whites and been fussed over at Philadelphia, and his perfectly sound warning that the Indians would lose if they went to war was ignored. The meeting broke up; the issue was to be settled by force of arms. There was only one way that could end. Washington sent General Anthony Wayne out with a 2,000-man army that crushed the Miamis at the Battle of Fallen Timbers in August, 1794, near the present site of Toledo, Ohio. When the beaten Indians ran to nearby Fort Miami and asked the British for shelter, they were refused entry. They must have seen the irony in that — their former allies locking them out on behalf of their former enemies.

The aftermath sent shivers up spines in Upper Canada. When Governor Simcoe heard that General Wayne was heading for Fort Miami, he thought the balloon had gone up on another war and marched off with a small army that would certainly have been whipped, as he later admitted, if it had encountered the Americans. "I think no force in this country could resist Wayne's direct attack,"[23] he wrote.

The Battle of Fallen Timbers and the scattering of the beaten tribes thereafter marked the end of effective resistance in the northwest to the onslaught of civilization. The embarrassment of British forts in American territory was settled by Jay's Treaty, and the Indians were left to fend for themselves.

When Brant returned to Brant's Ford, it was to find that Governor Simcoe saw the dark hand of conspiracy in his trip to Philadelphia, and Simcoe never trusted the Indian chief thereafter. He had been exposed to the dread disease of republicanism; perhaps he was infected. Simcoe issued a new proclamation stating that the Grand River land belonged to the Indians only as long as they remained on it. If they left it at any time, it would revert to the Crown. They could not, in any event, sell it or transfer it to others.

Brant protested—quite correctly—that this was a violation of the agreement made with Governor Haldimand, and he took his case to Lord Dorchester. Dorchester agreed with the Mohawk chief and suggested that the original "advantages" offered to the Indians by Haldimand should be unconditionally reaffirmed. However, Dorchester was overruled by the British government, and the land grants remained clouded.

Would the Indians Join the French?

When Simcoe left Upper Canada in a sulk in 1796, Peter Russell, a member of his executive council, took over the administration with the title of president of Upper Canada. Russell had been one of Sir Henry Clinton's secretaries. He had returned to England at the close of the war and came back with Simcoe as inspector general of Upper Canada. Brant thought he might be able to get from Russell what he couldn't get from Simcoe. Whatever anyone said about Simcoe, he was a bold, brave man, and Russell was not. So Brant unleashed a whole series of letters and speeches ridiculing Russell and complaining about the treatment of his people.

Somehow a rumor got started that Brant was about to muster his warriors and march on the legislature at York, and somehow Brant failed to quash it. It was a twitchy time. The French revolutionary war had broken out in 1792 and was going nicely. It seemed possible that the Indians, remembering their ancient friendship with the French, might take up the tomahawk on their behalf for the sake of scalps and auld lang syne. This was nonsense. Brant's entire career had been at the side of the British, and his first battle had been fought against the French at Lake George back in 1755. Just the same, there was Brant, tapping his foot and growling threats, and there were the French, waiting over the horizon. What was a body to do? Russell convinced himself that Brant would seize on "any feasible excuse" to join an invading French army. It could certainly be argued that snatching away his people's land in violation of the Haldimand agreement constituted a feasible excuse.[24]

So Russell called a special session of the executive council, which confirmed the original deeds. The British home secretary would later refuse to endorse the council's decision, but that was a bit late. Brant had already sold six blocks of land totaling 350,000 acres out of the original 570,000 acres. These sales became mired in endless confusion and misfortune.

A group of Indians who thought, perhaps with some reason, that Brant was doing rather better out of land dealings than they were, went to call on him to accuse him of misappropriating $38,000 (his "commission" on the land sales) and to tell him they had deposed him as a war chief of the Six Nations. Brant flew into a rage, heaped scorn on his tormentors, grabbed a tomahawk and chased them out of his house. The attempted coup was over. A meeting of sixteen chiefs signed a document proclaiming confidence in Brant's leadership, and runners were sent out to the outlying districts to put the message across.

Brant's old age was not a happy one. The land question continued to be unsettled, and he quarrelled bitterly with his oldest son, Isaac, a jealous and tormented man. The dispute ended in a knife-fight in which Isaac was badly wounded. He later died of infection from the cuts. Brant turned himself over to the authorities and won a ruling that the killing was justifiable homicide. On a number of occasions thereafter, Brant was found weeping in his bedroom, gazing at the dagger that had slain his son.[25]

He withdrew more and more from the active affairs of the Indian community, and his adopted nephew, Captain John Norton, a halfbreed (his mother was Scottish; his father Mohawk), took on some of his role but none of his prestige. It was Norton who went to England in Brant's place to argue in vain for freeing the Indian lands from all conditions. After the British refusal, Brant contemplated returning to the United States and sent Norton to call on the governor of New York state. However, the New Yorkers were unwilling to give up the large tracts of land Brant required, and nothing came of the proposal.

Brant withdrew from public life and settled down in Burlington, where he died in 1807.

The alienation of land from the Indians proceeded apace. Squatters moved in, lands were sold, traded and stolen. Brant's dream of a new confederacy had been crushed at Fallen Timbers. His dream of a prosperous Indian farming community along the Grand faded soon afterwards. By 1834 the lands were surrounded by such confusion that a full-scale inquiry was launched, which didn't do much to clarify the situation. In 1841 the Indians were told that the only way they could keep any land at all was to surrender it to the Crown, and they would be looked after. The Indians agreed and on January 18, 1841, gave up what remained of their lands except for those they were actually occupying and a 20,000-acre reserve.[26] The fight had gone out of them.

As Loyalists, the Indians received short shrift from beginning to end. They had not gone to war for the same reasons as their white neighbors. In most cases they had fought not to honor the king but in response to the plunder of their lands by the colonists, who happened to be mainly Patriots. The Brants played a key role in securing the Indians' loyalty, and it was loyalty to the Brants rather than to the Crown that probably kept most of them on Britain's side. As Daniel Claus, William Johnson's son-in-law and one of the prominent Indian agents, wrote, "A Joseph and Mary Brant will outdo fifty Butlers in managing and keeping the Indians firm . . . One word from Mary Brant is more taken notice of by the Five Nations than a thousand from the white man without exception."[27] Despite his old-fashioned insistence on calling Molly Mary and his refusal to accept the expansion of the Iroquois league to Six Nations, Claus had it worked out right.

The Brants, especially Joseph, did better when they struck their own deals and went their own way. Most of the Iroquois who moved to Brant's Ford sank slowly into poverty, as did most of those along the Bay of Quinte. Had they been given to introspection, they might well have wondered whether the intelligent course for them from the beginning might have been to make a separate deal with the rebelling colonies. Once the war began, they were doomed. Having taken the white king and his representatives at their word, the Indians committed themselves to the losing side. When the fighting was done, despite all the high-flown talk, they were at the mercy of the whites on both sides of the new border.

In the circumstances, it is perhaps astonishing that many of the Indian Loyalists fought vigorously on behalf of their newly adopted country when the War of 1812 broke out. They were led by John Brant, Joseph's son, who took over his role as war chief on his fathers death.

That war was to provide a crucial test for the Loyalists, and they passed it with flying colors.

16
Winners After All

"A Mr. Henry Hamilton killed Mr. Tarbox, an American citizen, with a saddler's knife, in Prescott, for which he was apprehended, tried and condemned, but not executed, because he only killed a damned Yankee."

Donald M'Leod, *A Brief Review of the Settlement of Upper Canada, 1841*

As the eighteenth century gave way to the nineteenth, and the Loyalists began to sink their roots into their new country, their influence struck the three main areas of Canada—the seaboard, Quebec and Ontario—in different ways, but in ways that all contained common elements— loyalty, conservatism and hard work.

Along the seaboard the struggle for power with the pre-Loyalist hierarchy ended with the triumph of the Loyalists. The old timers viewed the new arrivals with some apprehension, while the Loyalists suspected (or pretended to suspect) that many of the neutral Yankees were rebel sympathizers or republicans. (No smear was so effective on the heels of the Revolutionary War than the charge of republicanism, or "levelling tendencies.")

Gradually the Loyalists gained the ascendancy by virtue of their vigor, intelligence and self-righteousness. They were very sure that their wartime trials fitted them for the rewards of power, and they proceeded to take them. In the 1785 election for the Nova Scotia assembly, thirteen Loyalists and twenty-six pre-Loyalists were returned to office. The Loyalists also bagged what was, until responsible government became established decades later, the key post in the legislature—speaker of the assembly. That went to Sampson Salter Blowers, a Boston lawyer who had briefly been solicitor general of New York.

Blowers was an odd duck who believed that the secret to long life was never to wear an overcoat, no matter how cold it got. Maybe there was something to it; he died in 1842, in his hundredth year.[1]

Blowers also held the posts of attorney general and, later, chief justice, while the speaker's post continued to be filled by Loyalists. In fact Loyalists held the job for thirty of the next forty-five years.[2] They also provided the province with an influx of lawyers (there were only six when the Loyalists arrived), doctors and artisans.

The Loyalists inspired the founding of King's College at Windsor, Nova Scotia, in 1789, and made it an exclusively Anglican preserve despite the protests of many—including the high-Tory Anglican bishop of Nova Scotia. Because the Anglicans represented a minority of the provincial population, it seemed unjust to make the single university into a denominational institution. But the newcomers were having no truck with democratic tomfoolery, and they stuck to their Anglican guns. To gain entrance a student had to subscribe to the thirty-nine articles of the Anglican creed—the thirty-nine steps, as it were, to orthodoxy. The King's honor roll rang with the Loyalist names—DeLancey, Bliss, Arnold, Haliburton, Bayard, Courtland. The end result was that other faiths set up their own institutions of higher learning, whose students soon out-numbered (but never, my dear, outranked) the Anglicans. Later the university was moved to Halifax. Today, King's (where this book is being written) lives amicably with the much larger Dalhousie, on the same Halifax campus. We've learned tolerance over the years.

As the Loyalists first shared and then assumed power in the province, the tendency for politics to be merely a matter of connections was strengthened. In 1792 John Wentworth's ready assent to his wife Frances' liaison with Prince William landed him the lieutenant governor's job. When war broke out anew with France, Wentworth raised a regiment—the Nova Scotia Regiment of Foot—and had himself made colonel at full pay. The regiment's contribution to the war was the construction of a battery for cannon, which Wentworth named after himself, and he spent the war standing on guard.

In the spring of 1794 another of the royal princes arrived— Prince Edward, later the Duke of Kent. Edward was a tall, energetic and sober gent—unlike Silly Billy—and he had no need to make Frances Wentworth his mistress. He brought along his own—Alphonsie Thérèse Bernadine Julie de Montgenet de Saint Laurent—Madame St. Laurent, or Julie. Edward decided to convert Halifax from a shabby collection of wooden shacks to the fortress of the north, throwing up public buildings, barracks and batteries, workshops and a handsome townhouse for himself and Julie.[3] He leveled the old blockhouse on Citadel Hill, chopped fifteen feet off the top of the hill and built a fort there. He studded the place with fortifications, including three Martello towers, and built North America's first telegraph system, operating from semaphore towers.

A Love Nest for Julie

The money for all this came out of the British treasury—not happily, but, in view of Edward's position, inevitably—and was welcome indeed in Halifax, where the court circle, led by the prince and his lady, and the Wentworths and their friends, busied themselves with a round of levees, dinner parties, parades and balls. Wentworth gave Prince Edward some of his own land at Bedford Basin, where he built a little two-storey love-nest for Julie, with gravel paths and rides laid out to spell her name, and an artificial pond shaped like a heart.

Sir John—the title came in 1795—shifted his country estate to Preston on the hills behind Dartmouth and built a hilltop mansion suitable for entertaining royalty. When the prince and Julie came calling, a cannon on the terrace boomed out a salute. For excursions to visit the Prince at Beford Basin, there was a galley with a reclining lounge for Frances. Must have made her feel like Cleopatra. The oars were worked by slaves; Wentworth had fifty of them—part of a batch of five hundred Maroons shipped north from Jamaica in 1796. One of the Maroons became Wentworth's mistress, and they left behind a number of illegitimate offspring.[4] Things didn't work out so well for the rest of the Maroons. A tough bunch in their native Jamaica, they proved intractable in Nova Scotia as well, and were shipped off to Sierra Leone in 1800 to join the first black exodus from Halifax.

The Nova Scotia assembly resolved to build a decent legislature to replace the rented wooden building where it met, but Sir John got the money to build himself a new government house instead. (Province House was finally built in 1811.) It was supposed to cost £10,500, but cost almost three times that sum. This was not a bill the British government would pick up; it came straight from the pockets of Nova Scotians. The new building was dedicated by Prince Edward just before he departed to a new post in Gibraltar. The Wentworths were left to struggle with provincial society on their own.

Sir John used his post to deal out patronage to friends and relatives. He named his own son to the legislative council and got jobs for Frances' family, as well as their hangers-on. At last the assembly began to grow restive. Winkworth Cottnam Tonge (what lovely names these peoples had; this one is pronounced "tongue"), a naval officer, assemblyman and justice of the peace, began to build up a popular party. Tonge was not a Loyalist, needless to say, but he traveled among the Loyalists in the outlying towns, arguing that their needs were being neglected by Wentworth's Halifax clique, while they paid for the lieutenant governor's lavish lifestyle. For a time Tonge made some headway, enough to have himself elected speaker. But after a couple of stormy sessions Wentworth would no longer recognize him as speaker and had him dismissed from his naval post. Tonge left the province, and the popular movement died with him.

Wentworth was replaced in 1808 when the British government felt a younger and more military man was required for the post (the off-and-on Napoleonic Wars were on again). He retired to England with Lady Frances, bearing with him a pension from the grateful or at least supine assembly of £500 a year. (He returned to Halifax in 1814 and died there soon after, reduced to poverty by his and Frances' life-long extravagance.)

Wentworth's systematic milking of Nova Scotia aroused little ire. It took decades for the province to build up enough discontent to push for real self-government. Since an almost identical set of circumstances evolved in New Brunswick (which was ruled in absentia for fourteen years by Sir Thomas Carleton through a stand-in elite in Saint John) it is hard to escape the conclusion that the Loyalists' experience had conditioned them to put up with almost anything to avoid the scourge of mob rule.

In Quebec the situation was somewhat different, since the Loyalist influx was for the most part just passing through. While leading Loyalists had an undoubted influence—men like William Smith and Sir John Johnson were the governor's confidants—the real energy of the Loyalist thrust went westwards into Upper Canada. The Loyalist presence required the division of the province into two, and that was its major impact. In addition, the English Loyalists who did stay in Quebec helped to deepen the conflict, already underway when they arrived, between the French party and the English merchants. The struggle for self-government that erupted later turned, as does so much in Quebec's history, on the joined questions of language and religion, to which the Loyalists added a minor irritant rather than a major impact.

No Votes for les Yanks

The Eastern Townships, which Governor Haldimand wanted reserved for the expansion of the French Canadians, were opened to the English in 1791. No seigneuries had been erected in the area stretching from the Vermont border to the Richelieu River, which represented one of the richest farming regions in North America, so the 1791 decision to open it to freehold settlement brought a flood of land-hungry applicants. Many of these were Loyalists moving down from Nova Scotia; others were the "late Loyalists" pushing in from the northern United States in response to a sudden flood of affection for George III and his lovely, free land.

The Crown and clergy reserves provided in the Constitutional Act of 1791 impeded development here as in Upper Canada, and settlement was marked by land speculation on the part of Quebec's ruling elite, the so-called "Chateau clique." They managed to snap up huge blocks of territory. Another block against progress was the steadfast refusal of the Quebec assembly to provide anything in the way of roads, local courts or representation for "les Yanks," a term that included all the newcomers to the Eastern Townships. Despite these difficulties, the newcomers settled in, settled down and prospered. French Canadians did not begin to move into the region in significant numbers until much later and only became the majority when the twentieth century was well advanced. Today the Eastern Townships are one of the most attractive regions of the country, as well as a textbook example of the successful mingling of people of staunchly British and fiercely French ancestry. The Loyalists and late Loyalists deserve much of the credit.

In Upper Canada the Loyalists were in firm, triumphant power from the beginning. They converted a wilderness into a landscape of towns and farms in an astonishingly short time. This work took up most of their energies. Political development was hesitant and based on the solid conservative principles they had brought with them. God Save the King had a parallel, unspoken corollary—And Don't Rock the Boat.

They were not overly concerned with self-government. Under Simcoe and his successors it was the appointed legislative and executive councils—allied with the lieutenant governor and dedicated to the principles of firm hierarchical control—that ruled.

At the local level magistrates appointed by the executive council were in charge, making the key decisions on everything from law enforcement to repair and improvement of the streets, licensing taverns and regulating ferries. The magistrates met in each of the four districts in general quarter sessions of the peace, which issued regulations that had the effect of legislation, although there was none of the clutter of voting. It was the magistrates who levied local taxes. Property taxes in the home district around muddy York, Vaughan and Markham, came to a total of £25 16s 3d in 1798[5]—not enough to do much with even in 1798 prices. Setting a pattern that would become familiar to us all, the taxes collected did not cover expenditures.

It was the district quarter sessions that were responsible for such things as paying the salaries of the jailer and coroner, establishing a bounty on wolves, providing a pittance for the care of the poor and the insane, and hiring the high constable. The high constable in turn was assisted by unpaid constables named by the magistrates; refusal to serve was punished by a stiff fine of £2.

There were, to be sure, annual town meetings in some of the settlements of Upper Canada, but the major task of these meetings was merely to elect the town clerk, assessors, collectors, pathmasters and town warden who ran local affairs on lines laid down from on high. In York after 1804, one of the two town wardens was appointed by the Anglican minister. He was apparently qualified as a dispenser of power by virtue of his virtue.

In short, it is hard to show that the coming of the Loyalists "hastened the advent of free institutions" in Canada, as so many Loyalist historians (led by the redoubtable Stewart Wallace) have claimed. That argument is based on the fact that the Quebec Act, which smacked of feudalism, was scrapped after the Loyalists arrived, and representative assemblies were provided in both Upper and Lower Canada. Ergo, the Loyalists get credit for spreading democracy. Well, it's an argument.

However, representative government, even if it was hardly self-government in the full sense, was part of the pattern of all the British colonies. Presumably it would have to be extended to Quebec, whether or not the province remained in one piece. The Loyalists asked for the vote, certainly, but it was a part of their background, not a venture onto new ground. Patronage, connections and "douceurs" were the coin of politics, not votes.

The land bribes available to the friends of government ensured that the temptation to rebel was kept in check. When York received its first resident minister, Reverend Thomas Raddish, a friend of Chief Justice Elmsley, he was dealt 4,700 acres of land, including a large park lot intended for use as a glebe. Raddish sold it all to Elmsley and departed.[6]

This kind of transaction did not excite much comment because the *Upper Canada Gazette*, the preeminent newspaper, was not open to the kind of free discussion of political issues that had been common in the Thirteen Colonies. On March 22, 1800, the paper published a letter from "A Farmer" wondering about the political independence of an unnamed friend of government described as possessing "eminence of station." The executive council came down hard. The *Gazette* was threatened with immediate dismissal as king's printer and condemned as "highly culpable in having inserted such an Article . . . without authority."[7] The *Gazette* took the point, and future complaints about the paper were mostly to the effect that no one but friends of government could get a mention in its columns, even during elections.

Scotch Pedlars and the York Clique

As in Nova Scotia, the effective opposition came, when it came, from a non-Loyalist—Robert Thorpe, a judge appointed to the Upper Canada bench on the recommendation of Lord Castlereagh. Thorpe was apparently expecting to be named chief justice when Elmsley retired, and when that did not happen he went into opposition. He used his charges to juries to attack the new lieutenant governor, Francis Gore, appointed in 1806. Thorpe claimed that the "York clique" was surrounded by "Scotch Pedlars." He thundered that this "Shopkeeper Aristocracy has stunted the prosperity of the province and goaded the people until they have turned from the greatest loyalty to the utmost disaffection."[8]

It is interesting that Thorpe thought the safe argument to make was that the government, by its wickedness, was detaching the people from their loyalty. If it was, you couldn't prove it by the way the folks stood around looking at their shoes while the clique up top took care of Thorpe. He managed to get himself elected to the assembly, but Gore dismissed him, along with an ally, Charles Berton Wyatt, the surveyor general.

Then the executive council condemned Thorpe for his appeals to "Lower Classes of Individuals" and his "attempts to degrade, embarrass and vilify his Majesty's Servants," while Gore weighed in with the complaint that the real danger was that Thorpe might appeal to the people "in this Province, where Republican Principles prevail so much" and where the people were "impatient of control."[9] The essential charge against both Thorpe and Wyatt, when the verbiage was stripped away, was opposition to Gore and his government. Neither Thorpe nor Wyatt was ever reinstated, and Thorpe left the province.

At least Thorpe fared better than another of the few who dared oppose government. William Weekes, who made a public appeal "to those who may be inclined to think with freedom, and to act with independency," was successfully elected, but then shot in a duel with one William Dickson.[10]

Then there was Joseph Willcocks, another government opponent, but not a brilliant man. Thorpe once described him as "a good sportsman . . . who did not possess a sufficiency of brains to bait a mouse trap." He could be, and was, ignored. But no one could ignore the highly connected John Mills Jackson, an Englishman who visited the province and wrote a highly entertaining but scurrilous pamphlet called *A View of the Political Situation of Upper Canada* (his name was on the pamphlet; some argued it came from Thorpe). This document accused Gore and his adminisration of oppression, favoritism and land-jobbing. All of which was so patently true that it was necessary for the assembly to denounce the pamphlet as "a false, scandalous and seditious libel." The legislators passed an address to Gore, approving his administration and "testifying their abhorrence and detestation" of Jackson's criticisms.[11]

The fact is that any sort of criticism of government was seen as potentially dangerous in a province that viewed foreign invasion, internal insurrection and the onslaught of democracy with almost equal conern. The result was a piece of legislation which, even for its time, was astonishingly punitive. The Sedition Act, passed in 1804, (as relations with the United States began to slide toward war), provided that anyone who had not been in the province for six months, and who had not taken the oath of allegiance, might be arrested and called upon to prove that anything he said or did was not "intended to promote or encourage dissatisfaction." Under the act, anyone who raised a voice against government could be banished from the province. If he returned, he could be put to death. Gore, with the support of his executive council, ordered the magistrates not to "administer the Oath of Allegiance to any Person not holding Office in the Province, or being the son of a U.E. Loyalist,"[12] without his permission. In short, you had to swear an oath but were denied the right to swear it unless you were a proven Loyalist or government appointee. Any newcomer who kicked up a fuss could be chucked out, and no questions asked. (This iniquitous act was later used against Robert Gourlay in 1818. Gourlay was a troublesome Scot who wanted to forge closer ties between the colonies and the Empire, but who took a strong dislike to the Family Compact and all its members. They had him charged with sedition after he accused them of graft, patronage and land-jobbing. But two courts threw the sedition charges out, so that 1804 act was dusted off and banged on his head. As a matter of fact, he had taken an oath of allegiance, which should have protected him; but he didn't take it within the province, so he was caught on a technicality, slammed into jail and banished.)[13]

Gore's long rule in Upper Canada from 1806 to 1817 (although he decamped for England on a leave of absence during the War of 1812) marked the ascendancy of the Family Compact in Upper Canada, which put the province firmly in the hands of an oligarchy that looted the treasury, stole the lands, rewarded its friends and punished its enemies. Or, if you like, the Family Compact was the group that gave of their skill and industry to rule the unruly province, and happened to do well in the process.

The composition of the Family Compact tended to vary over the years, depending in part on who drew up the list of its members, but its key figures were identified by historian Robert Saunders as eight men. The leader was the Anglican cleric, John Strachan, who originally came to Canada from Scotland to educate the children of Richard Cartwright in Kingston. He hoped a district school and later a university would be established. When neither happened, he took orders, as the phrase went, and conducted a church and a school at Cornwall before moving to York in 1812 as Anglican rector and headmaster of a grammar school. Later he became an archdeacon and then a bishop. Strachan became the living embodiment of Simcoe's dream of the fusion of church and state. He ran both—with, through, around and over the lieutenant governor. The other seven key players in the Family Compact were William Allen, D'Arcy Boulton, Henry John Boulton, George Markland, Christopher Hagerman, William Dummer Powell and John Beverley Robinson.

Robinson was the most powerful member of the group, next to his mentor, Strachan. He was the son of Christopher Robinson of Virginia, who had served under Simcoe in the Queen's Rangers. John Beverley Robinson was born in 1791 in Lower Canada—of the truest, bluest Loyalist stock. Hagerman was also the son of a Loyalist and so, apparently was Markland, who was Strachan's pupil and protégé in Kingston. (His birth details are not firmly established.) Powell was a Loyalist who had gone from Boston to England during the war. Four of the eight members of the inner circle of the Family Compact were Loyalists or of Loyalist stock, which is hardly surprising.

When Gore decamped for England to sit out the War of 1812, Sir Isaac Brock, as military commander, took over in his stead and asked the legislature to suspend the writ of *habeas corpus*. The assembly gave him the polite but firm raspberry and continued to do so every time he raised the subject. Brock concluded that "the greatest influence which the vast numbers of settlers from the United States possess over the Lower House is truly alarming."[14] But that wasn't it at all; *habeas corpus* was not something the Loyalists, with their attachment to the wellsprings of their being, were willing to surrender. There was nothing American or radical about their refusal; it was in the finest Loyalist tradition. The hierarchy had privileges, but it also had responsibilities, and that was that.

A Damned Silly War

The War of 1812 found the Loyalists at their best. It was a damned silly war, provoked by Britain's policy of blockading American ports (to keep supplies from getting to Napoleon) and stopping and searching American vessels to remove and press sailors into her navy. Arrogance and bombast on the British side were reciprocated on the American side and eventually led to war.

However, when the guns began to fire, the Loyalists formed up and marched off. They didn't all go, by any means, and Brock continued to grumble that the people were "so sluggish and indifferent . . . that the artful and active scoundrel is allowed to parade the Country without interruption." Generals are never satisfied with the zeal of the population, which tends to shy away from being shot, but as Pierre Berton made clear in his two-volume history of the war, "the Loyalists were keen to fight."[15] It was the new settlers from the United States who, by 1812, made up sixty percent of Upper Canada's population, who were sluggish and indifferent. The fact that Brock was unable to secure a military appropriation from the house of assembly until two months after the Americans declared war was not the Loyalists' fault. The vote was finally carried by them acting en bloc.[16]

The ranks of the militia who fought beside the British regulars were chockablock with Loyalists—from Joseph Brant's son, who fought at Stoney Creek, to John Howe, who conducted intelligence-gathering missions just before the war from Halifax to Boston, New York, Philadelphia and Washington. (He warned that the Americans would invade Canada, expecting its conquest to be "perfectly easy.")[17] Loyalist George Chisholm served as a captain in the Regiment of York militia, and his three sons—John, William and George, Jr.—were all officers in the same outfit. John's son, in turn, served with him at Queenston Heights, where he was fatally wounded.

The Americans confidently expected Canada to fall to them because, as Howe reported, "They reckon . . . on a ready welcome from a number of Americans who have of late years become Settlers in Upper Canada."[18] That was a perfectly reasonable expectation, and, given a tendency on the part of the Atlantic region to sit out "Mr. Madison's War" (except for a flourishing privateer war conducted profitably out of the Nova Scotia ports), there was not much to stand in the way of an American takeover except the British regulars—who were stretched thin, and whom they had already licked in the Revolutionary War—and the Loyalists.

Perhaps if the Americans had fought a better and more aggressive war, things would have worked out as planned, but their blunders and the staunchness of the Loyalists turned the tide. Canada stood after the war exactly where she had stood before, except that she was imbued with a new sense of confidence and purpose. Much of the credit must go to the Loyalists and their memories, determination and, perhaps, lust for revenge. If the Battle of Waterloo was won on the playing fields of Eton, it is stretching things no further to say that the battles of Crysler's Farm and Lundy's Lane were won in the mob scenes of the American Revolution. (After Crysler's Farm, Dr. William Dunlop, serving the wounded, was afraid to allow Loyalists anywhere near the stricken Americans, for fear the Americans would be murdered.)

Peace in the Valley? Nope.

If this were a movie, we have reached the point where the camera should dolly in on the fearless yeoman—in this case a Loyalist—standing in the doorway of his cabin with one arm around the supple waist of his wife, the other raised to shade his eyes so that he can peer into the distance, past the yard where the children are playing contentedly, into the sun. He says, "Peace at last, Mary, peace in the valley." Fade to black. But history is not as neat as the movies, and what happened to the Loyalists as they scattered across the landscape was never uniform, never simple.

For many, life in the new land, after its harsh beginning, settled into a pattern something like the one they had known in their old homes. There was work to be done: there was church, gradually; there were schools, a social life and politics. For others, those early years were a bitter, endless battle to survive—a battle which not all won. For still others, the translation into a new land opened opportunities that had been blocked in America and wafted them to undreamt-of heights of power and affluence. And for a few, the change was made with comparative ease.

But there was, for every living Loyalist, the mark of what they had been through. How could it be otherwise? Gradually the scars healed, the memories dimmed, and the Loyalists became part of the mainstream of the new country and, in time, just another—though honored—minority. Their coming to Canada was another incident in the nation's history. After 1814 it becomes increasingly difficult to sort out the Loyalists from the streams of other immigrants who shipped in, sorted out and settled down.

And yet, and yet. The Loyalists brought with them the emotional and political, as well as the literal, baggage of their years of travail. Their strengths and weaknesses became woven into Canadian life and would never be eradicated. Historian Arthur Lower argues, "Canada, the modern version of the former British North America, is a by-product of the American Revolution. It originated in a lost cause, the other side of the Revolution."[19] A marvelously Canadian way of looking at the Loyalists. The losers. There is, however, another way to see them, without indulging in a sappy and romantic view. That is to see the Loyalists as losers who, defeated in one place, picked themselves up, dusted themselves off, moved north and transformed themselves into winners.

Unable to control the country in which most of them were born, they fashioned a new country closer to the heart's desire. They didn't do it alone, and they didn't do it without opposition, and from time to time they made a mess of it—as humans will. But the Loyalists put their stamp upon this land as surely as their old land had put its stamp upon them. Their strengths and weaknesses were reflected in the emerging country, gave it its new shape, created many of its problems, left it the legacy of a Loyalist underpinning, with all that implied for good and ill.

One measure of the importance of the Loyalists is to try to imagine what would have become of Canada without them. Imagine, just for a moment, if they had cowered at home rather than moving out, or scattered to the four winds (as the refugees of the French Revolution did later) and allowed Quebec and Nova Scotia to develop along the lines already laid down. Almost certainly the maritime area would have filled in with Americans, following the trend well established before the Revolutionary War. Ontario would have been swamped in the westward march of the American settlers, as Mexico was swallowed when they marched southwest. Would Britain have gone to war again to prevent the takeover of this area? Not likely. If Canada had been populated by a few hundred French fur traders, as western Quebec was before the arrival of the Loyalists, Britain would have attended to her other wars and allowed the Americans to get on with it. The western half of what is now Canada would have filled from the south, not the east, and Winnipeg would be stocked with Norwegians from Minnesota instead of Ukrainians.

The continental union so dear to the hearts of the men of vision in the Thirteen Colonies would have come into being, and if any independent nation existed in the northern half of North America, it would be Quebec. (There are times when this still appears a possibility to Canadian pessimists.)

Because of the Loyalists, the independent nation that emerged had a distinct and different flavor—more royalist, more British, more hierarchical and less inclined to kick over the traces. It had a strong penchant for the rule of law and a distaste for vigilante justice. It had less push and more tolerance than the Americans. It had less dash and more decency, less affluence and more—in every sense of the word—class.

Some of the blame for the revolutions of 1837 and 1838 must be laid at the door of the Loyalists, who accepted the ruling cliques' arbitrary measures with uncommon patience and tended to applaud the stern measures used to repress every form of dissent until it ripened into open rebellion. The long period of stultification in Nova Scotia and New Brunswick politics was also due in part to the Loyalist penchant for the status quo. Responsible government came painfully slowly because, as Esther Clark Wright commented, "There existed a deep and abiding loyalty to the British crown and the British government, and revolt . . . was unthinkable."[20]

This loyalty was not merely a knee-jerk reaction. The Loyalists were not wimps who could be bludgeoned into silence by fear of change. Their battle in the Thirteen Colonies had begun because they believed that—whatever the errors and transgressions of the British—there was a constitutional way to solve problems. The revolutionaries had all the bold slogans, but they also marched to a banner that never appeared in public— The End Justifies the Means. Tarring and feathering, confiscation, acts of attainder, murder—all were justified, time and again, by necessity. It was the Loyalist view that some principles were not divisible, and that even injustice was to be borne rather than substituting violence for debate, guns for resolutions, betrayal for loyalty.

It wasn't such a bad approach, and it has stood the test of time. It set the climate of opinion in this country in a way that has never—despite some close calls—been seriously changed.

When Confederation came to Canada in 1867, it was in part a response to fears of an American takeover of the west, in part a response to the intractable problems produced by legislative stalemate in the province of Canada (reunited in 1841), in part by a vision—a leftover, if you like, from the old continental vision—of a new continent-spanning nation. When the idea of reuniting Upper and Lower Canada was being discussed in 1824, John Beverley Robinson reacted with a counter-proposal—a "plan for a general legislative union of the British provinces of North America."[21] And that, forty-three years later, is what came into being with Confederation.

The new nation then devised was laid down on lines that the Loyalists drew when they first came here. It had their attachment to Britain, their respect for law, their penchant for tradition and their sense of fair play.

I do not claim that the Loyalists constructed the British North America Act (although many Loyalist descendants were numbered among the Fathers of Confederation). I do claim that Canada, if it existed at all today, would be a very different place indeed except for the Loyalists.

Their gift to their new nation was the nation itself.

Chapter Notes

Chapter notes can be very irritating, especially in a book that makes no pretence to be an academic study, so I have kept them to a minimum. I have left out general references that are available in a score of other places. My reason for including notes at all is twofold. First, the process of compiling such notes requires me to recheck original sources, which is good for the soul and will, I hope, help to reduce the number of egregious blunders. Furthermore, there is the hope that some readers will be stimulated to follow the same trails I followed.

Introduction

1. *American Archives*, 5th Series, Volume I, p. 98.
2. *Colombo's Canadian Quotations*, (Edmonton: Hurtig, 1974), p. 581.
3. Mary Beacock Fryer, *Loyalist Spy*, (Brockville: Beasancourt, 1974), p. 14.
4. Bruce Wilson, *As She Began*, (Toronto: Dundurn Press, 1981), p. 28.
5. William Stewart Wallace, *The United Empire Loyalists: A Chronicle of the Great Migration*, (Boston: Gregg Press, 1972), p. 13.
6. Claude-Anne Lopez and Eugenia W. Herbert, *The Private Franklin*, (New York: W.W. Norton, 1975), p. 51.
7. Wallace, *op. cit.*, pp. vi, vii.
8. Wallace, *op. cit.*, says, "Modern scholars estimate that the Tories comprised something closer to nineteen per cent of the total number of white Americans" (p. vi). But the estimates range from a low of 35,000 by Arthur R.M. Lower (*Canadians in the Making*, Toronto: Longmans, 1946, p. 122) to between 75,000 and 80,000 by Wallace (p. vii), to "between 80,000 and 100,000" by Bruce Wilson, *op. cit.* (p. 13). The *Oxford History of the American People* estimates that "about 80,000 departed with the British garrisons" (p. 286). When you get Oxford using "about," you know you're into the realm of speculation. As the historians delve ever deeper, they keep finding pockets of Loyalists in ships' manifests, muster rolls and on the demands for rations (sometimes inflated, just to make life difficult) for which the British officers indented.
9. When we break down the Loyalists by where they wound up in Canada, we get a table that looks like this:

Newfoundland	300
Cape Breton	500
Prince Edward Island	600
New Brunswick	14,000
Nova Scotia	20,000
Quebec	1,000
Ontario	12,000

That nets us 49,400, a suspiciously exact-looking figure. Call it 49,000. To this should probably be added as many as 20,000 late Loyalists. (The first five figures in this list are from a resource study prepared for Parks Canada in 1980 by historian Robert S. Allen, and published in *The Loyalist Ga-*

zette, Spring, 1982, pp. 5-6. The Quebec figure is my own estimate from the scanty numbers available, and the Ontario figure is set out in greater detail later in this book.)

Things are not a lot clearer when we try to decipher where the Loyalists came from. The largest traceable group to come to what is now Ontario, for example, came from New York state, and they are meticulously catalogued. Of the 7,500 accounted for in this group, 54 percent came from Tryon County, the westernmost county of New York, 25 percent came from Albany County (around Albany) and 14 percent from Charlotte County, which is now Vermont (Wilson, *op. cit.*, p. 13). But there were probably many others who came from all over the United States and straggled into Canada during the war.

10. Wilson, *op. cit.*, pp. 17, 18.
11. *Ibid*, p. 18.
12. *The World Almanac*, (New York: Newspaper Enterprise Association, 1984), p. 489.
13. This number, too, is an estimate, based more on mathematics and genealogical tables than statistically reliable data. It is the number usually quoted by officials of the United Empire Loyalists' Association of Canada. Allan Gould, in an article in the *Toronto Star*, May 26, 1979, wrote, "It has been argued that over four million Canadians are descended from those who came in the 1780s," but he doesn't say who argued it.
14. The quote is from Colonel Thomas Dundas' notes, reported in a monumental study of the Loyalist claims performed for the Ontario archives in 1904. The full title of the report is "Second Report of the Bureau of Archives for the Province of Ontario" by Alexander Fraser, provincial archivist, Toronto, 1904. The quote is from page 21.
15. *Historical Manuscripts Commission*, 14th Report, Carlisle Mss., V, pp. 356-7.
16. Wallace, *op. cit.*, p. 1.
17. Saul K. Padover, *The Washington Papers*, (New York: Grosset and Dunlap, 1967), p. 387.

Chapter One

1. Quoted in Bernard Bailyn, *The Ordeal of Thomas Hutchinson*, (Boston: Harvard University Press, 1976), p. 36.
2. *Ibid.*, p. 10, footnote.
3. Arthur M. Schlesinger, *The Birth of the Nation*, (Boston: Houghton Mifflin, 1981), p. 45.

4.*Ibid.*, p. 46.
5.John Brooke, *King George III*, (St. Albans: Granada, 1974), pp. 173-4.
6.Bailyn, *op. cit.*, p. 349.
7.*Ibid.*, p. 223.
8.*Ibid.*, p. 91.
9.Bruce Lancaster and J.H. Plumb, *The American Heritage Book of the Revolution*, (New York: Dell, 1979), p. 29.
10.W.S. MacNutt, *The Atlantic Provinces, 1712-1857*, (Toronto: McClelland and Stewart, 1977), p. 7.
11.Bailyn, *op. cit.*, p. 69.
12.*Ibid.*
13.*Ibid.*, pp. 36-7

Chapter Two

1. William E. Burroughs, *Vigilante*, (New York: Harcourt Brace, 1976), p. 36.
2.Esmond Wright, *The Fire of Liberty*, (London: The Folio Society, 1983), p. 86.
3.Bailyn, *op. cit.*, p. 275.
4.Wright, *op. cit.*, p. 19.
5.In the House of Commons debate, April 19, 1774.
6.Brooke, *op. cit.*, p. 276.
7.Lancaster, *op. cit.*, p. 60.
8.Sydney George Fisher, *The True History of the Revolution*, (London: J.B. Lippincott, 1902), p. 57.
9.Lancaster, *op. cit.*, p. 84.
10.Robert W. Coakley and Stetson Conn, *The War of the American Revolution, Center of Military History*, (Washington: United States Army, 1975), p. 85.
11.Fisher, *op. cit.*, p. 47.
12.*Ibid.*, p. 48.
13.*Ibid.*, p. 48.
14.Christopher Ward, *The War of the Revolution*, (New York: Macmillan, 1952), p. 10.
15.Fisher, *op. cit.*, p. 90.
16.Lancaster, *op. cit.*, p. 65.
17.Bailyn, *op. cit.*, pp. 133-4.

Chapter Three

1.Bailyn, *op. cit.*, p. 123.
2.*Ibid.*, p. 124.
3.*Ibid.*, p. 125.

4. Lancaster, *op. cit.*, p. 68.
5. *Ibid.*, p. 69.
6. Bailyn, *op. cit.*, p. 131.
7. *An Appeal to the World*, a pamphlet by Samuel Adams, (Boston, 1769), p. 32.
8. Bailyn, *op. cit.*, p. 132.
9. Lancaster, *op. cit.*, p. 69.
10. Bailyn, *op. cit.*, pp. 133-5.
11. W. Stewart Wallace, *The Macmillan Dictionary of Canadian Biography*, Third Edition, (Toronto: Macmillan, 1963), p. 224; see also Lancaster, *op. cit.*, p. 73.
12. Bailyn, *op. cit.*, p. 137.
13. *Ibid.*, p. 158.
14. Christopher Ward, *The War of the Revolution*, Vol. I, (New York: Macmillan, 1952), p. 12; see also Lancaster, op. cit., pp. 73-4.
15. Elizabeth P. McCaughney, *From Loyalist to Founding Father*, (New York: Columbia University Press, 1980), p. 56.
16. Wright, *op. cit.*, p. 9.
17. McCaughney, *op. cit.*, p. 58.
18. Bailyn, *op. cit.*, pp. 223ff.
19. Wright, *op. cit.*, p. 10.
20. *The Price of Loyalty: Tory Writings from the Revolutionary Era*, Catherine S. Crary, ed., (New York: McGraw-Hill, 1973), p. 16.
21. Lancaster, *op. cit.*, p. 78.
22. Crary, *op. cit.*, p. 21.
23. *Ibid.*, p. 23.
24. *The Loyalist Americans: A Focus on Greater New York*, Robert East and Jacob Judd, eds., (Tarrytown, N.Y.: Sleepy Hollow Press, 1975), p. 65.
25. Lancaster, *op. cit.*, p. 86.
26. Pauline Maier, *From Resistance to Revolution*, (New York: Knopf, 1972), pp. 274ff for all three quotes.
27. Wright, *op. cit.*, p. 7.
28. Coakley, *op. cit.*, p. 89.

Chapter Four

1. Nick and Helma Mika, *United Empire Loyalists*, (Belleville: Mika Publishing, 1976), p. 58.
2. Wright, *op. cit.*, p. 70.
3. *Ibid.*, p. 19.
4. Crary, *op. cit.*, p. 7.
5. Fisher, *op. cit.*, pp. 157ff.

6. *Ibid.*
7. Crary, *op. cit.*, p. 88.
8. All these examples were reported by the Loyalists, and are cited in Crary, *op. cit.*, p. 57.
9. *Ibid.*, p. 60.
10. *Ibid.*, p. 62.
11. Hereward Senior, "Portrait of a Quebec Loyalist: William Smith of New York," *The Loyalist Gazette*, Autumn, 1983. pp. 11-12.
12. Schlesinger, *op. cit.*, p. 243.
13. Lancaster, *op. cit.*, p. 86.
14. Maier, *op. cit.*, p. 282.
15. Lopez, *op. cit.*, pp. 123ff.
16. East, *op. cit.*, p. 64.
17. Bailyn, *op. cit.*, p. 214.
18. Fisher, *op. cit.*, p. 159.
19. Crary, *op. cit.*, p. 35.
20. Edward Alfred Johs, *The Loyalists of Massachusetts, Their Memorials, Petitions and Claims*, (London: Saint Catherine Press, 1930), p. ix.
21. Crary, *op. cit.*, pp. 236-7.
22. *The Diary of James Allen, Esq.*, Philadelphia, October 17, 1777; quoted in *Offbeat History*, Bulkley S. Guffin, ed., (Cleveland: World Publishing, 1967), p. 84.
23. Crary, *op. cit.*, pp. 36-8.
24. Brooke, *op. cit.*, p. 306.
25. Wright, *op. cit.*, p. 70.
26. *Ibid.*, p. 129.
27. *Ibid.*, p. 41.
28. *Ibid.*, p. 113.
29. Fisher, *op. cit.*, p. 295.
30. Wallace, *The United Empire Loyalists*, pp. 54-5.
31. Crary, *op. cit.*, p. 7.
32. Mika, *op. cit.*, p. 61.
33. Crary, *op cit.*, p. 138.
34. *Ibid.*, p. 155.
35. *Ibid.*, p. 63.
36. The best account of DeLancey I have come across is Catherine S. Crary's "Guerrilla Activities of James DeLancey's Cowboys in Westchester County: Conventional Warfare or Self-Interested Freebooting?" (Like so many historians, Ms. Crary asks the leading question, but doesn't answer it. Her article suggests the answer: both. This appears in *The Loyalist Americans*, edited by Robert East, pp. 14ff. The quotes are from this account.

37. Crary, *The Price of Loyalty*, p. 149. The Beverly Robinson mentioned is, of course, the ancestor of John Beverley Robinson of Upper Canada.
38. Wright, *op. cit.*, p. 71.
39. Crary, *op. cit.*, pp. 106-7.
40. *Ibid.*, p. 88.
41. Wright, *op. cit.*, p. 77.
42. *Ibid.*, p. 48.
43. *Ibid.*, p. 119.
44. Thomas Raddall, *The Path of Destiny*, (Toronto: Doubleday Canada, 1957), pp. 60ff.
45. Lancaster, *op. cit.*, p. 214.
46. Ward, *op. cit.*, pp. 496-8.
47. Raddall, *op. cit.*, p. 63.
48. Crary, *op. cit.*, p. 217.
49. *Ibid.*, pp. 220-4.

Chapters Five, Six and Seven

The American Revolutionary War has been explained, dissected, examined, reexamined and re-reexamined in thousands of books. Many of the major incidents—the evacuation of Charleston and Savannah, the siege of Boston, the surrender at Yorktown—have been documented so many times that I see no point in interrupting the text here with notes that are, in most cases, repetitions of notes that appear elsewhere. It seems to me more useful to list the baker's dozen of books, out of the 183 I consulted on this part of the war, that became major references for these three chapters. (A complete reference is given for volumes not previously cited in these notes.)

Crary, *The Price of Loyalty*. This is an invaluable collection of letters, diaries, journals, pamphlets and other material written by Loyalists at the time.

Wright, *The Fire of Liberty*. A similar collection of diaries, letters and excerpts from debates, but tilted in the opposite direction; that is, with most of its material from the Patriot side.

Lancaster and Plumb, *The American Heritage Book of the Revolution*. Condescending in tone and unabashedly "Patriotic" in outlook, but it contains a useful outline of the war.

Fisher, *The True History of the Revolution*. This is a cranky, unashamedly Tory view of the war, which blames everything on the wicked Whigs in England and America, but it contains material I have not seen elsewhere, including some of the contemporary quotes.

Ward, *The War of the Revolution*. A two-volume, exhaustive study of the military aspects of the war; useful, but tough reading.

Coakley and Conn, *The War of the American Revolution*. This is the U.S. Army's official history, and it gives the impression that no private moved without its permission. The bibliography runs to ninety-four pages, which impressed the hell out of me, with 1,200 reference books noted.

Allan W. Eckert, *The Wilderness War*. (Boston: Little, Brown, 1978). A made-for-TV version of the guerrilla war in the northeast. Eckert has reconstructed events into a sort of docudrama, with a day-by-day, you-are-there approach. However, he has compiled and worked into his narrative an impressive selection of original documents, which are most useful.

East and Judd, *The Loyalist Americans*. A series of essays on the Loyalists in the greater New York area.

Claude Halstead Van Tyne, *The American Revolution*, (New York: AMS Press, 1971). Leading up to the 1976 Bicentennial in the United States, publishers went back to the archives to re-publish earlier works. This one came out in 1905. It is a ponderous but fact-laden look at the Revolution and has the advantage of being very fair-minded. (Which means, of course, that I agree with most of it.)

Maier, *From Resistance to Revolution*. A treasure-trove of material on the early part of the war.

Sol Stember, *The Bicentennial Guide to the American Revolution*, (New York: Saturday Review Press, 1974). This wonderful three volume series of books was designed for people who would be driving over the United States during the Bicentennial year, and it covers, in loving detail, every skirmish, raid and battle, as well as much of the off-beat action. The volumes cover the war in the north, the middle colonies and the south. Much of the material—which is not annotated—is obviously taken from local histories, pamphlets and travel books. Stember gives explicit instructions on how to find sites that have become quite different since the eighteenth century, so you follow his lead through alley and hedgerow to where something happened two centuries or more ago (" Continue along 76 until it curves to the right and goes over a bridge with a cypress swamp to the right and an old frame building to the left. This is the site of Flood's Mill, now called Elliott's Mill."—that sort of thing.) Would that someone—Pierre Berton, perhaps—had the time, energy and money to do a series like this on Canadian history.

Bruce Bliven, Jr., *Under the Guns*. (New York: Harper and Row, 1972). A study of New York in 1775-76 that has much interesting material on the rest of the war.

Red, White and True Blue: The Loyalists in the Revolution. Esmond Wright, ed., (New York: AMS Press, 1976). A series of essays by various historical scholars on various aspects of Loyalism, edited by the indefatigable Esmond Wright and full of intriguing insights. There is, for example, an excellent portrait of the Loyalists who went to the West Indies, by Canada's own Wallace Brown.

1. The seven regiments were: Butler's Rangers, which was not a regular regiment, but operated as a guerrilla unit exclusively under Colonel John Butler; the King's Loyal Americans, organized by Ebenezer Jessup at the time of Burgoyne's abortive expedition in 1777 (it was reorganized with the Queen's Loyal Rangers into the Loyal Rangers); the King's Rangers, organized by Robert Rogers and later taken over by a regular British army officer, John Graves Simcoe; the King's Royal Regiment of New York; the Queen's Loyal Rangers, which was pretty well wiped out during a raid on Burgoyne's march; the Loyal Rangers, also called Jessup's Corps, organized by Edward Jessup; and the Royal Highland Emigrants. (This was a regiment formed by Colonel Allen MacLean of Highland veterans of the Seven Years War, and it became a regular British regiment—the 84th.) There were other groups like the Royal Fencible Americans, the New Jersey Volunteers, and the Guides and Pioneers, but these were not full-blown regiments and tended to fade as the war wore on.

Chapter Eight

1. Wilson, *op. cit.*, p. 52.

2. The phrase appears in the submissions of a number of the Loyalists to the royal commission on Loyalist claims.

3. Raddall, *op. cit.*, p. 73. Much of the description of early Halifax is taken from this book and from Raddall's equally fascinating *Halifax: Warden of the North*, (revised edition). (Toronto: McClelland and Stewart, 1971).

4. *Ibid.*, p. 86.

5. *Ibid.*, p. 87.

6. Raddall referred to the incident in his novel *His Majesty's Yankees*, written in 1942 and based on *The Neutral Yankees of Nova Scotia* by J.B. Brebner, and on the diary of Simeon Perkins. It has become part of the town lore and was told to me in graphic detail by a young woman in the travel booth.

7. Gorham kept a *Journal*, which tells this story from his side and contains the relevant details. It is available in the Colonial Office papers and is referred to as C.O. 217/53.

8. The story has been told often enough, but never better than in Raddall's *His Majesty's Yankees*, even if it is a novel.

9. Esther Clark Wright, *The Loyalists of New Brunswick*, (Hansport, Nova Scotia: Lancelot, 1981), pp. 31-2.

10. Sara Frost's journal has been widely quoted; I have used the version in *Pioneer Profiles of New Brunswick Settlers*, Charlotte Gourlay Robinson, ed., (Bellville: Mika, 1980), pp. 110ff.

11. *The Loyalist Gazette*, Spring, 1983. p. 8. The quote is in an article by Wallace Brown, called "The Loyalists and the Maritime Provinces."

12. Esther Clark Wright, *op. cit.*, pp. 85ff.

13. *Ibid.*, p. 166. The numbers are extremely confused, and it is especially difficult to say exactly how many went where or remained where they went. Wright, the quintessential author on the New Brunswick Loyalists, estimates that at least 13,500 went into the area that is now New Brunswick. She got this figure by going over all the army muster lists and civilian ration allotments, eliminating duplicates and then multiplying the 6,000 names she wound up with by 2.25 to allow for married men with families. She also found 1,020 officers and men on the army rolls listed as sailing for the St. John River area who never appeared on the lists there. Presumably they moved on.

14. Crary, *The Price of Loyalty*, p. 404.

15. Marion Robertson, *King's Bounty: A History of Early Shelburne, Nova Scotia*, (Halifax: Nova Scotia Museum, 1983), p. 22.

16. *Ibid.*, p. 33.

17.*Ibid.*, p. 50.
18.*Ibid.*, p. 52.
19.*Ibid.*, p. 55.
20.*Ibid.*, p. 57.
21.*Ibid.*, p. 72.
22.*Ibid.*, p. 125.
23.*Ibid.*, p. 128.
24.*Ibid.*, p. 129.

Chapter Nine

1. The conclusion is mine; the story is told substantially in *Canada's Smallest Province*, Francis W.P. Bolger, ed., (PEI Centennial Commission, 1973), pp. 47ff.
2. Gustavus Myers, *A History of Canadian Wealth*, Vol. I, (Toronto: James, Lewis and Samuel, 1972), p. 84.
3. Bolger, *op. cit.*, p. 53.
4. *Ibid.*, p. 57.
5. Donald Wetmore, *William Schurman of Bedeque*, in *Eleven Exiles*, Phyllis R. Blakeley and John N. Grant, ed., (Toronto: Dundurn Press, 1982), pp. 169ff.
6. Wallace, *The United Empire Loyalists*, p. 68.
7. D.G. Bell, *Early Loyalist Saint John*, (New Ireland Press, 1983), p. 87. This is another of the marvellous local histories Canadians keep spinning out while complaining that our history is dull. It is not dull—simply ignored. Most of the sections of this chapter on New Brunswick's foundation is drawn from this source and from *The Loyalists of New Brunswick* by Esther Clark Wright.
8. *The Loyalist Gazette*, Spring, 1983, p. 12. This is from "Winter of Discontent: The Loyalists' First Winter in Fredericton" by Earle Thomas.
9. *Ibid.*
10. Raddall, *Halifax*, pp. 103ff.

Chapter Ten

1. *American Colonial Documents to 1776*, (New York: Nelson and Sons), p. 752.
2. Lisa W. Strick, *The Black Presence in the Era of the American Revolution*, (Washington: Smithsonian, 1973), p. 22. There is a lot of information on the blacks in Shelburne, Nova Scotia, in *King's Bounty* by Marion Robertson, but most studies in this area have been done, alas, by Americans. The essential work, which forms the basis of the rest of this

chapter, is drawn almost exclusively from American and British documents. It is *The Black Loyalists*, subtitled "The Search for a Promised Land in Nova Scotia and Sierra Leone 1783-1870," by James W. St. G. Walker, (New York: Africana Publishing, 1976). The book is hard-sledding—Walker pulls all his punches—but it is jammed with quotes, the best of which I have borrowed. Unless otherwise noted, material in this chapter is from Walker, Strick and Robertson.

4. Walker, *op. cit.*, p. 3.
5. *Ibid.*, p. 10.
6. From the entry on Murray in *The Dictionary of National Biography*, E.T. Williams and C.S. Nicholls, eds., (London: Oxford University Press, 1982).

Chapter Eleven

1. Wallace, *United Empire Loyalists*, p. 92.
2. A.L. Burt, *The Old Province of Quebec*, Vol. II, (Toronto: McClelland and Stewart, 1968), pp. 84-5.
3. *Ibid.*, p. 86.
4. Gerald M. Craig, *Upper Canada: The Formative Years*, (Toronto: McClelland and Stewart, 1963), pp. 4-5.
5. *Loyalist Narratives from Upper Canada*, James J. Talman, ed., Champlain Society, Toronto, 1948, pp. 73ff.
6. Mika, *op. cit.*, p. 154.
7. Talman, *op. cit.*, p. xlvii.
8. *Ibid.*, p. xlviii.
9. Anderson, in *Loyalist Narratives*, p. 2.
10. *Testimonial of Roger Bates*, in *Loyalist Narratives*, pp. 30ff.
11. Burt, *op. cit.*, p. 95.
12. *Petition for an Assembly, 1784*, from *Canadian History in Documents 1763-1966*, J.M. Bliss, ed., (Toronto: Ryerson, 1966), p. 11.
13. Burt, *op. cit.*, p. 108.
14. *Ibid.*, p. 156.
15. *Ibid.*
16. *Sir Guy Carleton*, A.G. Bradley, (Toronto: University of Toronto Press, 1966), p. 260.
17. Craig, *op. cit.*, p. 14.

Chapter Twelve

1. *The Mark of Honour*, Hazel C. Mathews, (Toronto: University of Toronto Press, 1965), p. 133.
2. Burt, *op. cit.*, p. 96.

3. *Ibid.*, p. 98.
4. Talman, *op. cit.*, p. lvii.
5. *Ibid.*, p. 67.
6. Burt, *op. cit.*, p. 39.
7. *Ibid.*, p. 28.
8. *Ibid.*, p. 22.
9. *The Correspondence of Lieut. Governor John Graves Simcoe*, Vol. III, E.A. Cruikshank, edit., (Toronto, 1923), p. 235.
10. Burt, *op. cit.*, p. 25.
11. Wallace, *United Empire Loyalists*, p. 124.
12. *Ibid.*
13. Burt, *op. cit.*, p. 81.
14. Wallace, *op. cit.*, p. 124.
15. *Ibid.*, p. 125.
16. Myers, *op. cit.*, p. 83.
17. Arthur R.M. Lower, *Colony to Nation*, (Toronto: McClelland and Stewart, 1977), p. 118.
18. Arthur R.M. Lower, *Canadians in the Making*, (Toronto: McClelland and Stewart, 1958), p. 156.
19. Craig, *op. cit.*, pp. 20ff.
20. *Ibid.*, p. 29.
21. *Ibid.*, p. 31.
22. The numerous Simcoe biographies all deal with this quarrel, as do the biographies of Lord Dorchester. I have hewn to the cool and dispassionate account presented in A.G. Bradley's bloodless biography of Carleton, *Sir Guy Carleton*, *op. cit.*, pp. 292ff.
23. Bradley, *op. cit.*, p. 302.
24. *The Valley of the Six Nations*, Charles M. Johnston, ed., (Toronto: Champlain Society, 1964), p. xlv.
25. Cruickshank, *op. cit.*, Vol. II, p. 183.
26. *The Path of Destiny*, Raddall, *op. cit.*, p. 133.
27. *Ibid.*, p. 135.

Chapter Thirteen

1. Robert Gourlay, *Statistical Account of Upper Canada*, (Toronto: McClelland and Stewart, 1974), p. 96.
2. Wilson, *op. cit.*, p. 97.
3. Hugh Gillis, *Democracy in the Canadas*, (Toronto: Oxford University Press, 1951), p. 121.
4. Talman, *op. cit.*, p. 85.
5. *Ibid.*, p. 31.
6. *Ibid.*, p. 65.
7. *Ibid.*, p. 32.

8. Mathews, *op. cit.*, p. 134.
9. E.A. Owen, *Pioneer Sketches of Long Point Settlement*, (Toronto: William Briggs, 1898), p. 409.
10. *Ibid.*, pp. 403ff.
11. Wilson, *op. cit.*, p. 107.
12. Gillis, *op. cit.*, p. 113.
13. Lower, *Colony to Nation*, p. 118.
14. Wilson, *op. cit.*, p. 115.
15. *Ibid.*
16. Letter from Dundas to Lord Shelburne; cited in *Second Report of the Bureau of Archives for the Province of Ontario*, Alexander Fraser, public archivist, (Toronto, 1904), p. 22.
17. Talman, *op. cit.*, p. 75.
18. *Ibid.*, p. 85.
19. Craig, *op. cit.*, p. 31.
20. Lower, *op. cit.*, p. 160.
21. *Ibid.*, p. 161.
22. *Ibid.*

Chapter Fourteen

1. *The Royal Commission on the Losses and Services of American Loyalists 1783 to 1785: Being the Notes of Mr. Daniel Parker Coke, M.P.*, edited by Hugh E. Egerton, (Oxford, 1915), p. 5ff. Parker was one of the commissioners who kept notes, subsequently transcribed and edited. Except where noted, all the quotes in this chapter are from this document or from the Ontario Bureau of Archives second annual report, noted above, which consisted of a study of the Canadian Loyalist claims. These volumes, available in the British Museum in London and the Ontario Archives in Toronto, constitute the most usable available material from the claims. (The originals are stored in the Public Records Office in Kew Gardens, London.) The material is rich and varied, and formed the basis of Christopher Moore's *The Loyalists*, published by Macmillan in 1983.
2. L.F.S. Upton, "The Claims: The Mission of John Anstey," in *Red, White and True Blue*, p. 139.
3. Wallace, *United Empire Loyalists*, p. 117.
4. Upton, *op. cit.*, p. 142.
5. *Ibid.*, p. 141.
6. J.G. Taylor, *Some New Light on the Later Life and Last Resting Place of Benedict Arnold*, (London: George White, 1931), pp. 19ff.
7. Wallace, *op. cit.*, p. 114.

Chapter Fifteen

1. Johnston, *op. cit.*, p. xxxiv.
2. *The King's Friends*, Wallace Brown, (Providence: Brown University Press, 1966), p. 106.
3. A. Roy Petrie, *Joseph Brant*, (Toronto: Fitzhenry and Whiteside, 1978), p. 27.
4. Peter Marshall, "First Americans and Last Loyalists: An Indian Dilemma in War and Peace," in *Red, White and True Blue*, p. 49.
5. Francis Jennings, "Tribal Loyalty and Tribal Independence," in *Red, White and True Blue*, p. 21.
6. Helen Caister Robinson, *Mistress Molly*, (Toronto: Dundurn Press, 1980), p. 109.
7. Marshall, *op. cit.*, p. 42.
8. *Ibid.*
9. Johnston, *op. cit.*, p. xxxvii.
10. Marshall, *op. cit.*, p. 45.
11. Johnston, *op. cit.*, p. xxxviii.
12. Petrie, *op. cit.*, p. 48.
13. Marshall, *op. cit.*, p. 47.
14. Johnston, *op. cit.*, p. 52.
15. Robinson, *op. cit.*, p. 146.
16. Petrie, *op. cit.*, p. 31.
17. Jennings, *op. cit.*, pp. 19-20.
18. Marshall, *op. cit.*, p. 50.
19. The letter is quoted in full in Johnston, *op. cit.*, pp. 93-4.
20. *Ibid.*, p. 39.
21. Raddall, *The Path of Destiny*, p. 110.
22. *Ibid.*, p. 111.
23. *Ibid.*, p. 113.
24. Johnston, *op. cit.*, p. liii.
25. Petrie, *op. cit.*, p. 60.
26. Johnston, *op. cit.*, p. lxix.
27. Robinson, *op. cit.*, p. 89.

Chapter Sixteen

1. Brian Cutherbertson, "The Loyalist Ascendancy in Nova Scotia," in *The Loyalist Gazette*, Spring, 1983. p. 13.
2. *Ibid.*, p. 14.
3. Raddall, *The Path of Destiny*, p. 116.
4. *Ibid.*, p. 123.
5. *The Town of York, 1793-1815, A Collection of Early Documents*, Edith G. Firth, ed., (Toronto: Champlain Society,

1961), p. xlix.
6. *Ibid.*, p. lxxi.
7. *Ibid.*, p. 160.
8. *Ibid.*, p. lxvii.
9. Craig, *op. cit.*, p. 60.
10. Firth, *op. cit.*, p. lxvii.
11. Craig, *op. cit.*, p. 65.
12. *Ibid.*, p. 98.
13. Robert E. Saunders, "What Was the Family Compact?" in *Historical Essays on Upper Canada*, J.K. Johnson, ed., (Toronto: McClelland and Stewart, 1975), pp. 122ff.
14. Craig, *op. cit.*, p. 70.
15. Pierre Berton, *Flames Across the Border*, (Toronto: McClelland and Stewart, 1983), p. 23.
16. Mathews, *op. cit.*, p. 162.
17. John Grant, "John Howe, Sr.," in *Eleven Exiles*, p. 44.
18. *Ibid.*, p. 43.
19. Lower, *Colony to Nation*, p. 113.
20. Wright, *op. cit.*, p. 240.
21. Sir John Beverley Robinson, *Plan for a general legislative union of the British provinces of North America*, (London, 1824).

Index

Minute Men, 49, 95
Mississauga Indians, 172, 173, 229
M'Leod, Donald, 192, 239
mobs (mob rule), 15, 16, 20, 21, 22, 23, 24, 25, 27, 29, 30, 31, 35, 37, 38, 40, 41, 54, 56, 58, 59, 68, 78, 102, 103, 105, 106, 119, 147, 249
Mohawk Indians, 73, 76, 79, 82, 83, 118, 172, 209, 226, 227, 229
Montreal, 64, 118, 172, 190, 216, 217
Moore, Sir Henry, 30
Moore, Will, 22, 35
Morehead, William, 223
Morris, William, 131, 132
Murray, William, Earl of Mansfield, 165
Murry, Captain Robert, 143, 144
Mutiny Act, 30

New Brunswick, 5, 122, 149; election of 1785, 150-153; 164, 165, 201, 202, 217, 223, 242, 251
Newcombe, Silas, 57
New Hampshire, 38
New Jersey, 3, 28, 173
New Jersey Volunteers, 144
New London Gazette, 48
Newport, 15
Newport Mercury, 28
New Town, 83, 84
New York, 15, 26, 28, 39, 45, 65, 111, 120, 126, 140, 201
New York assembly, 33, 59, 60
New York State, 3, 28, 30, 45, 75, 103, 104, 173, 189
Niagara, 9, 131, 185, 192, 203
North, Lord, 32, 42, 43, 54, 63, 93, 108, 113, 136, 140, 171, 227, 228, 233
North Carolina, 3, 16, 39, 66, 90, 94
North Carolina assembly, 39
Norton, Captain John, 236, 237
Nova Scotia, 4, 5, 6, 15, 20, 39, 94, 109, 113, 117, 121-128, 133, 140, 141, 149, 153, 159, 160, 164, 167, 201, 216, 217, 242, 245, 251
Nova Scotia Regiment of Foot, 240

Odell, Johnathan, 149
Old Loyalist List, 183
Olive Branch Petition, 53
Oliver, Andrew, 21, 35, 43, 44, 153
Oliver, Peter, 45
Oliver, William, 151, 152, 153
Oneida Indians, 76, 226
Onondaga Indians, 76, 84, 229
Ontario, 4, 239, 251
Otis, James, 20, 21
Owen, E.A., 200, 208

Paine, Robert, 48
Paine, Tom, 26
Palmer, Alphea, 161
Parker, Captain John, 49

Parliament (Britain), 17-33, 37, 38, 42, 43, 45, 47, 53, 56, 85, 137, 181, 212, 217
Parr, Governor John, 121, 126, 129, 132, 133, 139-149, 153, 161, 163, 167
Parr Town, 139, 143, 144, 145, 149, 151
Patterson, Daniel, 93
Patterson, Walter, 135, 136, 137, 138, 139
peace treaties and negotiations, 101, 105-110, 158, 171, 172, 202, 219, 225, 226, 227, 233
Pembertson, Jeremy, 216
Penn, William, 16
Pennsylvania, 3, 16, 28, 38, 45, 46, 75, 173
Pennsylvania assembly, 32
Pennsylvania Chronicle, 32
Pennsylvania Ledger, 61
Perkins, Simeon, 163
Peters, Reverend Samuel, 46
Peters, Thomas, 164, 165, 166, 167, 168
Philadelphia, 15, 26, 45, 53, 61, 71, 122
Philipse, Frederick, 60, 220, 221
Pictou, 129, 204
Pincy Bottom killings, 93-94
Pitcairn, Major John, 49
Pitt, William, 25, 63, 108
Plains of Abraham, battle of, 5
Postell, Mary, 161, 162
Powell, William Dummer, 247, 248
Prescott, Samuel, 49
Preston, 129
Preston, Captain Thomas, 40, 41, 155
Prince, Zachery, 156
Prince Edward, 240, 241
Prince Edward Island, 39, 122, 125, 135, 139
Prince William, 153, 154, 240
Prince of Wales' American Regiment, 148
Proclamation of 1763, 46
Provincial Corps of the British Army, 80
Provost Dungeon, 97, 98, 102
Pullency, Sir William, 191
Purchas, Samuel, 231
Putnam, Clarissa, 76, 77
Putnam, General Israel, 7
Pynchon, Joseph, 130

Quartering Act, 45
Quebec, 5, 6, 15, 63, 109, 117, 121, 124, 131, 133, 169, 170, 175, 181, 194, 201, 216, 223, 228 239, 242, 251
Quebec Act (The Canada Bill), 46, 47, 48, 180, 193, 212, 244
Quebec City, 64, 70, 172, 173, 179, 217
Quebec Herald, 185
Queen's Rangers, 194, 195, 201, 247
Queenston Heights, 249
Quincy, Josiah, 41

Raddall, Thomas, 123, 131, 198
Raddish, Reverend Thomas, 245
Ramsheg, 129
Randolph, Peyton, 48